Living With Pottery

Foundations of Archaeological Inquiry

James M. Skibo, series editor

Expanding Archaeology
James M. Skibo, William H. Walker, and Axel E. Nielsen

Behavioral Archaeology: First Principles
Michael Brian Schiffer

Evolutionary Archaeology: Theory and Application
Michael J. O'Brien, editor

Unit Issues in Archaeology: Measuring Time, Space, and Material
Ann F. Ramenofsky and Anastasia Steffen, editors

Pottery Ethnoarchaeology in the Central Maya Highlands
Michael Deal

Pottery and People: A Dynamic Interaction
James M. Skibo and Gary M. Feinman, editors

Material Meanings: Critical Approaches to the Interpretation of Material Culture
Elizabeth S. Chilton, editor

Social Theory in Archaeology
Michael Brian Schiffer, editor

Race and the Archaeology of Identity
Charles E. Orser Jr., editor

Style, Function, Transmission: Evolutionary Archaeological Perspectives
Michael J. O'Brien and R. Lee Lyman, editors

The Archaeology of Settlement Abandonment in Middle America
Takeshi Inomata and Ronald W. Webb, editors

Complex Systems and Archaeology: Empirical and Theoretical Applications
R. Alexander Bentley and Herbert D. G. Maschner, editors

Essential Tensions in Archaeological Method and Theory
Todd L. and Christine S. VanPool

Archaeological Perspectives on Political Economies
Gary Feinman and Linda Nicholas, editors

Living With Pottery

Ethnoarchaeology among the Gamo of Southwest Ethiopia

John W. Arthur

The University of Utah Press
Salt Lake City

Foundations of Archaeological Inquiry
James M. Skibo, editor

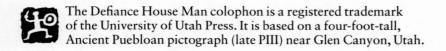 The Defiance House Man colophon is a registered trademark
of the University of Utah Press. It is based on a four-foot-tall,
Ancient Puebloan pictograph (late PIII) near Glen Canyon, Utah.

2006 07 08 09 10   5 4 3 2 1

LIBRARY OF CONGRESS CATALOGING-IN-PUBLICATION DATA

Arthur, John W.
  Living with pottery : ethnoarchaeology among the Gamo of southwest Ethiopia / John W.
Arthur.
     p. cm.
  Includes bibliographical references and index.
  ISBN-13: 978-0-87480-883-4 (cloth : alk. paper)
  ISBN-10: 0-87480-883-9 (cloth : alk. paper)
  ISBN-13: 978-0-87480-884-1 (pbk. : alk. paper)
  ISBN-10: 0-87480-884-7 (pbk. : alk. paper)   1. Pottery, Gamo.   2. Gamo (African
people)—Social life and customs.   3. Ethnoarchaeology—Ethiopia.   4. Ethiopia—Social
life and customs.   I. Title.
  DT380.4.G19A77 2006
  305.89'35—dc22   2006017549

To the Gamo People, Kathy, and Hannah

Contents

List of Figures   ix

List of Tables   xiii

Acknowledgments   xv

Introduction   1

1. The Gamo   10

2. Pottery Procurement and Production   29

3. Pottery Distribution   55

4. Pottery Primary Use   73

5. Pottery Use-Life   92

6. Pottery Mending and Reuse   102

7. Pottery Discard   121

8. Gamo Pottery and Its Implications for
     Ethnoarchaeology and Archaeology   135

References   141

Index   151

Figures

I.1. Map of the Gamo region within Ethiopia and Africa   4

I.2. A Gamo family with a portion of their household ceramic assemblage   5

1.1. View of the Gamo highlands overlooking the escarpment that extends down the Rift Valley and Lake Abaya   11

1.2. A farmer with his plow and enset, an indigenous staple, in the background   11

1.3. A woman scraping the corm of the enset   12

1.4. A woman grinding enset to prepare it for making fermented enset bread, *ooetsa*   12

1.5. View of the large Bodo (Dorze) weekly market   13

1.6. Map of markets associated with the villages of Zuza, Etello, and Guyla   14

1.7. A member of the *mala* caste who is also a *maka*, a person who sacrifices animals and prays for the people and their land   16

1.8. A member of the *mana* caste producing her wares   17

1.9. A member of the *degala* caste showing the abject poverty of his household   17

1.10. Map of the village locations of Zuza, Etello, and Guyla within the Gamo region   21

1.11. Map of households located within the Gamo village of Zuza   22

1.12. View of Zuza, illustrating the village location on top of a large ridge overlooking the Rift Valley   23

1.13. Map of households located within the Gamo village of Guyla   24

1.14. View from the meeting area (*dubusha*) in the village of Guyla   25

1.15. Map of households located within the Gamo village of Etello   26

1.16. A household in the village of Etello, with Tsudo Mountain in the background   27

2.1. A young girl helping with ceramic production by compacting the wall of a baking plate between the ground and hand stones   30

2.2. Zuza potters cleaning the three clays they have procured before they begin producing their vessels   32

2.3. A potter digging clay from a procurement area owned by a *mala* in the Ezo region   33

2.4. A potter digging from the *pullticalo* clay source in order to find clay suitable for producing pottery in the village of Guyla   33

2.5. A Zuza potter beating the clay with a large stick (*bookadoka*) before sifting the clay through a woven basket (*zizarey*)   35

2.6. A Guyla potter mixing the different clays together using her foot   36

2.7. Profile drawings of (A) narrow-mouth small jar, (B) large jar, (C) beer jar, and (D) narrow-mouth medium jar, which the Gamo potters produce   37

2.8. Profile drawings of (A) water pipe, (B) coffee pitcher, (C) coffee cup, (D) dish, and (E–F) bowl, which the Gamo potters produce   38

2.9. Profile drawings of (A) wide-mouth small jar, (B) single-handle jar, (C) foot-washing bowl (D) wide-mouth medium jar, and (E) baking plate, which the Gamo potters produce   39

2.10. A Guyla potter using a piece of leather (*gelba*) to shape the neck and rim of a jar   40

2.11. A Guyla potter using a bamboo tool (*mylee*) to thin the vessel wall   40

2.12. A Guyla potter starting to form the base by applying coils to the vessel   40

2.13. A Guyla potter forming the base by using the coil-and-scrape method   41

2.14. A Guyla potter compacting the walls of a beer vessel by using two hand stones   41

2.15. A Guyla potter shaping the interior of a bowl   41

2.16. A Zuza potter forming the rim of a baking plate using a piece of leather   42

2.17. A number of baking plates on a drying rack in a Zuza potter house   44

2.18. A Guyla potter burnishing a jar with a quartzite polishing stone (*elasucha*)   44

2.19. A Guyla potter prefiring the vessels before they are fired   49

2.20. A Guyla potter firing his vessels   49

2.21. Zuza potters preparing their vessels to be fired   50

2.22. View of a Zuza potter beginning to fire the vessels   50

3.1. Guyla potters preparing their vessels for the weekly market   56

3.2. The absolute frequency of vessels inventoried among 20 households in each of the three Gamo villages, demonstrating a greater number of vessels in the pottery-producing villages (Guyla and Zuza)   57

3.3. Relative frequencies of pots in 20 Zuza households by source of manufacture, illustrating their predominate use of Zuza and Ochollo district/*dere* pots   58

3.4. Relative frequencies of pots in 20 Guyla households by source of manufacture, illustrating that they tend to purchase locally made pottery (Guyla) even though they express preference for Birbir pots   61

3.5. Relative frequencies of pots in 20 Etello households by source of manufacture, illustrating that pots are purchased from many Gamo regions   62

3.6. Relative frequencies of pots in *mala* and *degala* households in Etello by source of manufacture (*n* = 220)   65

3.7. Relative frequencies of pots in *mala* and *degala* households in Guyla by source of manufacture (*n* = 412)   66

3.8. Mean cost (birr) of pots in Zuza, Guyla, and Etello by economic rank, illustrating that higher economic ranks generally spend more on household pottery   68

3.9. Relative frequencies of pots in Etello by economic rank and source of manufacture   69

3.10. Relative frequencies of pots in Zuza by economic rank and source of manufacture   70

3.11. Relative frequencies of pots in Guyla by economic rank and source of manufacture   71

4.1. Generalized spatial pattern of the pottery primary-use stage in the village of Zuza and the low-caste and poor households of Etello and Guyla   79

4.2. Generalized spatial pattern of the pottery primary-use stage in the villages of Etello and Guyla, including their high-caste and wealthy households   80

4.3. Generalized spatial pattern of the pottery primary-use stage in the potter households of Guyla   81

4.4. Mean number of primary-use vessels by caste and village   82

4.5. Mean number of primary-use vessel types by caste and village   83

4.6. Mean vessel volume by caste and village   85

4.7. Mean number of vessels by economic rank and village   87

4.8. Mean number of vessel types by economic rank and village   87

4.9. Mean vessel volume by economic rank and village   88

6.1. Women using jars to collect and transport water from a well in Zuza   103

6.2. A woman collecting and transporting water from a stream in Guyla   103

6.3. A large jar mended with enset leaves   106

6.4. A large jar mended with enset rope   106

6.5. A large jar reused to store water in a Zuza household   109

6.6. A large sherd and a jar reused as lids   111

6.7. Large sherds being used to form a beehive in the village of Guyla   111

6.8. Jar necks being reused to make openings for a beehive in the village of Zuza   111

6.9. Generalized spatial pattern of the pottery reuse stage in the village of Zuza and the low-caste and poor households of Etello and Guyla   112

6.10. Generalized spatial pattern of the pottery reuse stage in the villages of Etello and Guyla, including their high-caste and wealthy households   116

6.11. Generalized spatial pattern of the pottery reuse stage in the potter households of Guyla   117

7.1. A coffeepot sitting on a cooking hearth; after it breaks it usually cannot be reused and is immediately discarded   122

7.2. Generalized spatial pattern of the pottery discard stage in the village of Zuza and the low-caste and poor households of Etello and Guyla   123

7.3. Generalized spatial pattern of the pottery discard stage in the villages of Etello and Guyla, including their high-caste and wealthy households   124

7.4. View of pots being provisionally discarded in the household garden   125

7.5. View of provisionally discarded pots being stored adjacent to the house at a *halaka* household in Zuza   126

7.6. View of a typical Gamo village footpath where discarded sherds are often thrown   126

7.7. Mean number of discarded vessels by caste and village   127

7.8. Mean number of discarded vessel types by caste and village   127

7.9. Mean volume of discarded vessels by caste and village   128

7.10. Generalized spatial pattern of the pottery discard stage in the potter households of Guyla   130

7.11. Mean number of discarded vessels by economic rank and village   131

7.12. Mean number of discarded vessel types by economic rank and village   131

7.13. Mean volume of discarded vessels by economic rank and village   132

Tables

1.1. Social Hierarchy and Their Economic Associations in Gamo Society   20

2.1. Functional Attributes Ascribed to Clays and Temper by Zuza and Guyla Potters   34

2.2. Gamo Vessel Forms   36

2.3. Drying Location and Time for Specific Vessel Types Produced in Zuza   43

2.4. Drying Location and Time for Specific Vessel Types Produced in Guyla   43

2.5. Zuza Potters' Placement of Burnishing on Specific Vessel Forms   45

2.6. Guyla Potters' Placement of Burnishing on Specific Vessel Forms   45

2.7. Taxonomic and Gamo Names and Corresponding Elevational Ranges of Fuels Used to Fire Ceramic Vessels by Village, Demonstrating Primary Dependence on Local Resources   47

2.8. Zuza Potters' Placement of *Etema* on Specific Vessel Forms   47

2.9. Guyla Potters' Placement of *Etema* on Specific Vessel Forms   47

3.1. Geographical Distance between Pottery Producers and Markets   56

3.2. Large Markets in the Central Gamo Region and Their Corresponding Days   57

3.3. Each Guyla Households Generally Purchases Most of Its Guyla Pottery Vessels from a Single Potter   58

3.4. Reasons Given for Why Zuza Consumers (*n* = 44 Households) Prefer Zuza and Ochollo District/*Dere* Pots   59

3.5. Reasons Given for Why Guyla Consumers (*n* = 51 Households) Prefer Birbir and Guyla Pots   59

3.6. Reasons Given for Why Etello Consumers (*n* = 52 Households) Prefer Birbir and Zada or Guyla Pots   60

3.7. Cost of Vessel Types in Gamo Society   63

3.8. Mean Number of Wealth Attributes among Each of the Three Gamo Castes   64

3.9. Average and Range of Vessel Cost among the Nonpotter Groups   64

4.1. Gamo Vessel Types and Their Corresponding Primary Use and Capacity   74

4.2. Percentage of Primary-Use Vessel Types and Frequency of Primary-Use Vessel Types (Compared to Total Frequency of the Vessel Types) in the Entire Village Assemblage in Three Gamo Villages   75

4.3. Percentage and Number of Primary-Use Vessel Types in Three Gamo Villages   76

5.1. Vessel Cost and Use-Life in Three Gamo Villages (Correlations in Bold Are Significant at the .05 Confidence Level)   93

5.2. Zuza's Vessel Types and Their Use-Lives, Associated Volume Measurements, and the Correlations between Use-Life and Volume (Correlations in Bold Are Significant at the .05 Confidence Level)   94

5.3. Guyla's Vessel Types and Their Use-Lives, Associated Volume Measurements, and the Correlations between Use-Life and Volume (Correlations in Bold Are Significant at the .05 Confidence Level)   94

5.4. Etello's Vessel Types and Their Use-Lives, Associated Volume Measurements, and the Correlations between Use-Life and Volume (Correlations in Bold Are Significant at the .05 Confidence Level)   95

5.5. Vessel Use-Life by Functional Type and Village   95

5.6. Vessel Volume by Functional Type and Village   97

5.7. Vessel Use-Life and Volume by Functional Type and by Village and Caste   97

5.8. Vessel Cost and Use-Life by Village and Caste (Correlations in Bold Are Significant at the .05 Confidence Level)   98

5.9. Vessel Use-Life and Volume by Functional Type and by Village and Economic Rank   99

5.10. Vessel Cost and Use-Life by Village and Economic Rank (Correlations in Bold Are Significant at the .05 Confidence Level)   100

6.1. Reasons Why Vessels Break, with Their Corresponding Frequency and Percentage   104

6.2. Absolute and Relative Frequencies of Materials Used for Mending Pots   105

6.3. Types, Functions, Frequencies, Percentages, and Costs of Mended Vessels by Village, Illustrating That the Nonpotter Village (Etello) Has a Higher Frequency of Mended Pots   107

6.4. Percentage and Frequency of Broken Zuza Vessel Types Reused for Secondary Functions, the Same Function as before They Broke, and All Functions   107

6.5. Percentage and Frequency of Broken Etello Vessel Types Reused for Secondary Functions, the Same Function as before They Broke, and All Functions   108

6.6. Percentage and Frequency of Broken Guyla Vessel Types Reused for Secondary Functions, the Same Function as before They Broke, and All Functions   108

6.7. Average Number of Vessels per Household Reused for Secondary Functions, the Same Function as before They Broke, and All Functions by Village and Caste   113

6.8. Average Number of Vessel Types per Household Reused for Secondary Functions, the Same Function as before They Broke, and All Functions by Village and Caste   113

6.9. Average Vessel Volume (l) per Household of Vessels Reused for Secondary Functions, the Same Function as before They Broke, and All Functions by Village and Caste   114

6.10. Average Number of Vessels per Household Reused for Secondary Functions, the Same Function as before They Broke, and All Functions by Village and Economic Rank   115

6.11. Average Number of Vessel Types per Household Reused for Secondary Functions, the Same Function as before They Broke, and All Functions by Village and Economic Rank   118

6.12. Average Vessel Volume (l) per Household of Vessels Reused for Secondary Functions, the Same Function as before They Broke, and All Functions by Village and Economic Rank   119

7.1. Percentage of Discarded Vessel Types in Three Gamo Villages   122

Acknowledgments

I first would like to thank the Gamo people for their graciousness in allowing us to enter their lives and for their patience concerning my questions about their household pottery. Before I started this research, three people, James Neely, Robert Hard, and Steven Brandt, offered me exceptional guidance and support as I worked through my different degrees and gave me field experiences to develop my skills as an archaeologist and ethnoarchaeologist. I would like to thank these three mentors for their patience and knowledge and for allowing me to work with each of them in the field. There are a number of people whom I would like to thank for reading various versions of this manuscript and for providing critical editing and positive suggestions. These people include Steve Brandt, Abe Goldman, Bill Marquardt, Lynette Norr, Michelle Pudlak, Ken Sassaman, Peter Schmidt, Kathy Weedman, and two anonymous reviewers. This research started in summer 1995, when Steve Brandt took me to Ethiopia. While surveying the different ethnic groups in southwestern Ethiopia, I was introduced to the wonders of the country and to the continued importance of pottery production and use among all these groups. Peter Schmidt demonstrated to me the powerful need to listen to the African voice and provided a sound methodological framework concerning my ethnoarchaeological research. His research has directly affected my research methodology looking at the development of the Gamo caste system, and so

I have deep gratitude for his insightful use of archaeology, ethnoarchaeology, and oral history to achieve a more enriching understanding of the African past. Kenneth Sassaman has given me continued positive support throughout the writing of the different drafts, and his encouragement and optimism are a source that I continue to tap. I also thank Melanie Brandt for producing wonderful maps and illustrations for this book. I thank James M. Skibo for his positive suggestions concerning different aspects of my ethnoarchaeological research. I would like to thank two anonymous reviewers for taking the time to provide me with insightful and positive suggestions.

There are several Ethiopian institutions that made field research possible. I would like to thank Ethiopia's Authority for Research and Conservation of Cultural Heritage (ARCCH), the Southern Nations Nationalities and Peoples Regional Government (SNNRP) Bureau of Culture and Information, and the Institute of Ethiopian Studies (IES) and the Herbarium at Addis Ababa University. Certain individuals in these institutions helped facilitate the field research, therefore I greatly appreciate the support of Jara Haile Mariam (ARCCH, Director), Yonis Bayene (ARCCH, Director of Archaeology), Mulageta Belay (ARCCH, Field Representative), Tadale Tekiewe (CRCCH, Field Representative), Muluneh Gabre-Mariam (Director of the Ethiopian National Museum), Kebbede Geleta (ARCCH, Maps/Geographer), Yohannes

Hadaya Kanate and Solomon Tesfy (Heads of the SNNRP Bureau of Culture and Information, Awassa Office), Filamon Hadro and Ababanu Agabebo (Heads of the SNNRP Bureau of Culture and Information, Arba Minch Office), Zenebe Bonja Bonke (Chencha official), Dr. Abdul Samed (IES, Director), Taddese Bereso (IES, Assistant Director), Adane Dinku (Department of Soil and Water Conservation, Chencha Office), and Sebsebe Demissew and Melaku Wondafrosh (Addis Ababa Herbarium).

My research assistants and friends made fieldwork enjoyable and profitable. These people include Berhano Wolde, Gezahegn Alemayehu, Getacho Girma, Paulos Dena, and Ato Saleh. There are numerous friends that made life in the Gamo region a more enriching experience, and these include Tihun Mulushewa, Chunga Yohannes, Tesefaye Mekuria, Daniel Tadesse, and Ato Nega. I also would like to thank Calche Cara and his wife, Goonashay Dara, for providing my wife and me with a home in Doko Shaye. During my fieldwork, the Catholic Missions provided invaluable help in repairing our truck, therefore I greatly appreciate the help that we received from Father Denis and the people working at the Chencha and Arba Minch Catholic Missions. I thank John Fleagle for allowing me to use his generator, which provided much-needed electricity.

I would like to thank some extraordinary friends I met in Ethiopia, who made life away from home a fantastic journey. I am grateful to Declan and Kate Conway and Ibrahim Labouts for being my friends and experiencing life with me in Addis Ababa. They kept me motivated and gave me strength to finish my fieldwork. A special thanks goes out to Carlo Iori, my friend, supporter, and facilitator, who made research in Ethiopia possible by providing a vehicle and then his continued support throughout the two years, as well as today.

There are a number of institutions that provided financial support for my research. I would like to thank the National Science Foundation for funding this research. I also extend my gratitude to the five anonymous National Science Foundation reviewers, who provided me with insightful comments concerning my research. I would like to thank the Center for African Studies for furnishing me a travel grant in 1995, so that I was able to conduct pre-dissertation research in Ethiopia. The University of Florida College of Liberal Arts and Sciences McGinty Fellowship provided me with a scholarship to finish the manuscript. Finally, I would like to thank the Charles H. Fairbanks Committee for awarding me a scholarship to write the initial draft of this manuscript.

My family has continually supported my work in archaeology with their positive belief in my success. My mother, Frances Arthur, and father, Ray C. Arthur, provided an endless amount of kindness and support. My sister, Ellen LeBlanc, and my brother-in-law, Steve LeBlanc, helped me in many ways while I was living in Ethiopia, and for this a special thanks goes out to them. My brother, Jeffrey S. Arthur, has given me an unlimited amount of encouragement to achieve my goals.

My last acknowledgment goes to my wife and best friend, Kathy Weedman, and to my daughter Hannah. Kathy has insightfully commented on drafts of this manuscript and has given me strength and motivation each and every day for the last 16 years. Hannah makes every day brighter and happier than the day before.

Living With Pottery

Introduction

A potter once lived, by herself, on top of Tsudo Mountain.
The potter collected the clay from the mountaintop and made her pots. One
day she tested the strength of her pots, by rolling a pot down from the top
of Tsudo Mountain. When the pot reached the bottom of the mountain, it
still had not broken. Knowing that she would not make a living because her
pots were too strong, she left Tsudo Mountain, and that is why today no
potters live in the Gamo ritual-political district of Doko.[1]

This traditional story of a Gamo potter living in the southern highlands of Ethiopia epitomizes the interrelationships among social identity, economic wealth, and occupation in Gamo society. The potter was born into a low caste, and she will remain in this low caste until her death. The story also reflects the economic alienation of potters in Gamo society. Potters and other artisans usually have households located on poor agricultural land that are clustered together away from higher-caste households. In the story, the potter lives by herself on top of a mountain, which is an area of high soil erosion and unsuitable for farming. Without farmland, the potter's only means of a livelihood is to produce and sell her pots. She needs consumers to continue purchasing her pots after they break, but because her pots are too strong, she is forced to live in another ritual-political district among the Gamo. This story illustrates how pottery interfaces with many of the social and economic aspects of Gamo life.

THE CERAMIC LIFECYCLE AND SOCIAL AND ECONOMIC VARIABILITY

As the Gamo parable shows us, pots have their own life histories: pots are born, go through multiple life experiences of use, and eventually are discarded at their death. In this ceramic ethnoarchaeological study, I use the life history approach to understand how the lives of the Gamo people are reflected in their ceramics.

As early as 1886, Cushing (1886) made use of ethnoarchaeology (first termed by J. W. Fewkes [1900]) by drawing parallels between living Zuni potters in the American Southwest and ceramic vessel types in archaeological assemblages thought to belong to the ancestors of the living Zuni. More recent work by ethnoarchaeologists acknowledges pottery as a complex technology and emphasizes that we must not oversimplify the variability expressed in the relationships between people and their pots (Rice 1996:191). Whether focusing on present or past societies and their pots, researchers should address the regional, social, and economic context of ceramics. To provide a deeper understanding of the relationship between Gamo people and their pottery, in chapter 1 of this volume I discuss the Gamo people in terms of their environment, agriculture, markets, caste groups, diet, and political organization.

Linton (1944), Matson (1965), and Shepard (1956) were the first researchers to discuss pottery in terms of its lifecycle, function, and technology. These early studies inspired archaeologists to use ceramics to go beyond defining culture areas and chronological sequences. Subsequently, a number of ceramic ethnoarchaeologists showed that ceramics could help to distinguish inter- and intrasite variation by attempting to explore the relationship between ceramic style and social complexity (e.g., David and Hennig 1972; Deal 1998; DeBoer and Lathrap 1979; Deetz 1968; Hill 1970; Longacre 1968, 1970; Schiffer and Skibo 1997; Skibo 1999). Documenting and understanding the complexity of social and economic variation through pottery suggest that there is a need for multiple lines of evidence to control for socioeconomic variation. For instance, lifecycle studies are important to archaeologists because archaeologists often assume that the artifacts were in a state of discard. However, depending on a person's occupation, one may discard one's primary-use vessels or reuse vessels for a secondary function. Thus, understanding how to interpret the different lifecycle stages in the archaeological record may allow archaeologists to make more meaningful inferences delineating the social and economic context of prehistoric and historic sites. The lifecycle analysis is a flexible approach to understanding that objects go through different contextual meanings during their various stages of procurement, production, distribution, use, mending, reuse, and discard.

Ceramic procurement, production, and distribution provide the foundation for the use and eventual discard of ceramic containers within a village setting. Differences in the availability, type, and quality of raw materials needed for ceramic production and variation in potter production techniques significantly affect the types of vessels produced, the quality of the vessels, and their availability to consumers (Schiffer and Skibo 1987). In addition, nontechnological factors such as proximity to markets, vessel cost, and social relationships between the potters and consumers differentially influence the production and use of pottery in a cultural system (Aronson et al. 1994; Gosselain 1998). To address these issues, in chapter 2 I examine the social, economic, and geological conditions in which potters are situated within Gamo society and how this influences their procurement activities and the types of vessels they manufacture. And in chapter 3 I present the technological, social, and economic circumstances influenc-

ing ceramic distribution, including an overview of consumers' preferences and purchasing practices.

Ethnoarchaeological studies of household pottery use have provided archaeologists with models applicable to archaeological household subsistence, demography, social and economic status, and social interaction (e.g., Deal 1985, 1998; Deal and Hagstrum 1995; Miller 1985; Nelson 1991; Stanislawski 1969). Following Braun's (1983) concept that ceramic vessels are tools that are directly associated with people's actions concerning food preparation, consumption, storage, and transport, ethnoarchaeological research has focused on ecology and the technology of food processing in relationship to vessel frequency and type (Arnold 1985:127–144; Arnold 1991:64–65; Nelson 1991:168–169). Just as production and distribution influence each other, pottery use is an outcome of social and economic relations. Ethnographic studies indicate that the types of vessels used in preparing, transporting, and serving specific foods may provide a better understanding of the relationship among ceramics, foods, and the distribution of power and status (Goody 1982:37). Furthermore, there have been a number of studies outlining that the different items used in food preparation reflect the quality of diet and wealth in agrarian societies (Castro et al. 1981; DeWalt 1983; Lewis 1951; Otto 1984). Archaeological research also suggests that different ceramic assemblages may indicate dietary differences between low- and high-status residences (Cowgill et al. 1984). In addition to possible dietary differences among the distinct socioeconomic groups, differences also may exist concerning frequency of ceramic forms, discard rates, and taboos and proscriptive rules that limit use and ownership. In chapter 4 I examine ecology, diet, and social-economic factors influencing the primary use of Gamo pots.

The study of ceramic use-life from villages around the world remains an important methodological tool for interpreting the frequencies of types in the archaeological record. The variation of use-life among different types allows archaeologists to suggest the duration of occupation and population of a site (Foster 1960; Longacre 1985; Rice 1987:300). Researchers have gathered use-life information from 18 different ethnic groups that vary in terms of the longevity of functional classes of pots. Many factors can affect the use-life of a pot, including household size (Tani 1994), vessel size (Birmingham 1975:384; David and Hennig 1972; DeBoer 1985; de la Torre and Mudar 1982; Longacre 1985:340; Shott 1996), production methods (Arnold 1991:72; Bankes 1985:275–276; Deal 1983:155; Foster 1960; Okpoko 1987:452), and use (Bankes 1985:272; Foster 1960; Reid 1989; Tani 1994). This suggests that the circumstances that determine pottery use-life are complex, thereby strengthening the argument made here that it is important to document the different ceramic lifecycle stages to explore a society's social and economic variability. Although the role of socioeconomic status is mentioned as a factor that influences ceramic use-life (e.g., Rice 1987:300; Shott 1996:480), I am not aware of any studies that directly address the relationship between socioeconomic status and ceramic use-life. However, in chapter 5 of this volume, I explore how vessel use-life in the village, caste, and economic wealth contexts is affected by factors such as vessel volume, function, cost, social status, and wealth, as well as frequency of use and the potter's production methods.

Vessel reuse and eventual discard also have important implications for archaeologists attempting to decipher subsistence, food processing, activity areas, socioeconomic status, and the interactions between potters and consumers (Aronson et al. 1994; Arnold 1985; Arnold 1991; Deal 1985, 1998; Deal and Hagstrum 1995; Hally 1983; Miller 1985; Nelson 1991; Schiffer 1972). Archaeologists often neglect to discuss mending and reuse in their analysis, yet ethnoarchaeologists document that once vessels are broken people frequently mend them for use for the same function or for different functions. Reuse of a vessel is dependent on many factors, including the occupation and status of the vessel's owner. For example, vessels may be reused because the owners are too impoverished to purchase new

vessels, or the vessel may be reused because the owner has an occupation in which the reuse of a vessel serves a useful secondary function such as grain storage for farmers or grog for potters. Furthermore, vessels may be placed in "dead storage," indicating that currently they are serving no function but in the future they may be used again (Nelson 1991:171). Ethnoarchaeological studies also address questions of discard patterning through observing social rules and the location of activity areas versus discard areas (Deal 1998:83–89; Lindahl and Matenga 1995:106; Miller 1985:70–71; Reina and Hill 1978:247; Weigand 1969:23). In chapter 6 I discuss mending and reuse beginning with the different ways vessels break and the types of pots that the Gamo mend. I discuss two different ways that the various Gamo social-economic groups reuse vessels after they break for the same function and/or reuse pots for a secondary function. Furthermore, in chapter 7 of this volume, I end my lifecycle analyses with a study of Gamo ceramic discard by different villages, caste groups, and economic groups in terms of the frequency, type, volume, and spatial locations of the discarded vessels.

Pots are moved to different locations depending on their lifecycle stage and the social and economic status of the user. This book examines the spatial location of pots within each stage of the ceramic lifecycle. One of the most important criteria concerning the spatial locations of the ceramic assemblages is the organization of the household compound. The spatial location of pottery vessels can leave information concerning human behavior and help address archaeological formation processes (Deal 1998; Schiffer 1972, 1983, 1987). The organization of pots within the compound and their associated features should help to determine if the household belongs to a potter or a consumer and its social and economic status.

Household pottery is a reflection of the social and economic relations between people, because it is used in every household and each vessel tells its own life story as it travels from person to person, thereby representing the people in its different lifecycle stages. Thus,

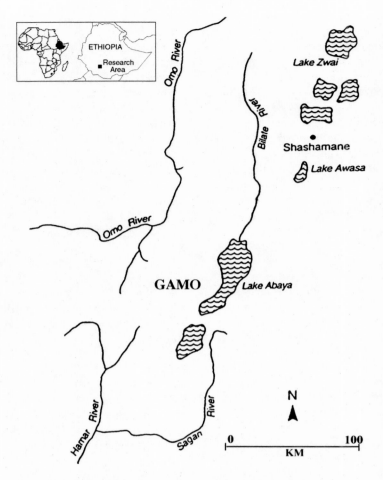

FIGURE I.1. Map of the Gamo region within Ethiopia and Africa.

household pottery is the perfect medium for exploring social and economic relationships. Therefore, my goal is to present a contemporary example that archaeologists can use in their pursuit of understanding the socioeconomic dimensions of each lifecycle stage.

THE LIFECYCLE APPROACH AND ETHNOARCHAEOLOGICAL METHODS

As the potter depended on her pots to break, archaeologists depend also on broken pots to help us understand social and economic variability. One of the most important aspects of ethnoarchaeology is to conduct research that will be useful to archaeologists as they are attempting to interpret their sites and material

culture (P. Arnold 2000:106; Arthur and Weedman 2005; Skibo 1992:16–17). Interpreting social and economic variation from pottery requires methods of analyses that are not direct or simplistic and requires linking the socioeconomic context with the ceramic lifecycle.

The Gamo are Omotic-speaking agriculturalists who live in the western highlands of the southern Ethiopian Rift Valley (Figure I.1). I chose the Gamo for my ethnoarchaeological research because they are one of the few peoples in the world among whom locally made pottery is a dominant material in their everyday life and has not been curtailed by the substitution of metal and plastic vessels.

They produce and use pottery on a daily basis for cooking, storing, serving, and transporting water and a variety of foods (Figure I.2; Arthur 1997, 2002a, 2003). At present, industrial vessels have not made a significant impact on household assemblages. The use of plastic water containers is just beginning to affect how people transport their daily water, especially in villages located near large towns. Plastic containers do not break as easily, and pottery transporting jars have a short use-life because people tend to drop their vessels when they slip and fall on the wet and slick footpaths, making plastic containers more popular. However, a 50-l plastic container costs approximately 25 birr (U.S.$4.00), whereas the average cost of a large jar is only 3.36 birr (U.S.$0.50). Therefore, most Gamo people continue to use pottery for the majority of their household needs rather than industrially produced wares.

Ethnoarchaeology undertaken in a society where people still use low-fired ceramics in everyday life provides a powerful contextual framework for archaeological inferences, especially because little behavioral information exists concerning the relationship among status, wealth, and household pottery. I believe the Gamo people of southwestern Ethiopia offer a unique opportunity for testing a range of hypotheses encompassing each lifecycle stage.

I spent approximately 20 months (September 1996–April 1998) living with the Gamo to understand the causes of ceramic variation within Gamo society. To provide archaeologists with a useful framework to analyze the social and economic variation, I collected information on 1,058 vessels from 60 households in three villages representing individuals and families of all the caste and socioeconomic groups in Gamo society.

Rapport and Village Selection

When I first arrived in the Gamo region it was important to me to develop a rapport with participants, as is essential to any ethnoarchaeological study (Arthur and Weedman 2005; Brumbach and Jarvenpa 1990; Gould 1971). I established rapport by hiring local

FIGURE I.2. A Gamo family with a portion of their household ceramic assemblage.

assistants, spending time with elders in the communities, conducting a census, and participating in community activities throughout my research study. I first discussed my research with the community elders to create awareness of my study, to ascertain social and economic information about villages, and to receive permission to work in their village. I found that most informants reacted very positively when I respected their schedules by making appointments with them and formally requesting their participation in the project rather than just assuming they had the time and interest to partake in my study.

Studies involving multivillage comparisons have led to an improved perspective concerning different stages of the ceramic lifecycle, use-life, and household and regional social and economic variation (Arnold 1991; Aronson et al. 1994; Deal 1998; DeBoer and Lathrap 1979; Gosselain 1998; Hayden and Cannon 1983; Longacre 1985, 1991; Longacre and Stark 1992; Nelson 1991; Reina and Hill 1978). Thus, I began my research by surveying the Gamo communities of Doko, Dorze, Ochollo, Kogo, Zada, and Borada in search of three villages, which I could use as an analytical basis for understanding the relationship between Gamo people and their pottery. During the survey, I compiled information in various villages concerning the different types of ceramic vessels; the presence of potters, farmers, and other artisans; and differences in ecological zones, crops, and foods. Subsequently, I selected the three Gamo villages of Etello, Guyla, and Zuza for in-depth study because I wanted to study pottery in diverse settings that included villages with resident and nonresident potters, villages in different ecological zones, and villages that were represented by peoples of varying social status, that is, caste groups.

One component of my research addressed whether differences occurred between the ceramic assemblages of pottery-producing villages, such as Guyla and Zuza, and non-pottery-producing villages, such as Etello. Previous ethnographic studies have found that non-pottery-producing villages have a larger number of vessels because of stockpiling (Aronson et al. 1994:101; Nelson 1991:171; Tani 1994:56). In order to test if the Gamo exhibit a similar pattern to the previous research, I investigated how they distributed their pottery in relation to these two village types. However, as I will demonstrate in the following chapters, in Etello, a non-pottery-producing Gamo village, households do not stockpile and have a smaller average household ceramic assemblage than pottery-producing villages.

The villages of Guyla and Etello are located in a highland environment (2,300–3,000 m), while Zuza is located in a lowland environment (1,500–2,300 m). The ecological setting of a Gamo village and its associated resources influence the types and number of ceramic containers that households use. Differences in village ecology and available foodstuffs affect the types of cooking vessels and their use within a village. The Gamo region is extremely mountainous, and the production

of agricultural crops corresponds to specific ecological zones governed largely by altitude. Researchers have not systematically explored the variability in ceramic use between settlements or socioeconomic households where people grow different crops in distinct ecological zones. Farmers located in different ecological zones often grow different types of crops because of environmental restrictions such as soil type and water availability. If we understand the movement of crops between villages located in different ecological zones and how people use ceramics to process, store, and transport these specific foods, then archaeologists will be better able to document socioeconomic variation based on ceramic function.

Each village I studied has a unique combination of individuals with different social and economic statuses. The Gamo are a three-tiered caste society, and in the village of Guyla all three caste groups are represented (*mala* farmers, *mana* potters, and *degala* hide workers), while in Zuza (*mala* farmers and *mana* potters) and Etello (*mala* farmers and *degala* hide workers) there are only two caste groups represented in each village. Other researchers have studied the relationship between ceramics and caste societies (i.e., Kramer 1997; Miller 1985; Sinopoli 1999), but there has not been a systematic study looking at the visibility of a caste system or an economic hierarchy based on a systematic study of each of the ceramic lifecycle stages. Caste membership in Gamo society is ascribed, endogamous, and occupational and has restrictions on commensality and concepts of purity and pollution. This study investigates the profound affect the caste system has on ceramic procurement, production, distribution, use, mending, reuse, and discard.

Village Census
After selecting the villages of Etello, Guyla, and Zuza for in-depth studies, I mapped each entire village and obtained census information from each household. During this time, I explained my research objectives, methodology, and the types of knowledge I wished the

individuals to share and allowed the members of the households to ask any questions and address any issues that concerned them.

I solicited information about each household, including members' names, clan, caste group, and the primary occupation of the head male and female of the household compound, as well as the other occupations conducted by household individuals. To assess the economic wealth of households, I also inquired about how many landholdings each owned and where they were located; the number of houses they owned; the type of crops they grew; where they obtained the majority of their food (i.e., the market or their farm); which markets they went to; and how many and what type of livestock they owned. The last part of the census questions pertained to the consumers' opinions concerning Gamo pottery. I asked which pottery they purchased (i.e., village or region) and what they thought was the best village or region for pottery production and why (i.e., answers usually referred to the work, clays, or firing process).

Household Pottery Study

After the census was completed, I chose 20 household compounds from each of the three villages to complete in-depth analyses of the ceramic assemblages. In each village, I stratified the sample to include the different caste groups. The only two conditions that were not random were that the households had to consist of the different caste and socioeconomic groups. I spent one day at each of the 60 household compounds interviewing the occupants about their ceramics and measuring and photographing every vessel.

I interviewed the head female of each household, as she was usually the person who purchased and used the vessels. At first, I used questionnaires to standardize my results, but as the research progressed I did not have to rely on the questionnaires and expanded questions as issues came forth. After each vessel was brought out into the compound, I would ask the informant about the history of each vessel, including, How old is the vessel? Where did you purchase the vessel, and which

village or region produced the vessel? and How much did the vessel cost? Informants also were asked to identify where each vessel was stored to document spatial changes in the location of vessels relative to their lifecycle (use, reuse, and discard) stages. I recorded the exact location of each vessel, including its specific placement within or adjacent to buildings and other features, as well as the specific function of buildings (e.g., kitchen, storage, weaving, or general living).

I recorded the use-life information for each vessel beginning with its production and ending when the vessel broke or was still being used when the interview was conducted. I wanted to know if the vessel was broken; if the vessel was broken, when and how it broke; and how the vessel was used before and after it broke. I consider primary-use pots as vessels that were not broken and were being used for their original function(s). Reuse vessels are broken pots that were reused for some function, either the original or a secondary function, before the vessel broke. Provisionally discarded pots were broken and at the time of analysis were not being used for any function, nor did the informant have a function in mind for the future.

After the vessel information was conducted, my assistant and I measured and photographed each vessel. Archaeologists use form to infer whether a vessel was used for serving, cooking, or storage (Arthur 2001; Braun 1980, 1983; Nelson and LeBlanc 1986; Plog 1980; Sassaman 1993; Steponaitis 1983). Each whole and broken vessel was measured within the household compound for rim diameter (both interior and exterior), rim thickness and height, neck diameter and height, vessel height (both interior and exterior), height from rim to maximum diameter, height from maximum diameter to base, vessel circumference and diameter at the maximum diameter of each vessel, and base diameter at its maximum point. In addition, I documented for each vessel the type of rim (i.e., direct, concave, or convex), the presence or absence of a base ring, handles, and interior and exterior decoration. The analysis of vessel form provides information concerning the variability and strength of vessel forms and how they are linked to different uses. In addition, based on the measurements from each vessel, vessel volume was gathered to determine the accuracy of earlier studies that suggest a relationship between volume and household population (Nelson 1981; Tani 1994; Turner and Lofgren 1966). The formula used for calculating the volumes of spherical vessels is $V = 4/3\pi r^3$ (Rice 1987:221). The formula used for calculating the volumes of ellipsoid vessels (i.e., *bache* or baking plates) is $V = 4/3\pi$ Vertical axis × Larger horizontal axis × Smaller horizontal axis (Rice 1987:221).

Gamo Potter Interviews

I conducted interviews with Gamo potters during two phases of my research. Initially, I interviewed potters during my survey of Gamo communities to understand the variation concerning pottery manufacture occurring in different Gamo regions. Later, during my in-depth studies in three Gamo villages, I also interviewed resident potters concerning the social and technological issues relating to ceramic procurement, production, and distribution. Furthermore, research focusing on Gamo potters allowed me to understand how the manufacturing and distribution of pots influence their use, reuse, and discard patterns.

In addition, to direct observations of potters producing their wares, I used open-ended interviews with the potters, and so each interview was structured differently. However, questions usually included the following: What village do you come from? (Gamo society is virilocal); From whom and at what age did you learn pottery production? Do you produce the vessels individually or with other people? and At which markets do you sell your vessels? In addition to documenting the production process, I investigated the potters' perceptions concerning the nontechnological and technological factors that influence the production process, such as (1) the clay sources and their use, owner, cost, and location; (2) the preferred clay sources and reasons why the potters prefer a given source; and (3) the

markets at which they sold their wares (Aronson et al. 1994). Additional information was collected on the fuelwoods used to fire the vessels; Adane Dinku from the Ministry of Agriculture, Department of Soil and Water Conservation, in Chencha and Dr. Sebsebe Demissew from the Addis Ababa University Herbarium identified the scientific taxonomy of the fuelwood samples I collected.

From the preceding methodological discussion, it should be clear that ethnoarchaeological research has the potential to make a substantial contribution to ceramic studies. In deriving social-economic information from pottery, it is especially important that the ethnoarchaeologist observe and that the archaeologists consider the life history of vessels in their specific social-economic household and village contexts.

PREMISE

The parable at the beginning of this chapter tells us the social and economic story of a Gamo potter and points to the life history of pots. From the time the potter produces and distributes her pots to the time the consumers use and discard their pots, each pot moves through a range of social and economic contexts that help to define Gamo society.

The stages of a pot's lifecycle are intertwined. Ceramic procurement, production, and distribution provide the foundation for the use, reuse, and eventual discard of ceramic containers within a village setting. Archaeologists must determine which household or community of people produced the pottery they find, which has important implications for understanding the social, economic, and political relationships between different households and communities. Each stage of the lifecycle reflects decisions made by specific individuals in a society (producers and consumers) and the socioeconomic context of those individuals. Demonstrating the impact that intervillage, social, and economic relations have on pottery vessels as they move from their birth to their death is a complex undertaking. Attempting to understand this complexity in the past provides an even more daunting task for archaeologists. Yet it is my goal in this volume to demonstrate to archaeologists that an ethnoarchaeological study of Gamo pottery can provide archaeologists with a framework for interpreting the behavior behind ceramic variation and distribution in archaeological assemblages.

Note

1. The story was told to me by a *maka* (a Gamo religious leader) living in Etello, a non-pottery-producing village and one of the three villages discussed in this analysis.

I

The Gamo

The Gamo people of southern Ethiopia, some 600,000 people strong, inhabit the mountains west of the Rift Valley lakes of Abaya and Chamo (Hasen 1996). The Gamo highlands rise from the Rift Valley lakes at an elevation of 1,160 m to a height of 3,540 m at Mount Tola (Figure 1.1). The dramatic rise of the Gamo highlands from the Rift Valley lakes of Abaya and Chamo provides a diversity in ecological conditions that affects regional climates and agricultural potential. The average rural population density is high, with some places exceeding 200 persons per square kilometer. The Gamo territory and peoples are subdivided into *deres* or districts, with each *dere* divided into *mota* or subdistricts, and *guta* or villages that are led by elected and hereditary elders (Abélès 1979, 1981; Cartledge 1995; Olmstead 1975; Sperber 1975). The focus of this book is on the ceramic assemblages of the three villages of Zuza, Guyla, and Etello. Each village exhibits differences in physical and social environments, and below I elaborate on their environments, agricultural production, markets, social organization, diet, and political organization to provide a basis for interpreting their residential pottery.

ENVIRONMENT AND AGRICULTURE
The Gamo region is extremely mountainous, and the production of agricultural crops corresponds to distinct ecological zones governed largely by altitude (Figure 1.2). The Gamo highlands have four major altitudinal

agroecozones traditionally identified in Amharic (the national language of Ethiopia) as (1) *qolla*, 1,160–1,500 m; (2) *woyna dega*, 1,500–2,300 m; (3) *dega*, 2,300–3,000 m; and (4) *wurch*, above 3,000 m (Cartledge 1995). However, the Gamo classify two distinct ecological zones, the *dega*, considered the highland region located between 2,300 and 3,000 m, and the *baso*, the lowlands situated between 1,160 and 2,300 m. These agroecozones vary in their annual amount of rainfall, which is dispersed over two biannual rainfall periods. The small rains occur from March to May, and the big rains occur from June to September, but it is also possible for the small rains to merge into the big rains, causing continuous precipitation from March to September (Westphal 1975:22).

In the *baso* zone, the principal crops are wheat (*Triticum savitum*), an indigenous Ethiopian grain called teff (*Eragrostis teff*), maize (*Zea mays*), and coffee (*Coffee arabica*). Secondary crops include enset (*Ensete ventricosum*) and barley (*Hordeum vulgare*). Enset is an endemic plant of Ethiopia that is farmed throughout southern Ethiopia. It is a large fibrous-leaf plant with the edible portions consisting of the roots, pseudostems, and leaf stems (Figures 1.3–1.4; Shack 1966; Westphal 1975:123). Enset is grown in every ecological zone from 1,200 to 3,100 m (Brandt et al. 1997:5; Huffnagel 1961; Westphal 1975). Many researchers believe that southwestern Ethiopia is possibly the region

FIGURE 1.1. View of the Gamo highlands overlooking the escarpment that extends down the Rift Valley and Lake Abaya.

FIGURE 1.2. A farmer with his plow and enset, an indigenous staple, in the background.

FIGURE 1.3. A woman scraping the corm of the enset.

FIGURE 1.4. A woman grinding enset to prepare it for making fermented enset bread, *ooetsa*.

where people began domesticating enset (Brandt 1984, 1997; Brandt and Fattovich 1990; Harlan 1969, 1992; Sauer 1952; Shack 1963; Simmons 1960; Vavilov 1926). However, no archaeological research to date has been conducted in the region to understand the development of enset and other types of food production.

In the *dega* zone, where the majority of people live, enset, barley, and Ethiopian cabbage (*Brassica integrifolia var. carinata*) are the primary crops. Secondary crops include Oromo potato (*Coleus edulis L.*) and castor bean (*Ricinus communis L.*).

The types of agricultural products greatly affect the types of pottery used in Gamo households. The variation in environmental zones and agricultural production requires regional differences in ceramic forms to accommodate processing, cooking, serving, and storage needs. Thus potters living in the different Gamo regions specialize in the production of different vessel types instigated by local consumer demand, which is contingent on variation in agricultural production.

MARKETS

The Gamo periodic markets are an important part of Gamo life for the dispersal of goods including pottery, craft goods, agricultural products, and to a limited extent imported national goods such as glass, plastics, and clothing throughout the landscape (Figure 1.5). The Gamo have an organized market system. The larger regional markets such as Bodo (Dorze), Tuka (Chencha), Pango (Doko Mesho), Zada,

FIGURE 1.5. View of the large Bodo (Dorze) weekly market.

and Ezo have permanent structures used by vendors, as well as sellers spreading their goods out on cloths or directly on the ground (Jackson 1971). People will barter with goods, but they also buy items using the Ethiopian national currency (birr). The use of the national currency has increased from 30 years ago when the Gamo market system had a limited participation in the cash economy (Jackson 1971). Jackson (1971) argues that the larger markets of Chencha and Ezo opened about 100 years ago, when the Gamo region was incorporated into the national political and economic systems as a result of Menelik II's conquest of the region in the 1890s. However, based on oral history in the Ezo region, I have located the original market site in Ezo, named Konafa, which may precede Menelik's conquest. This site had at least 14 permanent structures associated with the market that wealthy vendors used on market days. The Konafa market in Ezo was forced to move in the 1890s when Menelik II took control over the Gamo. Therefore, based on oral history, large markets occurred before the movement

of the Amhara people into the Gamo region, which indicates they have a considerable time depth.

Presently there are two types of markets in Gamo: regional and local. People living within a *mota*/subdistrict will visit the local market on specific days of the week. Here, local potters sell to their patrons, either new patrons or patrons who have been purchasing or exchanging food with specific potter families for generations, such as the case with the market in Leesha. The larger regional markets in Gamo also are organized according to the days of the week. Large markets in the central Gamo region such as Bodo (Dorze), Tuka (Chencha), Pango (Doko Mesho), Zada, and Ezo (Figure 1.6) are not open on the same day if they are located near one another. Furthermore, each of the larger markets specializes in specific products (Jackson 1971).

The only regional markets that are on the same day are Ezo and Bodo, which are 18 km apart and specialize in different materials. Bodo is known for its cotton, as many of the weavers live in and around Bodo. Ezo, how-

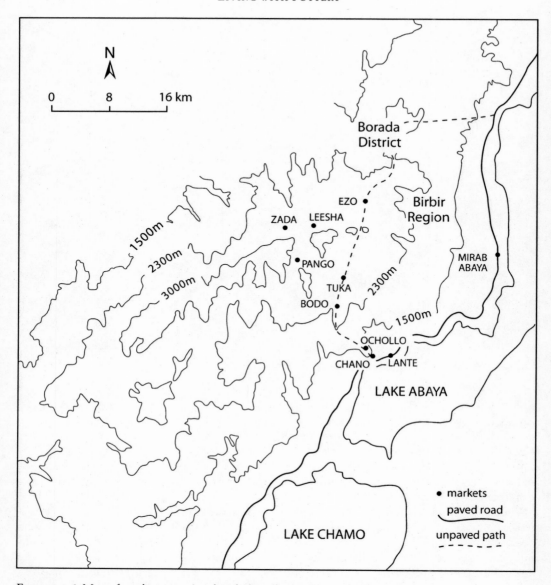

FIGURE 1.6. Map of markets associated with the villages of Zuza, Etello, and Guyla.

ever, is known for its pottery, because Birbir potters sell there, as well as potters from Zada, Leesha, and Borada. In addition, Ezo is known for selling high-quality milk, which Jackson (1971) also documented 30 years ago. Tuka's (Chencha) market has a variety of materials present, but it specializes in selling foods from the lowlands (e.g., bananas, maize, sweet potatoes, teff, etc.) and highlands (e.g., enset, barley, wheat, potatoes, cabbage,

etc.). In addition, potters from both lowland and highland areas sell their wares at the Tuka market.

Because markets are specialized to some extent, consumers decide to travel to markets based on the type of products they want to purchase. Some markets have cheaper prices for particular goods or better products compared to other markets. The potters take their wares to the market by tying the vessels together with enset rope and placing them upon their heads or upon a horse or donkey. Men and/or women transport the vessels to the weekly markets. Women will usually stay home if they have small children, because some markets are over 10 km one way from their household, which is too far for small children to walk.

The markets are the link between pottery producers and consumers, and they determine how pottery is dispersed over the landscape, for it is the markets where potters and consumers sell and purchase their pots. It is also at markets where the Gamo engage in social activities, such as trading, discussing local problems, and meeting potential spouses, an avenue for linking Gamo households.

SOCIAL ORGANIZATION AND CASTES

One of the most important and more difficult analyses in household archaeology involves interpreting the social position of each household. The analysis of socioeconomic levels within households is promising because many of the production and consumption activities take place within the household area and households differ based on specific cultural circumstances (caste, class, or occupation, to name only a few). In addition to indicating the specific socioeconomic position, the analysis at the household level allows for a larger view of the social, political, and economic conditions and changes that occur within agrarian societies (Smith 1987:298). Household ceramics are closely linked with the status of the household, because ceramics directly reflect the daily food preparations of all members of the household. Therefore, this ethnoarchaeological study of the Gamo, who have a strict social hierarchy, provides a valuable model for interpreting household social status in the archaeological record.

There is a debate concerning whether castes exist in Africa, as some researchers argue that castes can only be applied to southern Asia, where they are associated with the Hindu religion (Dumont 1957; Leach 1962). However, others clearly have demonstrated that castes are not confined to southern Asia but, rather, are present in many regions of the world including Africa (Haberland 1984; Hocart 1950; Hutton 1963; Levine 1974; Lewis 1970; Maquet 1970; Shack 1964, 1966; Sterner and David 1991; Vaughan 1970). It is difficult to proceed with a generalized notion of how to define castes, because the definition is dependent on spatial and temporal context. Most researchers agree that different occupations are generally associated with different castes. Caste groups are endogamous, and each caste group ranks differently on a hierarchical scale. Castes also are associated with purity and impurity, and each caste has its own perceptions and traditions associated with the caste system.

There also is debate in Ethiopia concerning the term to be used to refer to minority artisan groups; for instance, Cerulli (1956:61–62) uses the term *submerged*, Hamer (1987) simply refers to the division between cultivators and artisans as a twofold grouping, and more recently Pankhurst (1999, 2001:18–22) refers to them as "marginalised minorities." My work among the Gamo supports the work of other researchers (Cartledge 1995:40–43; Levine 1974:39; Lewis 1970; Silverman 1994; Todd 1978a, 1978b), and I propose that the Gamo have a strict social hierarchy and exemplify a caste system or what the Gamo term *burro*. One's caste membership in Gamo society is ascribed at birth, and there is nothing that one can do to change one's status. The northern and central regions of Gamo have a social organization that entails a rigid caste system consisting of three castes: in order of rank, (1) *mala* (Figure 1.7), (2) *mana* (Figure 1.8), and (3) *degala* (Figure 1.9). In the southern Gamo region, there are only two castes, *mala* and *mana*. The *mala* caste is the highest-status caste group. The *mala* caste members are farmers, weavers, merchants, elected officials, and sacrificers. While the men in the *mala* caste engage in the above activities, *mala* women usually farm, spin cotton, and produce beer. The women *mana* caste members are predominantly potters. Men who are in the *mana* caste farm if they are fortunate to own farmland; otherwise they help with different stages of pottery production (see chap. 2 for further discussion). The *degala* caste

FIGURE 1.7. A member of the *mala* caste who is also a *maka*, a person who sacrifices animals and prays for the people and their land.

is the lowest-status caste group, and *degala* men work as ironworkers, hide workers, and ground stone makers. *Degala* women spin cotton, decorate gourds, carry items to and from the market, and, if they have been granted farmland, help with farming activities.

Each caste is endogamous, and there are strict taboos against engaging in sexual intercourse with, living with, eating with, or marrying someone from another caste. If a taboo is broken, then the parties are ostracized from society. In addition, it is thought that if a person from the *mala* caste has sexual intercourse with either a *mana* or a *degala* member, death will occur for both individuals. Presently, this taboo is strictly enforced. I witnessed the punishment of a *mana* woman for flirting with members of the *mala* caste while she was ine-

briated. The woman was publicly ridiculed and then ordered temporarily to leave the village as part of her punishment. The Gamo feel that if a person from the high caste becomes intimate with a lower-caste person, such as a potter, then his or her fields and livestock will become infertile and sickness and death could come to the higher, *mala* caste group's family. When cultural rules are broken, the ancestors are upset and potentially cause disharmony, infertility, and illness. In addition, the artisan caste members are not allowed to attend important ceremonial functions or to eat with the higher *mala* caste members, because of this fear of being polluted by the lower-caste groups. This fear of pollution is even witnessed in the death of an individual, because *mala* caste members forbid the artisans from being buried within the *mala* cemetery, and artisans must bury their dead within their household land or in a separate artisan cemetery.

Another characteristic of the Gamo caste system is the economic relationship between the *mala* and artisans. This patron–client system (*mayla*) transpires between potter and consumer. In the past, before the integration of an Ethiopian currency, *mana* and *mala* individuals exchanged pots for food, but presently there is a mixture of exchange for food and purchasing with birr. However, the system remains as an important means of social and economic integration between the two castes (i.e., *mala* and *mana*). Neighbors of a potter usually will trade crops for the potter's vessels, which is an important component in the patron–client relationship because many potters do not have farmland. Thus, many potters are dependent on their *mala* clients. Hence, potters and other artisans have a less varied diet than the *mala* households because most do not own farmland.

DIET

There is a strong association between the use of pottery and food in Gamo society. Different ceramic forms are used to process a variety of Gamo foods for everyday consumption. Before discussing Gamo ceramics and their role in demonstrating regional, social, and

FIGURE 1.8. A member of the *mana* caste producing her wares.

FIGURE 1.9. A member of the *degala* caste showing the abject poverty of his household.

economic conditions, an understanding of the basic types of foods eaten in Gamo society is necessary.

The Gamo diet consists of a range of foods but depends, in part, on the seasonal availability of specific crops. The majority of meals eaten throughout the Gamo region are made with enset, which is available throughout the year. Different parts of the enset plant, which can be fermented, boiled, and/or roasted, are processed and prepared for making specific meals (Figures 1.3–1.4). One of the most common foods is the corm of a young enset plant. The Gamo prepare the enset corm by cutting it into a number of pieces and boiling it (*chaday*), usually with either cabbage or potatoes; also garlic and/or onions may be mixed into the cooking pot. Another common type of meal is prepared by fermenting enset by burying it for seven days, then trampling it with their feet, and then burying it again for another seven days. After two weeks, the enset has fermented and is made into bread that is cooked or mixed with a combination of grains (e.g., barley, wheat, maize, or sorghum) to make *ooetsa*. The Gamo cook all types of breads on the earthenware baking plate (*bache*). In addition, *enchila* (highland name) or *kashca* (lowland name) is made with fermented enset (*zaluma*) by mixing it with barley, wheat, maize, or sorghum flour. The *enchila/kashca* are formed into oval shapes, and to prevent them from sticking to the vessel wall, the cooking pot is lined with enset leaves. Another form of food prepared with enset is *patella*, which the Gamo make from enset boiled with salt and cabbage or potatoes. Gamo people also use enset to make *etema*, consisting of a white paste produced by squeezing the liquid out of the enset pulp. The Gamo consider *etema* the most prized part of the enset plant. It is eaten at special occasions, including births, feasts, and circumcisions (Cartledge 1995:187; Figure 1.2).

As mentioned above, grains such as barley, wheat, maize, teff, flax, and sorghum are grown and eaten by the Gamo. In the highland areas, most meals are made with barley and wheat, whereas in the lowland areas, maize and sorghum are more common. Gamo people consider barley the *baira* (senior) of cereals because of its importance in indigenous rituals, but wheat is a close second because of its use in Christian rituals (Christmas and saint days; Sperber 1975:212). An important barley food prepared and eaten during Meskal (Ethiopian New Year), Easter, local ritual-political feasts, and weddings is *gordo*, which is similar to porridge. The preparation of *gordo* is intensive. First, the barley must be pounded with a pestle in a wooden mortar to remove the husk. Then the barley is ground three or four times on a grinding stone to produce coarse flour. Every time the barley is ground on the grinding stone, it is sieved through a small woven basket (*zazarey*). After the barley is made into flour, water is boiled in a cooking pot, and milk and a small amount of the flour are added and stirred with a bamboo stick. Eventually all of the flour is added, and it is cooked for approximately one hour. Then the *gordo* is taken out of the cooking pot, placed in a large serving bowl, and mixed with butter. One of the most common forms of preparing and eating grains is by roasting them (*shasha*) and serving them in a ceramic bowl with coffee.

Meat is not a common food for the rural Gamo people, but it is an important food during religious holidays. Different animals are eaten during different holidays. A bull is purchased communally by several families and killed by the eldest of a lineage. The meat is usually prepared as a spicy stew (*ayshow wat*) or eaten raw with butter and spices. Chicken is eaten at Christmas and Easter in the form of a spicy stew (*cutoe wat*). Meat is an expensive item for the rural people of Gamo, and even during religious holidays, the artisans usually cannot afford to purchase meat. It is customary for the *mala* to give the *degala* the cow's head during Meskal. If the artisans do not receive meat from the *mala*, then they usually purchase with other artisans a bag of barley or maize, which they prepare and eat together.

Butter in Gamo society represents a direct measure of status and wealth and is tied to Gamo symbolic life. Households that own cows are the main producers of butter in

Gamo villages. The milk is separated after one week; the thick curd is placed in a jar, and then the jar orifice is securely covered with enset leaves. The jar is rocked back and forth in the compound for approximately eight hours. Potters make a small dimple in the upper portion of the jar neck so that the consumer can punch this dimple out and use it to see when the milk has changed to butter. Butter in Gamo society is placed on the heads of ritual leaders during both life and death ceremonies (Freeman 1997; Olmstead 1997:41, 49, 144–145; Sperber 1974:60–61).

Other types of foods cooked individually or in combination with other foods are cabbage and potatoes. Whereas cabbage and potatoes represent lower-income foods, the production and consumption of butter (oysa), beer (farso), and coffee (tukay) are associated with wealthy, high-status households. Beer is produced using a number of different grains such as barley, wheat, and maize. The grain is ground on a combination of grinding stones. First, water is boiled, then poured over the flour and stirred, and finally left to cool. Then it is left to ferment for five days, after which it is ready to be consumed.

Coffee is made by roasting and then grinding the beans on a mortar or a grinding stone. Water is boiled with ground coffee beans over the hearth. It is common in Gamo society to add salt to the coffee, instead of sugar. In addition, it is customary for a person to be served three cups of coffee in one sitting.

Food such as enset, potatoes, bread, porridge, and boiled enset are spiced with a liquid sauce (datsa), which is a combination of garlic, ginger, onion, red chili peppers, and salt. These foods are ground intensively on a special small grinding stone and put in a small pottery jar with water or milk. This jar is then sealed with an enset leaf. Peas and beans are also common foods in the Gamo diet. Lightly boiled peas and beans served with coffee in a small serving bowl is especially common. Another form of preparing beans and peas is called eretza, which is made by roasting them separately on a baking plate. After they are roasted they are mixed together and ground four times into a porridge. Then they are boiled with water and milk and cooked for ten minutes.

Most Gamo peoples eat products produced from enset; however, in the lowlands this diet is supplemented with maize and sorghum, and in the highlands, by barley and wheat. The types of foods prepared in each household are a reflection of the household's social and economic status. If people have the economic means, they are able to vary their diet by visiting markets and purchasing foods not grown locally. Although the market system expands the distribution of agricultural goods, most artisans subsist off the produce grown in their gardens or given in exchange for their craft goods. The environment, agricultural production, and social organization are interwoven and are directly reflected in the quantity and types of ceramic vessels in Gamo households.

POLITICAL ORGANIZATION

The strong political hierarchy within Gamo society should be clearly seen through the household assemblage of ceramics, because the variation in political power provides access to a different range of consumable goods and feasting responsibilities. There are several elected and hereditary leadership positions in Gamo society, including, in hierarchical order, the kao, dana, uduga, maka, and halaka (Abélès 1979, 1981; Bureau 1978, 1981; Halperin and Olmstead 1976; Olmstead 1975; Sperber 1975). A Gamo political leader (i.e., kao, dana, maka, uduga, or halaka) must be a baira, who is the senior male in his family and sometimes a member of a senior clan (Sperber 1975:212). These leaders settle disputes, perform sacrifices for the ancestors, and pray for the people.

The halaka has received the most attention from previous researchers (Abélès 1978, 1979, 1981; Freeman 1997; Halperin and Olmstead 1976; Sperber 1975). A halaka has been described as a man appointed by district assemblies, and he must be circumcised, married, wealthy, and morally respected (Sperber 1975:215). Halakas usually do not desire the appointment because becoming a halaka requires expending a substantial amount of

TABLE I.I. Social Hierarchies and Their Economic Associations in Gamo Society

CASTE	POSSIBLE SOCIAL LEADERS	POSSIBLE OCCUPATIONS
Mala	• *kao* • *dana* • *maka* • *uduga* • *halaka*	• farmer • merchant • government official • weaver • cotton spinner • market carrier
Mana	• *halaka*	• potter • farmer • cotton spinner • market carrier
Degala	• *halaka*	• hideworker • smith • ground stone producer • farmer • cotton spinner • market carrier

resources; however, it is taboo to refuse (Sperber 1975:215). Becoming a *halaka* is expensive because the candidate must give a series of feasts, one at his house and the other in the area of community gatherings or *debusha* (Freeman 1997:352). The last feast occurs when the *halaka* becomes an *ade* or *halaka-as-man*, where he provides a feast or senior's feast (*baira musa*) for four days that consists of beer and ceremonial Gamo foods (Freeman 1997). Pottery is an integral material for conducting *halaka* feasts, as it is the use of vessels that helps ferment the beer and cook the food given to the feast's participants. In addition, ceramic vessels generally are used to serve the food at the feasts, especially because people eat communally from large serving bowls.

The *mala* caste controls the Gamo political, economic, and religious systems (Table I.I). The *mana* and *degala* castes have no political control in Gamo society, except some *mana* and *degala* members may choose their own *halaka* (village sacrificer), but this *halaka* does not have the political influence of the *mala halaka*.

Gamo political organization is tied to the economic wealth of the household, especially regarding the induction of *halakas*. The "catching" of a *halaka* by the Gamo people is a result of his well-established reputation within the society—but also his wealth and whether the people believe he can afford to orchestrate the ceremonial feasts that are required in becoming a *halaka*. The economic wealth of a *halaka* and other households is signified through the quantity, types, and use of their household ceramic assemblages (Arthur 2003).

THE STUDY VILLAGES
I conducted the majority of my fieldwork in three villages: Zuza, Guyla, and Etello (Figure 1.10). This section discusses the context of each village concerning its environment, agriculture, markets, social organization and castes, diet, and political organizations.

Zuza, Ochollo
Zuza is located at an elevation of 2,100 m in the *baso* zone. It is located within Ochollo

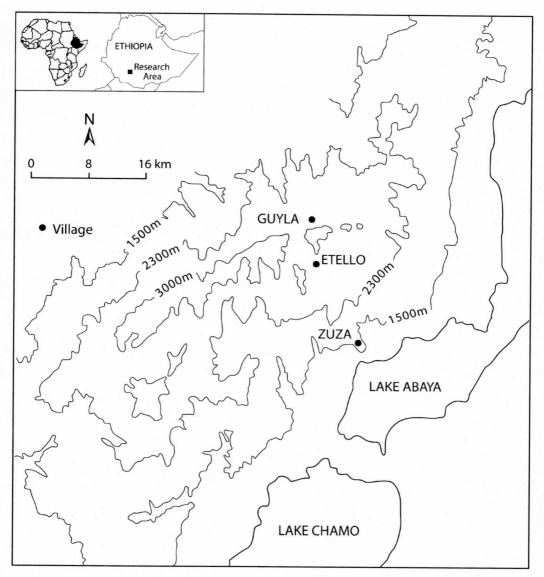

FIGURE 1.10. Map of the village locations of Zuza, Etello, and Guyla within the Gamo region.

district on a steep ridge overlooking the Rift Valley. The geographical location of Zuza on a hilltop restricts the size of the agricultural gardens adjacent to the households. Zuza garden plots consist of enset, corn, cabbage, peppers, and coffee. Thus, meals in Zuza mainly consist of enset, sweet potatoes, cabbage, maize, and sorghum. The majority of the land used for agriculture by the Zuza people is located away from the village, where they grow a number of lowland crops, including cotton. Likewise, the owning of livestock is minimal compared to that in the other two villages that I studied. Weaving and spinning cotton are two common types of nonagricultural work, which enhance household incomes. The people of Zuza usually visit the Bodo, Ochollo, and Lante markets, which specialize in the selling of raw and spun cotton. Many of the Zuza women spin cotton

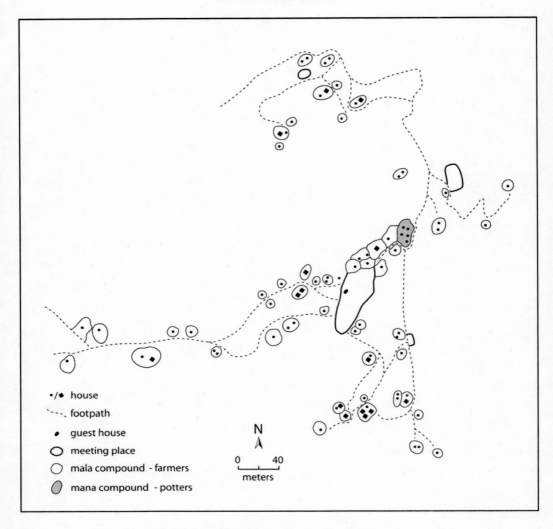

house
footpath
guest house
meeting place
mala compound - farmers
mana compound - potters

N

0   40
meters

FIGURE 1.11. Map of households located within the Gamo village of Zuza.

as a source of income, so at market they are either purchasing raw cotton or selling their spun cotton to weavers living throughout the region. The Ochollo potters sell at both the Ochollo and Lante markets and sometimes at the Bodo market. Within the three villages that I studied, both *mala* and artisan castes were present.

All of the Zuza *mana* households are located in one specific area, for it was a Zuza *halaka* that allowed them to live on this land, which the *halaka* controls. Because Zuza is located on top of a steep ridge, it is impossible to segregate artisans from the rest of the village population. There are a total of 57 households in Zuza with 198 people, averaging 3.5 people per household (Figures 1.11–1.12). The Zuza community consists of only *mala* (i.e., farmers and weavers) and *mana* (i.e., potters) households, and there are no *degala* hide workers or ironsmiths. Five households of potters live within one area, with a total population of 23 or 4.6 people per household, and the rest of the village households (*n* = 52) belong to farmers and/or weavers, with a population of 175 or 3.4 people per household.

FIGURE 1.12. View of Zuza, illustrating the village location on top of a large ridge overlooking the Rift Valley.

In Zuza and other villages, the presence of ritual-political leaders and their associated wealth affects the types and the number of pots present within the households. Among the Zuza *mala*, there is one *kao*, three *halakas*, and no *danas*, *makas*, or *udugas*. According to oral history, the Argama clan first inhabited Zuza, which was the first village inhabited in all of Ochollo district. There is only one *kao* living in Zuza, whose responsibility it is to speak first at meetings held at Bakero (i.e., the Zuza *debusha* or gathering place), where all of Ochollo meets. This is the only responsibility for the *kao*, because the responsibility of the *kao* in Ochollo has diminished. After the Ochollo *kao*'s father died in 1960, the eldest son became Ochollo's *kao* and had a feast for all of Ochollo. There are three former *halakas* living in Zuza, but at the time of my research, no one in Zuza was being initiated as *halaka*. In addition, there are no *danas*, *makas*, or *udugas* living in Zuza. I interviewed and studied the ceramic assemblages of 17 *mala* households, including the *kao* and three *hal-* *aka* households, and three *mana* households in Zuza.

Guyla, Zada

Guyla is situated in the *dega* zone at 2,600–2,700 m on the upper slope of a large valley providing enough land to conduct large-scale agriculture. Guyla is a village located on a well-drained mountainside, where several small streams provide ample drinking water. Except for the artisans, farming is the main occupation of the village, with weaving and cotton spinning providing secondary occupations. In Guyla, the farmers grow barley, wheat, enset, potatoes, cabbage, peas, and beans and tend to herds of domesticated stock. Meals include enset, potatoes, barley, wheat, beans, and peas. The Guyla people attend markets that specialize in the goods they produce, such as the Ezo, Zada, Pango, Tuka, and the small Leesha markets. In particular, the Ezo market is known for its sale of livestock products such as eggs, butter, and milk, and the Tuka market is known for its sales in

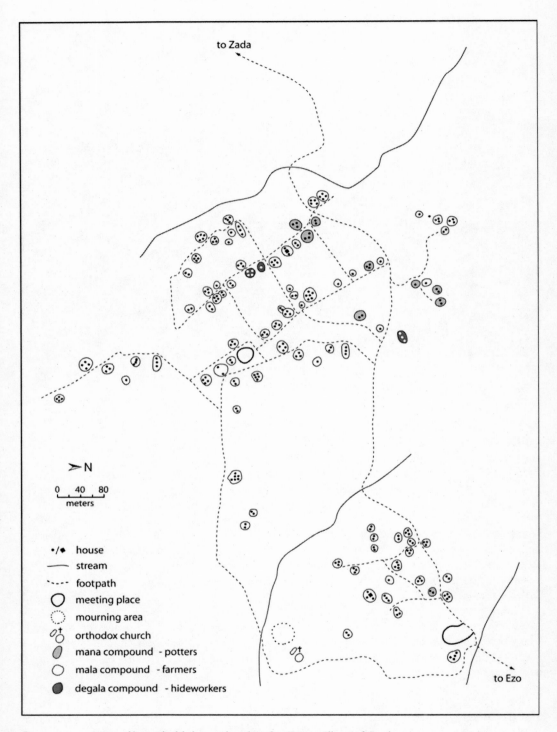

FIGURE 1.13. Map of households located within the Gamo village of Guyla.

FIGURE 1.14. View from the meeting area (*dubusha*) in the village of Guyla.

grains and meat (Jackson 1971:65–67). The potters sell their wares at the Leesha, Pango, and Zada markets and sometimes sell at the Tuka and Ezo markets, as well.

The majority of Guyla household compounds are situated in a grid pattern with footpaths running throughout. The Guyla *mana* and *degala* households tend to cluster in specific parts of the village but are not segregated in a remote part of the village. In Guyla there are 91 households with 342 people, with an average of 4.1 people per household (Figures 1.13–1.14). The Guyla community is represented by all three caste groups, including three *degala* hideworker households consisting of 13 people, or 4.3 people per household, and ten *mana* potter households scattered throughout the village, which represent 47 people, or 4.7 people per household. The remaining *mala* households of Guyla (*n* = 70) are inhabited by the farmers and/or weavers, a population of 282, or 4.0 people per household.

In the village of Guyla, which is located in Dita *dere*, the only leaders present are six former *halakas*. The people of Guyla repeatedly stated that they do not have enough wealth for someone to become *halaka*. However, there was one recently initiated *halaka* living in a village adjacent to Guyla. In Leesha *mota*, the first people inhabiting the area were from the Gawmala clan, and this is the reason the *kao* of Leesha is always from the Gawmala clan. However, it is not known which clan first inhabited the village of Guyla. There are presently no *danas*, but in the past the *dana* came only from Leesha, and his duty was to collect taxes. Presently in Leesha there is a *maka*, and his duties are to lead the people to the *debusha* Lalume, which the people consider an honored place. Lalume is an open field, and when people are walking through it to the market, they sit for a short time in respect to this honored land. The *uduga* in Leesha is from the clan Galomala, and his duties are to pray for the people and, during Meskal, to sprinkle honey in the Leesha market. I interviewed and studied the pottery in three *degala*, three *mana*, and 14 *mala* households, including two *halaka* households, in Guyla.

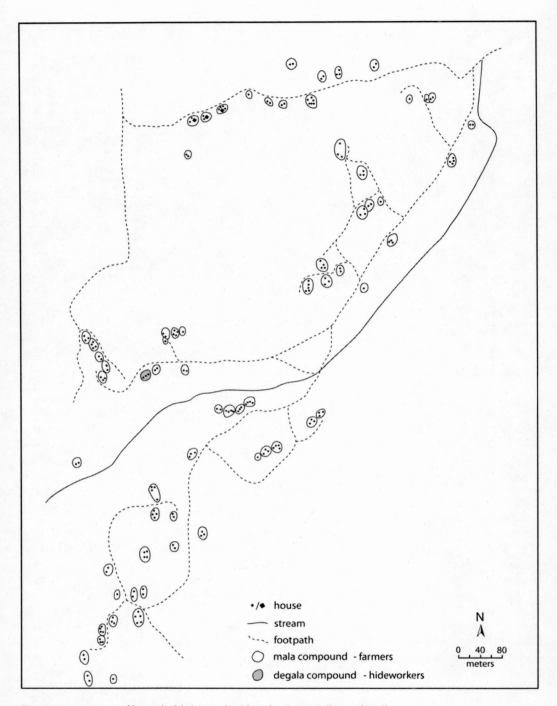

FIGURE 1.15. Map of households located within the Gamo village of Etello.

FIGURE 1.16. A household in the village of Etello, with Tsudo Mountain in the background.

Etello, Doko

Etello also is located in the *dega* zone but within a large valley, where the Itsamighty River provides enough well-watered land to conduct agriculture. The majority of households are situated adjacent to the Itsamighty River, where the village drinking water is gathered. Except for the hideworkers, farming is the main occupation of the village, with weaving and spinning cotton providing secondary occupations. The crops grown in Etello are similar to those grown in Guyla. In Etello, meals include enset, potatoes, barley, wheat, beans, and peas. In addition, the majority of people in Etello own some livestock. Etello is centrally located near many of the important Gamo markets. The villagers visit the Tuka (Chencha), Bodo (Dorze), Pango (Doko Mesho), and Ezo markets. However, the Tuka and Pango markets are the most commonly visited because of their size and proximity. Here the people sell and buy agricultural items and purchase ceramic vessels.

All three *degala* households are clustered together in one section of Etello, but they are not segregated from the rest of the village population. In Etello there are 68 households with 315 people, averaging 4.6 people per household (Figures 1.15–1.16). There are three hideworker households living in one concentrated area of the village with a population of 11 people, or 3.7 people per household. The rest of the Etello population (*n* = 65) is made up of farmers and/or weavers consisting of 304 people, or 4.7 people per household. Etello was chosen because it is a non-pottery-producing village. In the village of Etello, there are no *kaos*, *danas*, or *udugas*, although there are six former *halakas* and one *maka*. In the Doko district, where the village of Etello is located, the recent *dana* gave the people 10,000 birr, which is the equivalent of 99 oxen. The length of the *dana*'s term is dependent on whether there is another person who is qualified and has the wealth to donate either the oxen or the money to the people. The previous Doko *dana* was *dana* for 28 years until his death. The reason that the *maka* comes from this clan is that they were the first people to inhabit the village of Etello. In Etello, the *maka* explained that he has been a *maka* for seven years, and when he became *maka* by the people's wishes, he was given an ox from the seven *halakas* of the *dere*. In addition, every year for seven years the seven *halakas* gave the *maka* an ox, which they took to Tsudo Mountain in the forest. In the forest they slew the ox and prayed to God that the seven subdistricts in Doko would be productive and the people would have peace and health. In addition, they ate *gordo* that was given by the *dere*'s *uduga*. Currently in Doko, the *uduga* no longer collects the people's taxes. I interviewed and studied the pottery of three *degala* and 17 *mala* households, including one *maka* and two *halaka* households, in Etello.

CONCLUSION

The Gamo are a society with complex political, social, economic, and ecological structures that influence every aspect of daily life. Within Gamo society, cultural variation occurs between regions, affecting how the society produces, distributes, uses, mends, reuses, and discards its household ceramics. Gamo society provides an excellent setting in which to develop an understanding of how pottery variations reflect social, economic, and political diversity.

2

Pottery Procurement And Production

This chapter focuses on the first stages of the use-life cycle, procurement and production, by revealing the diverse set of strategies that Gamo potters use to produce their vessels. Previous research suggests that the cultural context of potters affects how and where they procure their clays, the types of vessels they produce, and their production techniques (D. Arnold 1985, 2000; Chávez 1992; Gosselain 1992, 2000; Kramer 1997:39–80; Nicholson and Patterson 1992; Stark 1992, 1994; Stark and Longacre 1993). In addition, the consumer also has an important voice concerning how Gamo potters produce their wares, because the potters are continually trying to attract new customers. The Gamo learning process, clay and temper acquisition, and forming, drying, decorating, firing, and post-firing of the vessel are all explicitly affected by the social and economic conditions in which the potters live.

THE LEARNING PROCESS

Women make pottery in Gamo society. Women work on all aspects of the production and marketing of their wares, including digging the clay, carrying the clay and wood, forming and firing the vessels, and carrying the pots to market. Depending on the household, men do help with some production tasks such as digging and cleaning the clay, collecting the wood, firing the pots, and carrying the vessels to market. The potter women store their materials, produce vessels, and dry, prefire,

and fire their vessels within their family compound. Wealthier potters have more land and small specialized potting workshops adjacent to their houses, whereas the poorest potters work either in their compound or in the house vestibule.

Gamo potters are full-time specialists. Potters produce pots to sell or barter to nonpotter households, and there are no Gamo potters who produce pots only for their own households. The potter's status in the Gamo social hierarchy is ascribed and determined by birth, and no action may change the hierarchical positioning of individual potters or other craft specialists. The craft of pottery production is generally transferred from mother to daughter. Potters believe that they must teach their daughters how to produce pottery because the limited amount of farmland prevents most *mana* caste members from owning enough farmland to meet household subsistence needs. Seventeen potters whom I interviewed learned from their mothers and one from her father's second wife. However, postmarital residence in Gamo society is virilocal; thus after marriage a potter woman moves to live with her husband's father's kin, and in one instance I recorded a potter learned from her mother-in-law. When a woman moves to live with her husband, she may encounter a range of economic conditions. A woman potter may find herself in a family that has farmland, or she may find that her new family owns only the land on which the house is situated. Even

FIGURE 2.1. A young girl helping with ceramic production by compacting the wall of a baking plate between the ground and hand stones.

if the husband has farmland, it usually does not produce enough food for the family. Those *mana* households (47 percent) that have been given farmland from the *mala* caste usually are able to build a small separate structure to use as a workshop (55 percent); however, this does not indicate a higher level of production. Learning how to produce pottery provides a potter woman with an important skill, which significantly contributes to the household's economic livelihood.

Gamo potters learn how to produce pottery when they are six to 13 years old (Figure 2.1). Informal instruction usually last for three years or until the daughter is married. Girls begin learning the production process by helping their mothers mine and carry the clay from the clay sources to the household. Using a large jar, they also transport water from the well or stream to mix the clays. In addition, they help with cleaning the clay of stones, grinding the clay, and selecting grog temper from broken vessels that cracked during either the drying or the firing process. Af-

ter they become more experienced with all of the production activities, they practice producing small vessels.

Potters are dependent on their craft to make a living because they rarely have more than their household garden to produce food. Although some potters can afford to build a small structure used as a workshop, this does not suggest that their level of production is significantly higher than that of potters who do not have a workshop. Some potters have been fortunate to receive farmland from *mala* caste members and therefore can produce enough food to be able to afford building a small structure.

The majority of Gamo potters, with the help of their daughters and/or daughters-in-law, produce pots by themselves. Sometimes two wives of the same husband work together, as one family does in Guyla. Some potters who are friends travel to the clay sources together to procure the clays. In addition, sometimes a mother or daughter will travel to the other's village and stay for a week or so and help the host potter manufacture pots. There are competitive feelings between different potter families, even if they are friends, and so the majority of potters work alone or with their own family members.

The potters stated that they produce their vessels much like the person who taught them (e.g., mother or mother-in-law). However, a new locality, family, friends, and different consumers often influence changes in pottery production. Although the majority of the learning process is conducted at the mother's household, once the potter moves to her husband's household she learns how to produce and distribute her vessels from her husband's relatives. The new potter has to learn where the clay and temper sources are located. She has to learn what proportion of the different clays work well together, as some clays do not work well in the shaping of specific vessel forms. She needs to know if the drying process is the same as in her childhood village, as the temperature and precipitation patterns may be different if her new village is in a different ecological zone. In addition, she has to learn what types of fuelwood are accessible and how her new village potters prefire their vessels. The learning process not only influences the potter's production methods but also has direct implications toward how the potter forms and decorates the vessel, and this affects the vessel's style. The majority of potters believe rim shape is the most important attribute in discriminating their vessels from their teachers' vessels. Other attributes that potters think are different from their mothers' are the type of formal decoration (e.g., appliqué, comb-stamping, and incising) and the shape of the vessel. After potters marry, they begin to reflect their new villages and regions regarding ceramic style in order to compete with other potters and to comply with consumer expectations. A potter also needs to learn which weekly markets are best to sell her wares and if the prices for different forms are different from those in her former childhood village. Thus, there are two subsystems in the learning process among Gamo potters, a potter's childhood village and her husband's village.

CLAY AND TEMPER ACQUISITION
Methods and Distance to Sources

Among the Gamo potters, relations with landowners, geological constraints, and proximity are the primary reasons given for deciding where to mine clay. Each village has its own set of clay sources, which are mined either by individuals or with other potters in the village. One reason that potters mine at particular sources is the relationship between the clay source's landowner and the potter. Archaeologists are able to measure the physical attributes of clays such as elasticity, hardness, particle size, and so on, but we usually are unable to measure the social conditions that influence a potter's choice in clay procurement (Aronson et al. 1994). Thus, understanding both the social and the physical conditions in the mining of clay can aid us in understanding the potter's decision-making process.

Proximity to the clay source is an important factor for Gamo potters, because potters carry the clay in baskets (*tiseti*) on their backs. Guyla potters mine their clay from sources that are less than 6 km from their village. They collect three of the five clays and one temper (nonplastic material) between 1 and 6 km, and the remaining two sources are within 1 km of the village. Guyla potters who collect the *ano* temper and *poze* and *ooka* clays walk six hours (round-trip) to transport all three materials. However, one potter family in Guyla obtains their *zoo* clay directly from their household property, and the *caretsa* clay is located adjacent to the eldest potter's household land.

All three clays used by the Zuza potters are between 1 and 6 km of their village. The time it takes for Zuza potters to transport their clays both ways is five hours each for the *walle* and *kura* clays and three hours for the *mochollo* clay (Figure 2.2). Potters living in the villages of Denkarar and Keya (less than 1 km from Zuza) use different clay sources than those in Zuza, indicating that each village within a region decides independently where the potters should mine their clay. When potter women marry and move to Denkarar, Keya, or Zuza villages, they are taught by the older potters in the new village where to extract clay.

FIGURE 2.2. Zuza potters cleaning the three clays they have procured before they begin producing their vessels.

Other factors that influence where potters may obtain clay and temper are their relations with the landowners of the clay sources and village elders' decisions on where potters may mine clay (Figure 2.3). The majority of Guyla potters belong to two families. One potter family extracts all of its clays from its own land. The other potter family collects only one clay from its land, and the *poze* clay is collected from a *mala*'s land. However, both families do mine from the same temper source (*ano*) located outside of Guyla approximately 4 km to the northwest. The two families do not share their clay sources with each other to protect the source(s) from becoming depleted. Two landowners, who are *mala* farmers, will not allow the Guyla potters to mine their clay. Several of the Guyla potters complained that they are not treated well by the *mala* because of the potter's low status within Gamo culture. One Guyla family that uses a clay source named *pullticalo* (after the landowner's name) has problems with the water table flooding the hole. This is especially a problem during the rainy seasons, which limits the frequency of production among this family of Guyla potters. The *pullticalo* clay is extracted approximately 4–5 m from the surface, with the majority of the clay lying just above and below the water table (Figure 2.4). An adjacent source was abandoned after a potter was killed in 1996, when the wall of the clay pit collapsed. This potter's family is uncertain about their future because the *pullticalo* clay source is becoming too dangerous and it is difficult to find a landowner within the proximity of Guyla willing to let the potters mine clay.

Since 1974, more than ten potter families have moved from the highland region to the lowland areas where there are no clay sources. Efforts by the national government to move people from the highlands to the lowlands adjacent to Lake Abaya took place during the Derg government between 1974 and 1991. The Derg government established lowland villages, and its socialist ideology advocated that all people have access to farmland. Al-

FIGURE 2.3. A potter digging clay from a procurement area owned by a *mala* in the Ezo region.

FIGURE 2.4. A potter digging from the *pullticalo* clay source in order to find clay suitable for producing pottery in the village of Guyla.

TABLE 2.1. Functional Attributes Ascribed to Clays and Temper by Zuza and Guyla Potters

TYPE OF CLAY/TEMPER	ATTRIBUTES
Zuza	
Kura (clay)	Provides elasticity to the vessels and is the most important clay.
Mochollo (clay)	When mixed with the *kura* clay, the two protect the vessels during the firing process. *Mochollo* is the second most important clay.
Walle (clay)	Provides color to the vessel and is the third most important clay.
Guyla	
Ano (temper)	Provides elasticity and strength. Provides strength during firing.
Zoo (clay)	Provides form to the vessel especially during the dry season but does not provide enough strength if it is the only clay.
Caretsa (clay)	The best clay because of its elasticity and keeps the vessel from falling when wet.
Pose (clay)	Stonelike quality. Stops cracking during the drying period.
Ooka (clay)	Provides elasticity. Stops cracking during the drying period. Vessel will break easily without mixing *ano* and *pose* clay.

though the potter families have farmland in the lowlands, there are no clay sources in the lowland region. Potters from Fura Mandita walk six hours round-trip (approximately 14 km round-trip) up to the highland Donay region to obtain their clays.

Technical Factors in Clay and Temper Selection

Whereas social conditions tend to influence where potters extract their clay, once the clay has been mined technical factors predominate concerning how the potters manipulate their clays and tempers (Table 2.1). The Gamo potters are concerned more with how the clays and temper perform when being processed during production than with how the clays react when used by consumers. The potters have specific reasons for using their selection of different clays and tempers (Arthur 1997).

The majority of potters state that it is important to mix the correct combination and proportion of the clays and tempers to achieve the proper result. In Guyla, potters state that if they just use the *zoo* clay the vessel will not be strong, and they have to mix the *ooka* clay with temper and *pose* clay or the pot will break. In Zuza, the *mochollo* and *kura* clays have to be mixed so that the pots will not

break during the firing process. In addition, important factors for using specific clays and tempers during production are clays that provide elasticity when forming the vessel, curtail cracks during the drying period, and provide protection against the firing process.

Every Guyla potter uses the *ano* temper, indicating that this temper is an important technological component of their pottery production. This is supported by the fact that the *ano* temper source is located farther than that of any other material. The *ano* temper is an important resource in protecting the vessels during firing. One Guyla potter stated that before placing the pots in the fire she covers them with the pumice *ano* temper, which keeps them from breaking during firing. The *walle* clay is the only material that has a nontechnological role by providing color to Zuza pots. The potters' clay and temper descriptions provide an emic perspective concerning what clay and temper attributes are necessary for production.

Gamo potters mix three to four types of clay together to produce all of the vessel forms. Naturally mined temper (nonplastic inclusions) and/or grog (small pieces of broken pottery) also are added to the clays. Except for the grog, Zuza potters do not use

FIGURE 2.5. A Zuza potter beating the clay with a large stick (*bookadoka*) before sifting the clay through a woven basket (*zizarey*).

additional temper because enough temper occurs naturally in the Zuza clays. The potters remove the pebbles and other impurities from the clay to prevent production problems. After the clays are cleaned, they are pounded with a large stick (*bookadoka*) and sifted through a woven basket (*zizarey*; Figure 2.5). The *zizarey* also serves to aid in measuring the proportion of each clay in the final clay mixture. All vessels are made with the same proportion of clays. The potters mix the clays by stomping on the clay with one foot (Figure 2.6). Once the clays, tempers, and water have been mixed together, in their proper proportions, the potters can begin to form the vessels.

FORMING THE VESSELS

Gamo potters produce 14 different vessel forms (Table 2.2). The number of pots manufactured by potters varies with each potter, with a range of five to 70 vessels per week. Gamo potters usually specialize in the production of one or two vessel types even though they can usually produce all types. Sometimes the clays used in a village are not suitable for the production of particular vessel types. For example, Guyla potters state that they do not usually produce baking plates because their clay is not adequate for this type of production.

The Gamo potters produce a range of vessel types to process various crops. For example, they produce five types of multifunctional jars (single-handle jar, wide-mouth small jar, wide-mouth medium jar, narrow-mouth medium jar, and large jar), a beer jar for storing beer, a coffee pitcher, a narrow-mouth small jar for drinking, and a baking plate for roasting. They also make serving bowls and dishes and water pipes for smoking tobacco. Protestant potters will not produce water pipes, because it is not allowed by their religion. The less commonly produced types include the foot-washing bowl and coffee cups, which generally have been replaced by imported Chinese porcelain cups. Only one traditional coffee cup was found during my vessel inventory of 60 households in three villages. Figures 2.7–2.9 indicate the types of vessel forms manufactured by Gamo potters.

Vessels are formed using a combination of hand-building, coil-and-scrape, and paddle-

FIGURE 2.6. A Guyla potter mixing the different clays together using her foot.

TABLE 2.2. Gamo Vessel Forms

EMIC NAME	ETIC NAME	TYPICAL USES
Kolay	single-handle jar	multifunctional jar used for cooking and serving
Tayche	wide-mouth small jar	multifunctional jar used for cooking and serving
Tsua	narrow-mouth small jar	drinking
Diste	wide-mouth medium jar	cooking and storage
Tsaro	narrow-mouth medium jar	multifunctional jar used for cooking, storing, and transporting
Otto	large jar	multifunctional jar used for cooking, storing, and transporting
Batsa	beer jar	fermenting beer
Shele	bowl	communal eating and storing food
Peele	dish	communal eating
Bache	baking plate	roasting foods and baking breads
Jebana	coffee pitcher	boil coffee
Sene	coffee cup	drink coffee
Guya	water pipe	smoke tobacco
Gumgay	foot-washing bowl	wash feet

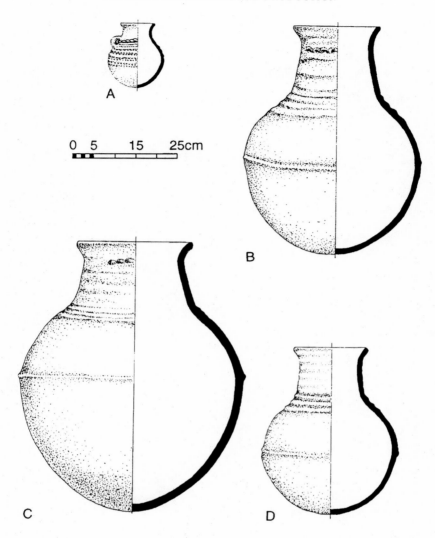

FIGURE 2.7. Profile drawings of (A) narrow-mouth small jar, (B) large jar, (C) beer jar, and (D) narrow-mouth medium jar, which the Gamo potters produce.

and-anvil techniques. The type of vessel construction is dependent on the vessel form. While the vessels are still wet, a piece of leather (*gelba*) or cloth is used to help form the clay rim and neck (Figure 2.10). The exterior of the vessel is thinned using a bamboo stick (*mylee*; Figure 2.11). The interior of the vessel is thinned and smoothed with the outer covering of half a seedpod (*kayshe* tree [*Jacaranda mimosifolia*]) that is obtained from the lowland area adjacent to Lake Abaya.

The jars (e.g., narrow-mouth small jar, narrow-mouth medium jar, large jar, and beer jar) are formed by drawing the clay up to produce the upper part of the body; then the neck and rim are formed using the coil-and-scrape method. Once the top half of the vessel is formed, it is turned upside down on its rim and placed on a piece of enset leaf to keep it from touching the ground. Then the rounded base is formed using the coil-and-scrape method until the base is eventually closed up

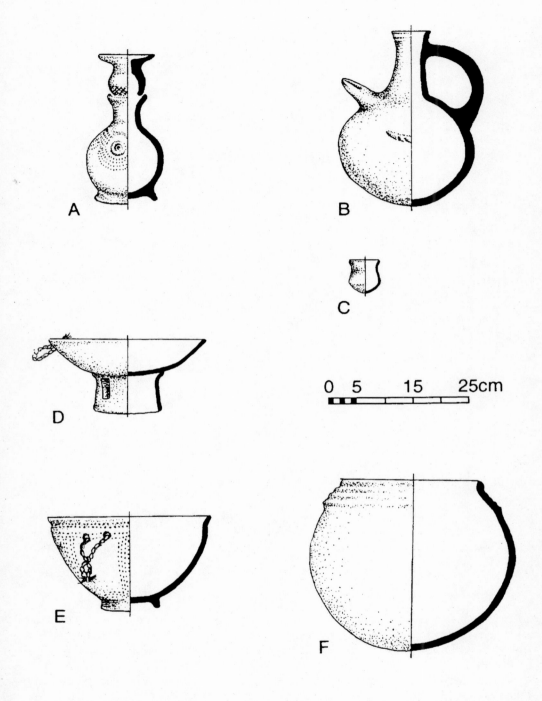

FIGURE 2.8. Profile drawings of (A) water pipe, (B) coffee pitcher, (C) coffee cup, (D) dish, and (E–F) bowl, which the Gamo potters produce.

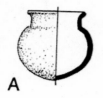

A

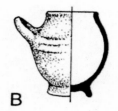

B

C

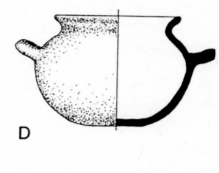

D

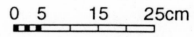

0 5   15   25cm

E

FIGURE 2.9. Profile drawings of (A) wide-mouth small jar, (B) single-handle jar, (C) foot-washing bowl (D) wide-mouth medium jar, and (E) baking plate, which the Gamo potters produce.

FIGURE 2.10. A Guyla potter using a piece of leather (*gelba*) to shape the neck and rim of a jar.

FIGURE 2.11. A Guyla potter using a bamboo tool (*mylee*) to thin the vessel wall.

(Figures 2.12–2.13). The wide-mouth medium jars are formed as the other jars are, except that the base of the wide-mouth medium jar is flat instead of round. The production process is more elaborate for beer jars. After the upper half is formed, the vessel's exterior is scraped to thin the walls. Then the potter uses two hand stones, one in the interior and one on the exterior, to pound and compact the walls of the beer jar (Figure 2.14).

Small- to medium-sized bowls and serving dishes are formed by pounding a fist into a lump of clay. Then the potter moves around the lump, shaping it until it is formed into a bowl or dish (Figure 2.15). Although large bowls are produced much like the jars, by forming the upper half first and then the base, some bowls and dishes have base stands attached to the body that are formed after the body is shaped into its final form.

The *bache* is formed from a lump of clay that is pounded with the fist until it begins to take the shape of a baking plate. Then the potter moves around the vessel, slowly work-

FIGURE 2.12. A Guyla potter starting to form the base by applying coils to the vessel.

FIGURE 2.13. A Guyla potter forming the base by using the coil-and-scrape method.

FIGURE 2.14. A Guyla potter compacting the walls of a beer vessel by using two hand stones.

FIGURE 2.15. A Guyla potter shaping the interior of a bowl.

FIGURE 2.16. A Zuza potter forming the rim of a baking plate using a piece of leather.

ing on the shape of the rim with a wet piece of leather or cloth (Figure 2.16). After the baking plate dries in its first stage (i.e., 15 days), the exterior of the plate is scraped with a bamboo stick, and then it is laid upon a grinding stone and pounded with a hand stone to compact the vessel wall. The interior of the baking plate is burnished, whereas the exterior is left rough and plain in appearance. The coffee pitcher is produced by forming the base and body in a way similar to how the small- to medium-sized bowls are made. Then the neck is produced using the coil-and-scrape method. The spout is formed by attaching a small coil on the upper part of the body. A small stick is used to hollow out the spout, which is then shaped into its final form.

Each potter uses a complex set of techniques to form the different types of vessels. The types of vessels that a potter produces are dependent on a number of factors, including the learning history of each potter, suitable clays, and consumer demands.

DRYING THE VESSELS

The vessels are dried from three days to two months depending on the potter's preference, which is based on the type of clays, type of vessel, and season (Tables 2.3–2.4). One problem that Gamo potters have is a lack of space to dry their vessels. They usually dry the vessels within their houses, which restricts the amount of vessels they can produce at any given time. The majority of vessels are first dried on the ground and then placed on an elevated rafter situated over a hearth, where they will sit until they are ready for firing (Figure 2.17). During the two rainy seasons (i.e., March–April and June–September), vessels are dried for a longer period of time, which reduces the number of vessels produced. Although some potters use the same types of clays, there is variation in the amount of time to dry specific vessel types. Zuza potters also hang their baking plates with enset rope from the interior wall of their house until they are leather hard. It is not uncommon to see more

TABLE 2.3. Drying Location and Time for Specific Vessel Types Produced in Zuza

VESSEL TYPE	INTERIOR HOUSE DRYING LOCATION	LENGTH OF DRYING TIME
Baking plate (*bache*)	house wall	15 days
	rafter	7 days
Wide-mouth medium jar (*diste*)	rafter	11 days
Bowl (*shele*)	rafter	11 days
Large jar (*otto*)	rafter	11 days
Beer jar (*batsa*)	rafter	28 days

TABLE 2.4. Drying Location and Time for Specific Vessel Types Produced in Guyla

VESSEL TYPE	INTERIOR HOUSE DRYING LOCATIONS	LENGTH OF DRYING TIME
Coffee pitcher (*jebana*)	ground	7 to 14 days
	rafter	7 days
Wide-mouth medium jar (*diste*)	rafter	7 (dry season) to 14 days (rainy season)
Large jar (*otto*)	ground	14 days
	rafter	7 days to 1 month
Narrow-mouth medium jar (*tsaro*)	ground	10 days (dry season)
	rafter	7 (dry season) to 14 days (rainy season)
Bowl (*shele*)	rafter	7 days to 1 month (depends on vessel size)
Baking plate (*bache*)	ground	7 days
	rafter	3 to 7 days
Narrow-mouth small jar (*tsua*)	ground	3 to 7 days
	rafter	4 to 7 days
Upper part of beer jar (*batsa*)	ground	4 to 5 days
Complete beer jar (*batsa*)	ground then rafter	2 to 3 weeks (ground) to 1 to 2 weeks (rafter)
	rafter	1 month
Water pipe (*guya*)	rafter	1 month
Dish (*peele*)	rafter	7 to 14 days
Foot-washing bowl (*gumgay*)	rafter	2 to 3 weeks to 1 month (depending on weather conditions)
Pot supports (*mestakalay*)	rafter	7 (dry season) to 14 days (rainy season)

FIGURE 2.17. A number of baking plates on a drying rack in a Zuza potter house.

FIGURE 2.18. A Guyla potter burnishing a jar with a quartzite polishing stone (*elasucha*).

than a dozen baking plates hanging from the house walls within each of the Zuza potter's houses.

DECORATING THE VESSELS

After the vessel is dried, the potter then burnishes it with a quartzite polishing stone (*elasucha*) either on both the interior and exterior walls or only on one side of the wall (Figure 2.18). The location of the burnishing relies on the vessel type (Tables 2.5–2.6). Potters stated that burnishing gives the pots "a bright color." The Guyla potters decorate the vessels with a combination of appliqué, incising, and rippling, whereas the Zuza potters decorate their pots only with appliqué.

The type and placement of decoration are dependent on the vessel form and, most important, the individual potter. Appliqué rings (*shetoti*) that encompass a vessel are common on jars. Usually one *sheto* is placed on the maximum circumference of the jars, but the beer jars may have two or three *shetoti* placed on their maximum circumference. Three *shetoti* are placed also on the upper body of the

TABLE 2.5. Zuza Potters' Placement of Burnishing on Specific Vessel Forms

VESSEL FORM	INTERIOR	EXTERIOR	INTERIOR AND EXTERIOR
Wide-mouth medium jar (*diste*)			x
Bowl (*shele*)			x
Dish (*peele*)			x
Coffee pitcher (*jebana*)		x	
Narrow-mouth small jar (*tsua*)		x	
Water pipe (*guya*)		x	
Baking plate (*bache*)	x		
Large jar (*otto*)	x		

TABLE 2.6. Guyla Potters' Placement of Burnishing on Specific Vessel Forms

VESSEL FORM	INTERIOR	EXTERIOR	INTERIOR AND EXTERIOR
Wide-mouth medium jar (*diste*)			x
Narrow-mouth medium jar (*tsaro*)			x
Bowl (*shele*)			x
Dish (*peele*)			x
Coffee pitcher (*jebana*)		x	
Narrow-mouth small jar (*tsua*)	x (interior neck)	x	
Water pipe (*guya*)		x	
Baking plate (*bache*)	x		

beer jars. A *sheto* is also found on the base of serving bowls, which serve as foot rings, but sometimes *shetoti* can begin at the maximum circumference of the serving bowl and continue either to the base or to the rim.

Another appliqué type of decoration is *temo*, which are small (numbering three to nine) projections found on the upper exterior wall of the jars. Sometimes potters put a series of *temoti* on the upper body of the wide-mouth medium jars, which otherwise are undecorated. A second type of decoration is rippling (*kansa*), which is when the potter forms grooves on the exterior wall. Rippling is found on the necks of jars and serving vessels. The rim on all jars and the majority of bowls also is referred to as *kansa*.

Comb-stamping (*beesho*) vessels is usu-ally practiced in the central Gamo region, such as Guyla, but is rarely done by Zuza potters. The incised designs are made with either sheep teeth attached to a stick or two iron prongs attached to a wood handle (both tools are named *chechamarcho*). The *beesho* can be applied on the interior and/or exterior of the serving bowls and dishes, the exterior of the narrow-mouth small jars, and the exterior of the water pipes. The individual potter and the larger village/regional stylistic traditions dictate this type of decoration. In addition, potters often discussed how comb-stamping is a time-consuming activity. Potters spend more time on comb-stamping than any other type of decoration because they comb-stamp large sections of the interior and/or exterior. Therefore, potters comb-stamp a vessel more if it is being sold at a market than if it is sold to a specific individual (Arthur 2002b). Potters at the markets are competing against other potters for the consumer, and therefore they invest more labor time to produce comb-stamped vessels. Serving vessels produced in the central Gamo region may have a combination of all types of decorative styles, based on the individual potter, the village, and the regional style.

Gamo potters name pots with human anatomical features. The top of the rim is called the mouth (*dona*), the neck is also called the neck (*core*), the body is called the stomach (*oolo*), and the base is called the anus (*tache* in Zuza or *meskatay* in Guyla). Specific types of decoration correspond to particular anatomical features, such as *dansa*, which translates as "breast." This rare type of appliqué is a large oval that points upward and is placed on the upper body of cooking jars. Water pipes (*guyas*) usually have a specific decoration called *pigay* that is only placed on this vessel form. Pigay translates as a "scar" and is associated with scars created by burning the skin, believed to heal wounds and pains. In addition, the hole, where the hollow bamboo stem (*pikay*) is used to suck the smoke from the water pipe, is called the drinking place (*owezaso*). Besides giving potters classifications for specific parts of the pot, the naming of anatomical features suggests a symbolic importance to Gamo potters. Because the majority of potter families rely on the manufacturing of pottery vessels for their sole livelihood, potters take the clay and temper, what the *mala* consider dirty work, and bring them to life in the form of a pot. The pottery vessel can be used to bring sustenance to the potter family by selling it or exchanging it for food—and even processing that food into an edible form.

FIRING THE VESSELS
Fuelwood

Gamo potters select particular fuelwoods to prefire and fire their vessels. The selection of fuelwoods by Gamo potters is determined by their village's ecological location (Table 2.7). For example, because Zuza potters live within the *baso* ecological zone and are socially tied to other lowland communities, they collect their fuel from the lowlands. The area surrounding Zuza is dense with grass and trees, and it is much easier to obtain fuel for the Zuza potters than it is for Guyla potters who live in the highland or *dega* ecological zone. Fuelwood shortages commonly were mentioned by Guyla potters as causing production problems. There are forested areas in the highland region, but these are sacred areas and potters are forbidden to collect fuelwood from sacred forests. If a potter were caught collecting fuelwood from a sacred area, she would be forced to leave the Gamo area and never allowed to return. These sacred forests are places where the animal sacrifices take place to protect and provide fertility to the area's people.

Guyla potters use cow dung (*osha*) and/or horse dung (*fando*) if they are not able to find enough wood or grass. Because the Guyla village is located in the *dega* ecological zone, which is more densely populated and farmed than the Zuza hinterland, the Guyla potters gather some of their fuels from the *baso* ecological zone (e.g., *gargecho* and *odora* trees). Potters from both villages have favorite types of fuels that are based primarily on technological rather than nontechnological factors.

Zuza potters pay 5 birr (U.S.$0.75) per bundle, which will provide for one firing, for all of their types of fuels. They use ten types of fuels collected individually from the lowlands adjacent to Lake Abaya but prefer seven fuel types. The fuel types they prefer are *shankara*, *shobo*, *checha*, *omazey*, *galas*, and *goganza* trees and *gata* grass. They prefer the *goganza* and *galas* trees because the fire will burn longer than with other types of fuel.

Guyla potters communally buy fuelwood that costs between 14 and 40 birr (U.S.$2.00–6.00) per tree depending on the type of fuel. They use between two and 11 fuel types that are all found within 6 km of Guyla. The types of fuels are *fando* (horse dung); *osha* (cow dung); *kashelo* (bamboo leaves); *barzaf* (eucalyptus tree); and *gedema*, *borto*, *anka*, *shenato*, *tseda*, and *gargecho* trees. The two rainy seasons affect the types of fuelwood

TABLE 2.7. Taxonomic and Gamo Names and Corresponding Elevational Ranges of Fuels Used to Fire Ceramic Vessels by Village, Demonstrating Primary Dependence on Local Resources

VILLAGE	TAXONOMIC NAME	GAMO NAME	ELEVATIONAL RANGE
Zuza (lowland)	*Hyparrhencei* sp.	*gata* (grass)	1,100–3,000 m
	Acacia nilotica (subalata)	*checha* (tree)	900–1,000 m
	Terminahei sp.	*galas* (tree)	250–2,200 m
	Olea africana	*wera* (tree)	(not published)
	Ficus sycomorus	*lafo* (tree)	500–2,000 m
	?	*shankara* (tree)	(not published)
	?	*omazey* (tree)	(not published)
	?	*goganza* (tree)	(not published)
	?	*bolala* (tree)	(not published)
Guyla (highland)	*Erythrina abyssinica*	*borto* (tree)	1,300–2,400 m
	Erythrina brucei		1,400–2,600 m
	Myrica sahcifolei	*shenato* (tree)	1,750–3,300 m
	Eucalyptus sp.	*barzaf* (tree)	(not published)
	Arundinaria alpina	*wesha* (bamboo tree)	2,200–4,000 m
	Dombeya sp.	*anka* (tree)	850–3,100 m
	Maesa landeolata	*gargecho* (tree)	700–1,700 m
	Acacia brevispica	*odora* (tree)	900–2,000 m
	Hyparrhencie sp.	*gata* (grass)	1,100–3,000 m
	Cupresse lustanica	*tseda* (tree)	(not published)

used, because certain woods dry faster during the rainy seasons than others. The Guyla potters prefer *anka, barzaf, barto, shenato, gata,* or *kashelo* fuel. Two reasons were given as to why certain fuels were best. First, they believed that *anka, shenato, barto,* and *gargecho* woods are best because they burn longer than other fuel types, especially during the dry season. Second, the eucalyptus or *barzaf* tree was considered the best during the rainy season because it dries fast. Potters from both villages stated that it is more important to have a fire that burns for a long time than a fire that is very hot.

Prefiring and Firing the Vessels

After burnishing and decorating the pots, potters prefire vessels on top of a wooden rack (*afansha*) located in the workshop or potter's house or placed around a small hearth at the same location where the potter will fire the vessels (Figure 2.19). The vessels are slowly smoked and heated for approximately four hours, before being put in an open fire located outside in the compound. The construction of the open fire begins by placing a layer of either ash or eucalyptus leaves on the ground. This is done to provide a buffer between the ground and the vessels, as the ground may be moist, which will cause the vessels to crack. A layer of wood is carefully laid on the ash or leaf surface. Then the vessels are placed on top of the wood, and finally, dried grass is applied. During the firing of the vessels, more grass is placed onto the fire, and the potter eventually pokes a stick at the base of the grass heap to make a hole so she can see how the vessels are firing. This also provides more oxygen to the fire, which will ignite the remaining portion of the grass. The open fire lasts approximately

TABLE 2.8. Zuza Potters' Placement of *Etema* on Specific Vessel Forms

VESSEL FORM	INTERIOR	EXTERIOR	INTERIOR AND EXTERIOR
Coffee pitcher (*jebana*)		x	
Water pipe (*guya*)		x	
Narrow-mouth small jar (*tsua*)		x	
Narrow-mouth medium jar (*tsaro*)		x	
Baking plate (*bache*)	x		
Large jar (*otto*)	x		
Wide-mouth medium jar (*diste*)			x
Bowl (*shele*)			x
Dish (*peele*)			x

TABLE 2.9. Guyla Potters' Placement of *Etema* on Specific Vessel Forms

VESSEL FORM	INTERIOR	EXTERIOR	INTERIOR AND EXTERIOR
Coffee pitcher (*jebana*)			x
Wide-mouth medium jar (*diste*)			x
Narrow-mouth small jar (*tsua*)			x
Narrow-mouth medium jar (*tsaro*)		x	
Large jar (*otto*)	x	x (above maximum diameter)	
Baking plate (*bache*)	x		
Bowl (*shele*)			x
Dish (*peele*)			x
Water pipe (*guya*)			x

two hours (Figures 2.20–2.22). Potters usually fire between four and 30 vessels on a specific day every week. Generally the vessels are fired the day before they are taken to the market.

Vessel Postfiring Treatment

Immediately after removal from the fire, a coating of *etema* (i.e., liquid from the enset plant) is applied to the exterior and/or interior of the vessel (Tables 2.8–2.9). Gamo potters believe *etema* gives the vessel strength and beauty. In Zuza, they put *etema* on the same vessel side that they burnish, which they state provides a reflection and is a type of decoration. In addition, cow dung is applied on the exterior of jars from the base to the maximum diameter. The application of cow dung provides added protection against cracking while on the hearth. Furthermore, potters cover a vessel's surface with leaves, which produces a smudged surface treatment, changing the vessel color from a red to black. They also reduce bowls and dishes for decoration because consumers expect their serving vessels to be black.

FIGURE 2.19. A Guyla potter prefiring the vessels before they are fired.

FIGURE 2.20. A Guyla potter firing his vessels.

FIGURE 2.21. Zuza potters preparing their vessels to be fired.

FIGURE 2.22. View of a Zuza potter beginning to fire the vessels.

GAMO POTTERY PROCUREMENT AND PRODUCTION IN CROSS-CULTURAL PERSPECTIVE

This study of Gamo pottery procurement and production provides insights for archaeologists concerned with regional and socioeconomic relationships. Gamo potters belong to a submerged caste group that manufactures pottery vessels full-time throughout the year. Production decreases only during the second (heavy) rainy season. Potters living in other regions of the world often have a low status (Behura 1978:32–36; Blurton 1997; David and Kramer 2001:215–216; Foster 1965; Frank 1993; Gelbert 1999; Gupta 1969:21; Herbert 1993; LaViolette 2000:91; London 2000:105; Mitchell 1979; Sillar 1997:7; Silverman 1994:174; Stark 1995; Thompson 1974:121, 123, 130). Gamo potters manufacture pots for their economic needs, but most important, they are socially linked to the occupation of potting by their caste. Because many potter households do not own farmland to fulfill their economic needs, mothers and mothers-in-law teach their daughters and daughters-in-law how to manufacture pots. This ensures that their daughters will have an economic livelihood, while they are apprentices and when they move to live with their husbands' fathers' kin. In other cultures such as the Tzeltal Maya of Mexico, Deal (1998:29–30) reports that two generations ago Maya potters were more likely to learn from their mothers-in-law because they married at age 11 or 12, but presently a majority of potters have learned from their mothers. Herbich's (1987:200) research among the Luo of Kenya indicates that women marry young and learn how to manufacture pots from their mothers-in-law, rather than their mothers. Gamo potters learn first through informal instruction by watching and conducting chores such as gathering water and cleaning and pounding the clay. This type of informal instruction also is present among the Achuar and Quichua in the Ecuadorian Amazon (Bowser 2000), the Maya (Deal 1998:27; Hayden and Cannon 1984), the Kalinga of the Philippines (Longacre 1981:60), the Huichol of northern

Mexico (Weigand 1969:31–32), the Atzompa of southern Mexico (Hendry 1992:100), and the Hopi of the American Southwest (Stanislawski and Stanislawski 1978:72). Children begin to become potters by learning the different types of work involved in making pots. Over time they practice through more formal instruction by first learning how to make small pots and then learning how to produce larger vessels.

Even though potters learn two different microtraditions, one from the mother's household and village and one from the mother-in-law's household and village, the pottery forms and designs reflect the tradition of the place in which they reside. The majority of Gamo potters believe they produce pots similar to those of their teachers (e.g., mother and mother-in-law), but the rim and decorations are indicators of their own individuality. When they marry and move to another village that is located in a new region, they begin to produce vessels that are similar to those of their new village/region rather than where they first learned how to produce pots. While this is a form of resocialization, it is not as strong when compared to practices of the Luo of Kenya, who discourage their daughters from learning how to make pots until they are married and learn from their mothers-in-law (see Herbich 1987). Because daughters of Gamo potters learn at an early age all aspects of pottery production, when they marry into a new village and household, they already have learned the basic techniques of pottery production. Therefore, they learn new techniques such as stylistic attributes, clay selection, and new distribution networks, but they always have their knowledge from their natal household concerning potting techniques. Proximity and access to clay sources and consumer demands are the reasons why potters conform to their new village's techniques of producing vessels. Gamo potters tend to work alone or with their family members, which is similar to Maya potters, except that there are two exceptions among the Maya of Guatemala, the communities of Rabinal and Santa María Chiquimula, where potters manufacture "in an almost assembly-line manner" (Reina and Hill 1978:21). Hence, archaeologists looking at pottery materials should be able to discern the village or regional origin of earthenware materials based on form and decoration.

It should be possible for archaeologists to determine the range of socioeconomic relations in a region based on pottery analysis (Stark et al. 2000). D. Arnold's (2000) article clearly states in detail the important issues related to paste variability, which should prompt archaeologists to begin to ask more contextual questions of their assemblages concerning why potters used or did not use specific clays. D. Arnold states that "without more study of the relationship between past variability and the geological, social, and behavioral variables of raw materials selection, procurement, and paste preparation in ethnoarchaeological contexts, the use of paste data to infer production organization within the community of potters is premature" (2000:363). He continues by stating, "Although the composition of ceramic pastes cannot tell us much about production organization, they can tell us a great deal about the organization of ceramic distribution with regional surveys by identifying source communities and their rise and fall through time" (2000:370). In Gamo society, potters are full-time specialists, and a majority of society is dependent on these potters to obtain their household pottery. The issue of the variability of Gamo clays needs to be addressed in the future; I collected 27 clays and one temper from 11 potters living in seven villages that need to be analyzed to explore the variability of clays mined by potters living in different villages and regions. Thus, the analysis of the ceramic paste will determine if there is more heterogeneity of clays and tempers in nonpotter villages, where consumers obtain their pots from diverse potters at markets, compared to pottery-producing villages, where the patron–client system occurs.

The factors affecting the use of Gamo clays indicate that there is a complex array of issues related to the geological, social, and behavioral factors that affect where Gamo potters obtain their clays and tempers and confirm

that the social context of a society will have more to say concerning the distribution of pots rather than the organization of ceramic production. Gamo potters living in the same village often procure their clays and tempers from the same sources. However, some potters living in the same village mine their materials from two distinct sources. The Guyla potters do not share their clay sources because of competition and the fear that the clay source will become depleted. Both Guyla's and Zuza's potters extract their clays and temper from within 6 km of their village. Therefore, the mining of clays and tempers is tethered to where specific potters live. This agrees with D. Arnold's (1985:35–57, 1993:200–204, 2000: 343) worldwide sample of potters that indicates a majority of potters collect their clays and tempers within 7 km of their villages and 33 percent of the world's potters collect within 1 km of their production site. This is not surprising given the amount of labor involved in transporting clay from the sources.

Archaeologists should be aware that ethnographic studies indicate that potters will select lower-quality clays that are closer to their production area rather than clays that are of higher quality but farther away (Arnold 1991:23; Davison and Hosford 1978; Haaland 1978:49; Rye and Evans 1976:126). Hence, proximity of the clays and tempers may be more important than their quality. Gamo potters use different clays and tempers based on several social, economic, and technical factors. The low social status of Gamo potters makes it difficult for some potter communities to find suitable clays because some *mala* will not allow potters to dig for clay on their farmland. One example illustrates this point: the potters of Ezo Shasha, who do not have farmland, used four clays to produce their vessels, but in 1991 the *mala* stopped giving permission to the potters to mine the clays. Since 1991 the Ezo Shasha potters had to switch from four clays to only one clay that they had never used before. The Ezo Shasha potters complain that since they started using the new clay, the pots break more easily than when they used the four clays prior to

1991. Guyla potters also complained that the control of farmland by the *mala* makes it difficult for them to obtain permission to dig on the land for suitable clays. Although D. Arnold (2000) discusses that the control of clay sources by elites has caused potters in Ticul, Mexico, and Chinautla, Guatemala, to stop using specific sources, those potters have expanded, rather than limited, their use of clay sources. However, because the Gamo potters are part of a strict caste system, they have not been able to find alternate clay sources. Other conditions that affect the types of clays used are geological factors such as the high water table flooding sources used by the Guyla potters. One Guyla potter died because the wall of the clay quarry collapsed, which also has been reported in Ticul, Mexico, where at least a half dozen potters have died from collapsing mines (D. Arnold 2000). In addition, Gamo potters stated that it is important to acquire the right mixture of clays and temper or else the pots will break during production. The proximity and quality of clay sources, as well as landownership, are important components in the use of particular clay sources throughout the world (Arnold 1993:64, 66; Aronson et al. 1994:88; Handler 1963:315–316; Lauer 1974:143–144; Neupert 2000:253; Van de Velde and Van de Velde 1939:22). Thus, this study of the Gamo concurs with D. Arnold's (2000) assessment that changes in the mining of clays are caused by environmental processes, landownership, and the exhaustion of sources.

Gamo potters have a limited amount of land, and the drying of vessels limits the amount of pots produced. This also is found among the potters in Ticul, Mexico, who found that the limited amount of interior space is a crucial factor in the amount of vessels that potters can produce (Arnold 1999:70). The Gamo allocate a considerable amount of time for drying, which can range from seven to 28 days depending on the size of the vessel. This compares to potters living in the Los Tuxtlas region of Mexico (Arnold 1991:50–51), the Mixco society of Guatemala (Arnold 1978:342), or the Bailén community of Spain (Curtis 1962:493), where potters dry their vessels for only one day. Comparable drying times to those used by the Gamo occur in Nigeria (20 days; Wahlman 1972:324), New Guinea (one–two weeks to many months; Kakubayashi 1978:138; Lauer 1974:72; Smith 1967:12; Tuckson and May 1975:169; Watson 1955:123), New Hebrides, Melanesia (two–three weeks; Shutler 1968: 17), Micronesia, and Pakistan (11–16 days; Rye and Evans 1976:74; see Arnold 1985:66–70 for a list of cross-cultural drying times). Raw material and weather can affect the drying rates (Arnold 1985:62–77), and the Gamo live in an environment, especially from May to September, where the weather is humid, moist, cold, and cloudy, which increases the drying time.

Gamo potters reduce their vessels during the postfiring, and this treatment is similar to the process found among the San Nicolas potters in the Philippines, where they reduce their cooking pots because they believe it makes the pots more beautiful and durable (Longacre et al. 2000). These postfiring methods attract the attention of the consumers, helping the potters to sell their wares. This smudging of the vessel does not necessarily make the vessel stronger, but it does help the vessels to be more resistant to surface abrasion, which may affect the use-life of the vessel (Longacre et al. 2000; Schiffer and Skibo 1987).

Difficulty in acquiring fuelwood also appears to be a common issue for potters. The Gamo potters living in the highland village of Guyla complained about problems finding fuelwood because of deforestation and are unable to collect fuel from sacred forests. The lack of fuelwood has been documented from other potters such as those living in Acatlan, Mexico, where they have been forced to use trash, sugarcane, cornstalks, cactus, and rubber tires (Lackey 1981:59–60); and potters living in Los Pueblos, Michoacan, Mexico, have used sawdust or tires or had to resort to obtaining wood from 80 km away (Papousek 1981:84–85, 114).

In sum, Gamo pottery procurement and production reflect trends in other parts of the world and yet are clearly influenced by the unique cultural lifeways and traditions in which they are embedded. The next chapter focuses on distribution and illustrates that archaeologists should be able to further understand the social and economic context of a society by studying the ceramic variation witnessed within distinct villages and households.

3

Pottery Distribution

The types of ceramics found in individual households in a region are influenced by a wide array of cultural and environmental factors, such as the geographic distribution of potters, the availability of good potting clay, the types of crops grown and food prepared, the type of economy (e.g., market verses patron–client), vessel cost, and the social-economic standing of the household (D. Arnold 1985, 1993, 2000; Chávez 1992; Kramer 1997:109–133; Stark 1992, 1994). Thus, understanding how potters distribute their wares throughout the region and who lives in each household and village should help archaeologists understand variation in household assemblages. The social makeup of a village strongly determines how pots are distributed, as a non-pottery-producing village purchases pots produced throughout the Gamo region, whereas a pottery-producing village obtains a majority of its pots from resident potters. Two questions may lead to an understanding of how to differentiate between pottery-producing and non-pottery-producing villages. First, how do nontechnological factors (e.g., proximity to markets, vessel cost, social relationship between potters and consumers) found in different villages influence the distribution and use of pottery in a cultural system (Aronson et al. 1994; Gosselain 1998)? Second, are the differences in the potters' production techniques or materials used in different villages significant enough to influence which vessel consumers select (Schiffer and Skibo 1987)? These ques-

tions are important because archaeologists are not always able to identify the technological and nontechnological factors that influence the distribution of ceramic production and use within a region. The goal of this chapter is to present the different factors that lead to how Gamo pots are distributed, such as consumer preference, vessel cost, and household social and economic characteristics.

VILLAGE ANALYSIS

The Origin of Pottery in Gamo Households
Potters supply their village with pots through the patron–client (*mayla*) system, but also they are free to sell at weekly markets, providing nonpotter villages access to vessels (Figure 3.1; Tables 3.1–3.2; see chap. 1). Pottery consumers in the villages of Zuza and Guyla purchase their pots either from markets or directly from the potters' households. The inhabitants of Etello must travel to markets to purchase vessels because there are no potters living in the village or within the larger associated region of Doko. Figure 3.2 illustrates the differences in the frequency of pots in Etello, a nonpotter village, compared to Zuza and Guyla, which have potters living within them. When comparing the 20 households from each of the three villages, Zuza and Guyla have a mean of 17.3 and 24.5 pots per household, respectively. In contrast, Etello has only a mean of 11.1 pots per household. Thus, households in the non-pottery-producing village have smaller inventories than households

TABLE 3.1. Geographical Distance between Pottery Producers and Markets

GAMO POTTERY-PRODUCING VILLAGE/REGION	MARKET	DISTANCE (ONE WAY)
Guyla	Leesha	less than 1 km
	Pango (Doko Mesho)	6 km
	Tuka (Chencha)	12 km
	Ezo	9 km
	Zada	4 km
Zuza	Ochollo	less than 1 km
	Chano	6 km
Birbir	Ezo	9 km
	Charey	less than 1 km
	Mirab Abaya	13 km
Ezo	Ezo	less than 1–3 km
	Tuka (Chencha)	12 km
	Bodo (Dorze)	18 km
Borada	Ezo	12–18 km
Zada	Pango (Doko Mesho)	6 km

FIGURE 3.1. Guyla potters preparing their vessels for the weekly market.

in pottery-producing villages. Furthermore, the Guyla households that purchase their vessels from Guyla potters buy or exchange mostly with a single Guyla potter (Table 3.3). Information was not gathered on whether Zuza consumers knew which pots were produced by specific potters. However, the majority of Zuza consumers purchased their pots from Zuza potters (Figure 3.3). Etello consumers only knew from which village or region their pots were made and rarely knew the potter by name. Therefore it is impossible to conclude if Etello consumers were obtaining their pots from a single potter or not.

Consumer Pottery Preferences

Census information collected from the villages of Zuza, Guyla, and Etello indicates that consumers prefer vessels made in particular regions for both technical and nontechnical reasons. Each household was visited in each village, and the eldest woman of the household was asked two questions relating to pottery: (1) Which pottery region or village

TABLE 3.2. Large Markets in the Central Gamo Region and Their Corresponding Days

MARKET	DAYS
Bodo (Dorze)	Monday and Thursday
Tuka (Chencha)	Tuesday and Saturday
Pango (Doko Mesho)	Sunday
Ezo	Monday and Thursday
Zada	Tuesday

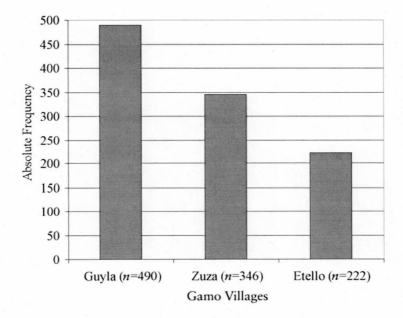

FIGURE 3.2. The absolute frequency of vessels inventoried among 20 households in each of the three Gamo villages, demonstrating a greater number of vessels in the pottery-producing villages (Guyla and Zuza).

produces the best pottery? and (2) Why do you prefer pottery from that region or village? Comparison between the villages reflects regional differences in consumer preference. In general, consumers say they prefer local ceramics, which they can purchase at markets close to their own village.

Consumers in the village of Zuza prefer either Zuza pottery or a combination of Zuza and other pottery found in villages that are part of Ochollo district/*dere* (Table 3.4). Ochollo has a market every Sunday with all

Ochollo potters attending to sell their wares. The consumers prefer Ochollo potters for technological and nontechnological factors. Most people believe that the Ochollo pots are stronger (technological), meaning they last a long time or are more durable. Other important technological factors include the quality of the clay, the quality of the work, and/or the length of time the potters take in drying their pots. Proximity was the only nontechnological answer given by the Zuza consumers. The Ochollo market is located within the

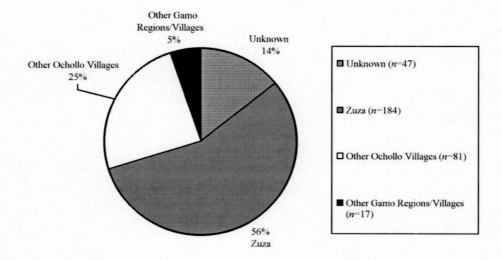

FIGURE 3.3. Relative frequencies of pots in 20 Zuza households by source of manufacture, illustrating their predominate use of Zuza and Ochollo district/*dere* pots.

TABLE 3.3. Each Guyla Household Generally Purchases Most of Its Guyla Pottery Vessels from a Single Potter

HOUSEHOLD ID NUMBER	NUMBER OF PRODUCERS REPRESENTED IN HOUSEHOLD INVENTORY	% POTS FROM SINGLE PRODUCER
39	1	100
15	1	100
55	2	95
25	2	91
47	2	64
53	2	54
66	2	50
31	3	88
65	3	50
3	4	56
28	4	40
5	5	70
56	5	36
45	6	63
19	6	35
17	6	27

TABLE 3.4. Reasons Given for Why Zuza Consumers (*n* = 44 Households) Prefer Zuza and Ochollo District/Dere Pots

REASON	% PREFERRING ZUZA POTS (*n* = 24)	% PREFERRING TWO OR MORE OF THE OCHOLLO *DERE* POTS (ZUZA, KIA, DENKARAR, DOMA) (*n* = 20)
Stronger: last a long time, more durable	29	40
Proximity	25	15
Clay quality	17	15
Quality of work	17	
Dried for a long time	17	5
No reason	8	35

TABLE 3.5. Reasons Given for Why Guyla Consumers (*n* = 51 Households) Prefer Birbir and Guyla Pots

REASON	% PREFERRING BIRBIR POTS (*n* = 36)	% PREFERRING GUYLA POTS (*n* = 15)
Stronger: last a long time	56	56
Quality of clay	39	7
Fired for a long time	6	
Proximity		20
Able to exchange food for pots		7
Only buy Guyla pots		6

boundaries of two adjacent villages, Zuza and Doma.

The majority of Guyla consumers said they prefer pottery based on technological aspects. Consumers who prefer pots from either Birbir subdistrict/*mota* or the village of Guyla stated that they were strong pots that lasted a long time (Table 3.5). All of the Guyla consumers who prefer Birbir pots selected them based on their technological qualities of either pottery use (i.e., strong: last a long time) or production (i.e., clay quality and fired for a long time). Among the Guyla consumers, 7 percent stated that they prefer Guyla pottery because they could exchange food for the pots (a nontechnological reason).

Thus, we have two groups of consumers in Guyla: (1) the group that prefers Birbir pots and is more interested in the technological aspects of pottery use and production and (2) the group that prefers Guyla pots and has mixed opinions about the technological and nontechnological elements concerning pottery production and distribution. Consumers who purchase Birbir pots must walk 10 km one way to the weekly Ezo market, where Birbir potters sell their pots. Consumers who live in Guyla can visit the small weekly Leesha subdistrict/*mota* market located in the village of Guyla to buy or exchange food for Guyla pots.

In Etello, consumers travel to markets to purchase pottery because there are no potters living in the village. The patron–client

TABLE 3.6. Reasons Given for Why Etello Consumers (*n* = 52 Households) Prefer Birbir and Zada or Guyla Pots

REASON	% PREFERRING BIRBIR POTS (*n* = 40)	% PREFERRING ZADA OR GUYLA POTS (*n* = 12)
Stronger: last a long time	50	25
Quality of clay	30	8
Quality of work	13	7
Quality of fuelwood	7	
Proximity		50
Only buy Zada or Guyla pots		17
Cheap		8

relationships that are found in the pottery-producing villages of Zuza and Guyla do not exist in Etello. Etello consumers buy from specific potters who are selling their wares at the markets but still are more likely to purchase pots made in a specific village or region. There is a direct relationship between which market the Etello consumers visit and the kind of pottery they can purchase, as Gamo potters usually go to specific markets.

In the 52 Etello households surveyed, 77 percent (*n* = 40) prefer Birbir pots, and only 23 percent (*n* = 12) prefer either Guyla or Zada pots. Consumers who prefer Birbir pots provided only technological reasons for their preference (Table 3.6). These reasons are related to either use (i.e., stronger: long lasting) or production (i.e., quality of either the clay, the potter's work, or the fuelwood). Etello consumers who prefer Birbir pots must go to Ezo, which is the closest market for the sale or trade of Birbir pots but is a 14-km walk from Etello. The majority of consumers who prefer Guyla or Zada pots do so because of proximity. The Guyla potters usually go to the Leesha (8 km from Etello), Pango (Doko Mesho; 3 km from Etello), or Zada markets (9.5 km from Etello), and so the Etello consumers who prefer Guyla or Zada pots (*n* = 12) must go to one of these three markets. These markets are closer to Etello than the Ezo market. Another nontechnological reason for preferring Guyla or Zada pots is that they are cheaper than Birbir pottery. Reasons for preferring Guyla or Zada pottery are based either on distribution (i.e., proximity), production (i.e., stronger: long lasting or the quality of the potter's work or clay), tradition (i.e., only buy Zada or Guyla pottery), or economics (i.e., inexpensive).

Preference versus Actual Purchase

My research indicates that individuals do not always purchase pots from the particular potter/village that they prefer. Although consumers may prefer nonlocally produced pottery, they are not always able to purchase these pots because of a number of reasons, including (1) distance and household responsibilities, especially childcare; (2) cost constraints; (3) a long-term patron–client relationship; and (4) household economics. The ceramic inventory from 20 households in each village indicates that despite preferences, consumers actually purchase locally made ceramics more frequently.

Zuza consumers' preference for Zuza pots is reflected in their actual use of Zuza vessels. Figure 3.3 illustrates the number of pots and their manufacturing location among the 20 Zuza households. From the 346 pottery vessels inventoried, I was able to obtain information on 329 vessels concerning where they were manufactured. Just over half (55.9 percent) of the vessels were manufactured in Zuza. This reflects the strong patron–client

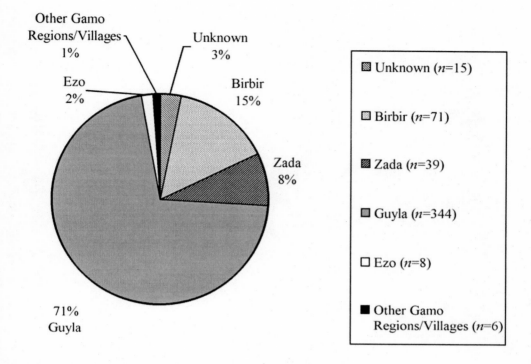

Other Gamo
Regions/Villages
1%

Unknown
3%

Ezo
2%

Birbir
15%

Zada
8%

71%
Guyla

Unknown (*n*=15)

Birbir (*n*=71)

Zada (*n*=39)

Guyla (*n*=344)

Ezo (*n*=8)

Other Gamo
Regions/Villages (*n*=6)

FIGURE 3.4. Relative frequencies of pots in 20 Guyla households by source of manufacture, illustrating that they tend to purchase locally made pottery (Guyla) even though they express preference for Birbir pots.

relationship that occurs in Zuza between the *mala* and *mana* households.

The unknown category reflects the fact that informants do not always know where a pot was manufactured, primarily because the informant's mother-in-law had purchased the pot. In addition, almost a quarter of the pots (24.6 percent) used in Zuza came from Ochollo district/*dere* potters, which indicates that consumers and potters living in Ochollo do most of their purchasing of pots in the Ochollo market. Only 5.2 percent of the pots inventoried came from areas outside of Ochollo.

The household inventory of pots from 20 households in Guyla indicates that almost three-fourths (71 percent) of the pots were produced in Guyla. Although consumers in Guyla say they prefer Birbir pots (see Table 3.5), only 15 percent of the pots were pro-

duced in the Birbir region (Figure 3.4). This indicates that among Guyla consumers proximity is a stronger determinant for the purchase of pots than technical qualities. In addition, the patron–client relationship between the *mala* and *mana* is long-standing in Guyla, resulting in *mala* households purchasing a majority of their pots from a specific Guyla potter (see Table 3.3).

Consumers in Guyla had the lowest percentage of pots that were in the unknown origin category (3 percent) compared to Etello (13 percent) and Zuza (14 percent). This is related to two factors. First, in Guyla many mothers-in-law, mothers, and their unmarried daughters, who purchased the pots, were still living in the village. In Zuza and Etello many of the daughters were married and had moved to their husbands' households; thus they were not present to tell me the origin

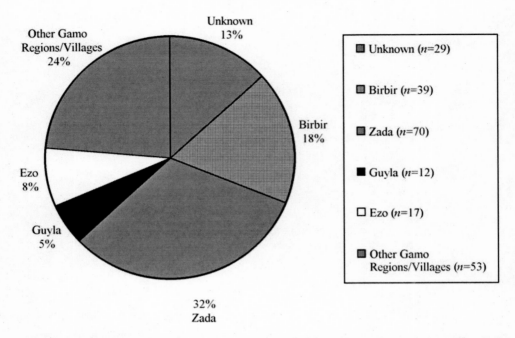

Other Gamo
Regions/Villages
24%

Unknown
13%

Birbir
18%

Ezo
8%

Guyla
5%

32%
Zada

| Unknown (n=29) |
| Birbir (n=39) |
| Zada (n=70) |
| Guyla (n=12) |
| Ezo (n=17) |
| Other Gamo Regions/Villages (n=53) |

FIGURE 3.5. Relative frequencies of pots in 20 Etello households by source of manufacture, illustrating that pots are purchased from many Gamo regions.

of the pots they had purchased. Second, the Guyla women who bought the pots were still alive, while in Etello and Zuza most women who had purchased the pots were deceased and thus not around to tell me the origin of the pots they purchased.

The pottery inventory data indicate a difference between the preference and the actual use of pottery among Etello consumers. The household inventory of pots from 20 households in Etello indicates that the highest percentage of pots were manufactured in Zada (32 percent; Figure 3.5). This is a result of women traveling to the closest market, Pango, where the majority of Zada pots are sold. Although the majority of the Etello consumers prefer Birbir pots (see Table 3.6), less than one-fifth (18 percent) of the consumers from Etello use Birbir pots. This study indicates a purchasing preference for locally made ceramics, which may reflect that women are purchasing pots from their natal regions.

Gamo women purchase most of their pottery vessels from the markets. Therefore, where women grow up and then live after

marriage may affect their market choice. The majority of Etello women come from either Etello or neighboring villages (within the Doko Gambela or Pango regions of Doko) and market at Pango, Tuka, or Ezo, yet they prefer Birbir pots. There are several possible reasons why the use of Birbir pots in Etello does not correspond with the percentage of consumers who prefer Birbir vessels. First, because Birbir pots are sold only at the Ezo market (10 km away), distance may be a problem. Women who have small children stated that they cannot travel to distant markets like Ezo because of the time it takes away from child care. In addition, elderly women who have health problems stated that they are not able to travel to Ezo and must purchase their pots at closer markets such as Pango (3 km) or Tuka (4 km). Second, Birbir pots are more expensive than pots made in other regions such as Guyla. The majority of the Guyla women were born in villages near to Guyla; therefore they are familiar with the use of Guyla pots. As with the Etello consumers, Guyla women are not always able to travel to the Ezo mar-

TABLE 3.7. Cost of Vessel Types in Gamo Society

VESSEL TYPE	n	COST (BIRR)		
		MEAN	MEDIAN	RANGE
Coffee pitcher (*jebana*)	50	1.43	1.50	0.50–3.00
Wide-mouth medium jar (*diste*)	49	1.81	1.50	0.40–6.00
Large jar (*otto*)	240	3.36	3.00	0.30–11.00
Narrow-mouth medium jar (*tsaro*)	131	1.14	1.00	0.10–8.00
Bowl (*shele*)	141	2.12	1.50	0.10–18.00
Baking plate (*bache*)	31	3.91	3.00	1.00–15.00
Narrow-mouth small jar (*tsua*)	56	0.55	0.50	0.10–2.00
Beer jar (*batsa*)	48	14.02	10.50	0.35–50.00
Water pipe (*guya*)	21	1.85	2.00	1.00–3.50
Dish (*peele*)	28	2.18	1.75	0.10–6.00
Foot-washing bowl (*gumgay*)	4	3.12	3.50	0.50–5.00
Single-handle jar (*kolay*)	2	0.5	0.50	0.10–1.00
Wide-mouth small jar (*tayche*)	3	0.56	0.50	0.50–0.70
TOTAL	804	2.94	2.00	0.10–50.00

ket where Birbir pots are sold because of their household responsibilities.

Vessel Cost

Information on vessel cost was obtained by asking potters and consumers for information about the cost of each vessel during the household ceramic census. The cost of pottery is dependent on where it is manufactured. The majority of transactions are conducted with the Ethiopian national currency, the birr (1996–1998, 8 birr = U.S.$1.00). However, in the small village markets and between patron and clients the vessels may be traded for a certain volume of a specific crop.

The most expensive pots, based on a sample size of 804 vessels, come from the Birbir region, with a mean cost of 4.39 birr (*n* = 20). The region that produces the least expensive vessels is Zuza, with a mean cost of 1.81 birr (*n* = 226). The reason for the high cost of Birbir pots is partly based on their popularity with consumers. A majority of Guyla and Etello consumers prefer Birbir pots (see Tables 3.5–3.6). In addition, the number of

Birbir beer jars, the most expensive type of vessel, was less than the number of beer jars manufactured by Zada and Guyla potters. This is because the majority of consumers could not afford beer jars produced by Birbir potters but can afford beer jars manufactured by Zuza and Guyla potters.

The cost of a vessel also varies depending on its type. Beer jars are expensive to buy because they are the most expensive and labor-intensive to manufacture (Table 3.7). The production of beer jars requires potters to procure more clay than other vessel types. Potters dry beer jars for one month and use more fuel-wood to fire them than other vessel types. In addition, after considerable investment in the production process of beer jars or any other type of vessel, there is no guarantee of a successful firing. The average price for beer jars among Zuza, Etello, and Guyla consumers is 14.02 birr (*n* = 48). This compares to 2.22 birr for the average price of 756 vessels of all other types of pots from the three villages. Cost data were not available for vessels purchased before the wife came to live in the household,

TABLE 3.8. Mean Number of Wealth Attributes among Each of the Three Gamo Castes

CASTE	FARMLANDS	OCCUPATIONS	LIVESTOCK	HOUSES	WIVES
Mala (n = 48)	3.4	1.5	2.7	2.3	0.9
Mana (n = 6)	1.5	1.5	0.7	1.5	1.2
Degala (n = 6)	1.5	1.8	0.3	1.7	0.8

TABLE 3.9. Average and Range of Vessel Cost among the Nonpotter Groups

VILLAGE AND CASTE	VESSEL COST (BIRR)	
	AVERAGE	RANGE
Zuza mala	1.84 (n = 226)	0.10–15.00
Etello mala	2.82 (n =197)	0.10–30.50
Etello degala	2.21 (n = 19)	0.25–4.00
Guyla mala	3.93 (n = 315)	0.20–50.00
Guyla degala	2.26 (n = 47)	0.20–10.00

purchased by someone who had died before I conducted the household inventory, or purchased through barter.

CASTE GROUP ANALYSIS

There are three Gamo caste groups, *mala*, *mana*, and *degala*, which have different occupations, access to land, and social and economic standing (Table 3.8; see chap. 1). The *mala*, *mana*, and *degala* purchase a variety of pot types from different villages/regions because of their social status, income, and marriage patterns (i.e., wife's origins).

Vessel Expenditure

The mean expenditure on pots by specific caste households suggests that the *mala*/farmer households spend more on pots than the *degala*/hide-worker households. All *mana*/potter households in both Zuza and Guyla villages use their own wares, so it is not possible to compare them to other caste households. Generally, except for the Zuza *mala* caste, artisans buy less expensive pots than the *mala* caste (Table 3.9). Zuza pots have a low cost because potters have access to abundant fuelwoods, which lowers the production costs. However, in areas where artisans own more

land and are subsequently wealthier, they are able to purchase more expensive vessels.

The Origin of Household Pottery

The patron–client system is very strong in Guyla (Figure 3.4) and Zuza (Figure 3.3), and for this reason, a high percentage of the *mala* pots originated in Guyla and Zuza, respectively. Almost two-thirds (64 percent) of the Guyla *mala* pots come from Guyla potters. The largest number of non-Guyla pots that Guyla *mala* buy are from the Birbir region (20 percent), which they prefer for their durability. The Guyla *mala* can afford the high cost and have family members who are able to walk to the Ezo market to purchase the vessels. Guyla hideworkers cannot afford to purchase Birbir pots even though they may travel to the Ezo market. In contrast, in Zuza only 5 percent of the Zuza *mala* pots came from outside the Zuza/Ochollo region, indicating that consumers prefer Zuza/Ochollo pots not only because of their proximity but also for their durability (Table 3.4). Zuza *mala* travel to the Bodo (Dorze) market, but they often stated that pots manufactured by Bodo potters are poorly made. Even the Bodo potters admit that the clays in Bodo are difficult to work

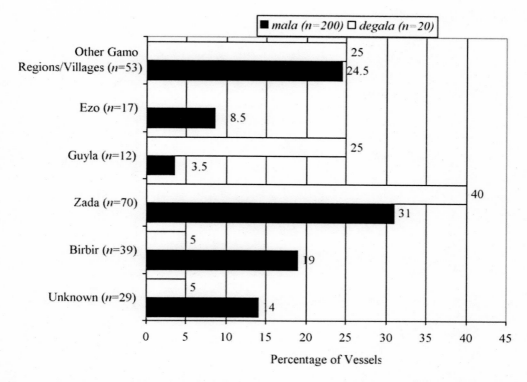

FIGURE 3.6. Relative frequencies of pots in *mala* and *degala* households in Etello by source of manufacture (*n* = 220).

and not as durable as clays that they used in their parents' villages. In contrast, in the non-potter village of Etello, the *mala* households purchase a high percentage of their pots (19 percent) from Birbir potters at the Ezo market (10 km away). Like the Guyla *mala*, the Etello *mala* purchase Birbir pots, which are expensive and available at markets located far away. In addition, the Etello *mala* households have a high percentage of vessels that are older than the vessels in *degala* households. The reason *mala* households have older vessels is that they use large storage vessels for brewing beer and storing crops, which the *degala* households cannot afford to purchase. Storage vessels have a longer use-life than other types of vessels (see chap. 5).

The *degala* in Etello tend to buy pots produced in Guyla (25 percent) at the Pango market (6 km away), which is closer in proximity and has less expensive pottery. Only a few of the vessels (5 percent) in *degala* households

(see Figure 3.6) come from Birbir. While there is a sharp contrast in the origin of pots between *mala* and *degala* households in Etello, in Guyla the differences between *mala* and *degala* distributions of pottery containers are not as dramatic (Figure 3.7). This is because Guyla has potters that both castes can purchase pots from, and Guyla's *degala* households own farmland and are not as economically deprived as are the hideworker households living in other Gamo villages (i.e., Etello's *degala*). Although Guyla's *degala* have farmland and have more economic opportunities than other artisans, they still are considered as social outcastes by the Guyla *mala*.

In villages with potters, the patron–client system takes precedence over other decisions, and most pots are locally produced and consumed. The patron–client system reflects the larger caste hierarchy within Gamo society, which influences the distribution of ceramics across the landscape.

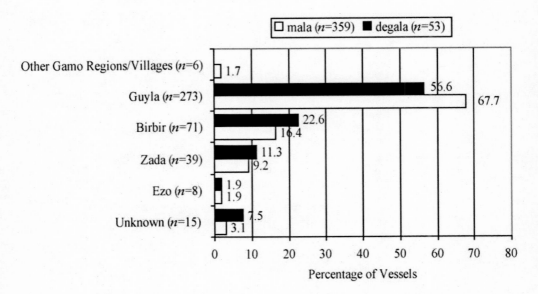

FIGURE 3.7. Relative frequencies of pots in *mala* and *degala* households in Guyla by source of manufacture (*n* = 412).

ECONOMIC RANK ANALYSIS

Identifying economic differences in the archaeological record provides a view of a society's organizational structure. The analysis of spatial patterns of households and their material culture, such as household ceramics, allows archaeologists to re-create the economic hierarchy of a society. Ceramic vessels are an important medium for interpreting household wealth because of their close association with subsistence and their durability against post-depositional factors. The different lifecycle stages of production, distribution, use, mending, reuse, and discard of Gamo household ceramics may reflect different household patterns based on economic wealth.

Wealth in Gamo society is dependent on the household's developmental cycle, as well as one's social placement. Social status and wealth are not isomorphic, as a household's economic wealth may be higher than that of another household that may belong to a higher caste. For example, some potter households do not have farmland, but because there are a number of people generating income, they are economically wealthier than households inhabited by *mala* widows. Thus, the developmental cycle in terms of who is living within the household and their associated occupation(s) directly affects a household's economic status. Therefore, it is important to analyze the households within both an economic and a caste context to better define household social and economic wealth using household ceramic assemblages.

The Gamo economic wealth analysis is based on emic descriptions derived from interviews obtained during my household census in the three villages. The Gamo people base economic wealth on a number of conditions that are both associated and not associated with the caste system. They assess the wealth of a household in terms of (1) the amount and quality of house construction, (2) the amount of land farmed, (3) the type and number of livestock owned, (4) the number of wives within each household including the senior family and their extended family, and (5) the type and number of occupations people are engaged in. These emic factors are the basic tenets of whether a household is wealthy or not. Although it may seem unpalatable to Westerners that the number of wives is given as an economic condition of wealth, it is among the Gamo patriarchal men who have access to the majority of political and economic wealth.

A Gamo man can only marry more than one woman if he can afford to support them all. Women are not viewed as property, but wives are a symbolic indicator of a man's wealth.

Because the Gamo are an agrarian society, land is one of the most important measures of wealth. Some *mana* and *degala* households own land that they either obtained from the *mala* or received through land reallocation instigated by the National Marxist government beginning in 1974. In 1991, when the new Ethiopian government took control, the Gamo began to reinstate their traditional ideals, resulting in some *degala* families losing their farmland. The *mana* and *degala* households that do not have land to farm are economically disadvantaged because they must rely only on the selling of products that they produce to provide income.

If the residents of a household have more than one type of occupation, then the amount of economic wealth increases as it provides economic/occupational diversity. A household that consists of a husband and wife or wives, because the Gamo practice polygyny, also provides the household with more economic opportunities. The types and number of houses within a household are an indicator of wealth, as the construction of a traditional Gamo house is a considerable economic burden. In addition, building a nontraditional house constructed with wood, mud, straw, and corrugated tin sheets is an economic indicator of a wealthy household among the Gamo peoples. Another important indicator of economic wealth are the type and amount of livestock that a household may own. Livestock are an important indicator of wealth for a household because livestock can provide a more varied diet such as eggs, butter, and milk, which are expensive food items. Livestock make the farmland more productive by providing manure for fertilizer and draft power for plowing.

All three villages have households that represent the various economic ranks, with Guyla having the wealthiest households among the three villages. Among the Gamo, the wealthiest households generally belong to the political elite. However, some of these titles indicate social and political roles rather than economic wealth. The *kao*, *uduga*, and *maka* sacrifice animals for the well-being of the people that live in their *mota*. And while the *dana* and *halaka* must pray for their people, they also must give feasts that require substantial wealth.

Caste and economic rank do not always coincide, so that the lowest caste group does not always belong to the lowest economic rank. Surprisingly, there are *degala* households that are members of the wealthiest economic group, as well as some *mana* and *degala* households situated within the average economic group. This indicates that there is no one-to-one relationship between social status such as caste group membership and economic wealth.

In order to measure the emic perception of Gamo economic wealth, I developed a point system (Table 3.8). I gave one point for each occupation within a household. If the household owned only one house, then it received no points. If a household owned two houses, then it received one point, and so forth for each additional house. If the household did not own farmland or livestock, then it received no points for either category, but if the household owned farmland or livestock (excluding chickens), it received one point for each category. If a widow or widower occupied the household, the household received no points for the marriage category. Households with one wife received one point, and if they had more than one wife, they received two points. I tabulated and averaged all five categories for each household from the three villages. Based on the ranges and the mean rank score from the three villages, I determined three ranks. The poorest rank ranges from one to three points, the middle-income rank ranges from four to six points, and the wealthiest rank ranges from seven to ten points.

Vessel Expenditure
As with the caste households, wealthy households spend on average more on each vessel than households with less wealth. This holds true for Zuza and Guyla, but in Etello, the rich households spend less on pots than the poorer

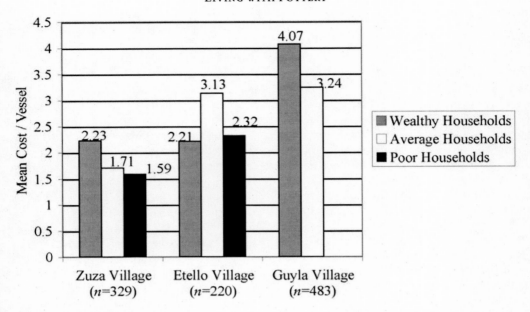

FIGURE 3.8. Mean cost (birr) of pots in Zuza, Etello, and Guyla by economic rank, illustrating that higher economic ranks generally spend more on household pottery.

households. In Etello, the poorest households spend 2.32 birr, the middle-income households spend 3.13 birr, and the rich households spend 2.21 birr on average for a pot (see Figure 3.8). Therefore, in Etello, economic position does not influence how much people pay for their household pots, which may be a reflection of potters not living within the village or region. As discussed above in the caste section, Etello *mala* purchase almost one-fifth of their pots from Birbir potters, who charge more than other Gamo potters. Although the wealthier households of Etello buy more pots from Birbir, the middle-income Etello households purchase Birbir pots that are more expensive on average. Fifty-five percent of Etello *mala* are considered middle-income households in terms of wealth, and it is these households that travel to the Ezo market and purchase more expensive pottery such as the Birbir pots.

The Origin of Household Pottery
The poorest households purchase a higher percentage of cheaper pots than the wealthier households. However, the origins of household pottery are related also to where the wife

of the household was born and raised before moving to her husband's household.

In the nonpotter village, the wealthier households purchase more expensive pottery from more distant resources, while in potter villages the patron–client system prevails. In Etello the wealthiest households have a higher percentage of vessels purchased from Birbir and Ezo potters than either the middle-income or the poorest households (Figure 3.9). However, they purchase less expensive Birbir pots (2.4 birr) on average than the middle-income households, which spend 3.0 birr on average for Birbir pots. Only five of the 20 households are wealthy, whereas 11 households are considered middle income, thereby increasing the number of consumers who travel to Ezo and purchase expensive Birbir pots. In Guyla, the wealthiest households also purchase a little over twice as many of their vessels from Birbir potters as the middle-income households. In contrast, in Zuza, most of the wealthiest and poorest households maintain the village trend by purchasing Zuza pots.

The middle-income households purchase less expensive pottery from a variety of sources. In Etello, the middle-income and

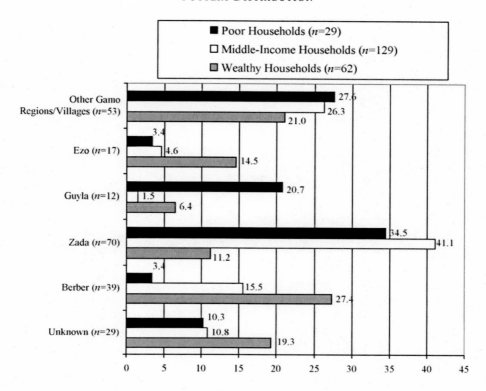

FIGURE 3.9. Relative frequencies of pots in Etello by economic rank and source of manufacture.

poor households have a higher percentage of vessels from Zada, which is closer and has less expensive pots than those purchased by Etello's wealthy population. In Zuza, the households with middle-income wealth purchase fewer pots from Zuza potters and more pots from other potters (Figure 3.10). When looking at the social makeup of the middle-income households it becomes clear that the reason they have fewer pots from Zuza is because they have stronger social ties to other Ochollo regions. One household's mother's brother is the *kao* (ritual sacrificer) of Ochollo, and so they have social obligations not only to Zuza but also to all Ochollo villages. A middle-income household informant who has no Zuza vessels was raised in Ochollo Dinkarar/Moye and has a number of pots from that village even though she prefers Zuza pots. Another informant, who has no Zuza vessels, prefers Ochollo Kia pots and so purchases her vessels from Kia potters at the

Ochollo market. In contrast to Zuza, in Guyla the middle-income households purchase a higher percentage of their pots from Guyla potters, but the consistency between the two economic ranks concerning who they purchase pots from is remarkable (Figure 3.11).

The poorest households purchase their pots through the patron–client system and buy low-cost local wares at nearby markets. In Zuza, the poorest households maintain the village trend by purchasing Zuza pots. The poor Etello households purchase more of their vessels from the Pango market, where both Zada and Guyla potters sell their wares.

There are only two economic ranks in Guyla based on the criteria discussed above, which indicates that Guyla households are generally wealthier than Zuza and Etello households. The economic wealth of Gamo households influences the purchasing of a household's pottery assemblage. The dispersal of household wealth throughout the village reflects

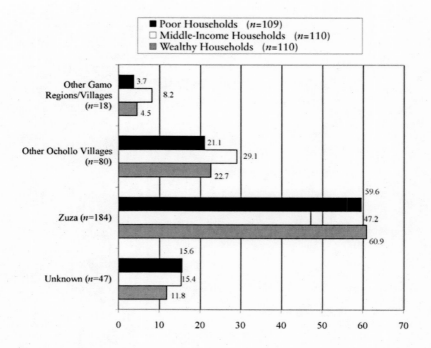

FIGURE 3.10. Relative frequencies of pots in Zuza by economic rank and source of manufacture.

differences in the distribution of pottery that is manufactured and sold in various Gamo villages or regions.

GAMO POTTERY DISTRIBUTION IN CROSS-CULTURAL PERSPECTIVE

Archaeologists examining household pottery within a village should be able to determine the presence of a patron–client system through examination of the clay, form, and decoration at different households. A strong emphasis on local purchases in a society with a market economy where potters are full-time craft specialists may suggest the presence of a patron–client system. Village households engaged in the patron–client system should have a majority of their household pottery assemblage manufactured by a single potter living within the same village. Gamo villages with resident potters have a patron–client system (*mayla*; e.g., Zuza and Guyla), but villages without potters do not have patron–client relationships (e.g., Etello); that is, wealthy individuals in villages without potters do not es-

tablish patron–client relationships with potters in other villages. The Gamo patron–client system in villages with potters has important ramifications for the origin of household pottery. In pottery-producing villages, most non-potter households purchase the majority of their pottery from a single potter. A strict caste hierarchy with a strong patron–client system also is found in the Rajasthan (Kramer 1997) and Malwa (Miller 1985) regions of India. Kramer (1997) has found a contrast between the two cities of Jodhpur and Udaipur in Rajasthan regarding ceramic visibility. Jodhpur has more pots and more types coming from a wider array of potters than Udaipur because middlemen are involved in Jodhpur pottery distribution. In addition, the caste relationship between potters and vendors is more important to their economic transaction, indicating the importance of the patron–client relationship (Kramer 1997:109–133). In Rajasthan, and the Malwa regions of India, pots are sold in the village and at weekly markets (Kramer 1997:123–124; Miller 1985:82–93),

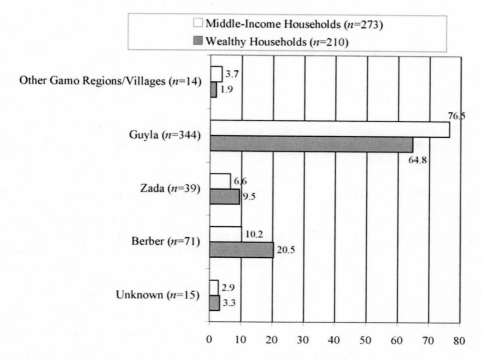

FIGURE 3.11. Relative frequencies of pots in Guyla by economic rank and source of manufacture.

but the scale is much larger than the Gamo distribution pattern, for there are large cities and pots are transported using modern technology. Gamo potters sell both to their village and at weekly markets to nonpotter villages, which are also conducted in the Rajasthan and Malwa regions of India. In contrast to the caste system found in South Asia and among the Gamo, other types of relations can affect the distribution of pottery, such as the kin- or *suki*-based social relations between Kalinga potters and consumers (Stark 1992). Social relations and their economic ties, rather than proximity, dictate the movement of pots from potter to consumer among the Kalinga. The above examples indicate the importance of socioeconomic relationships concerning the variation we see in the distribution of material goods.

The Gamo example indicates that non-pottery-producing villages like Etello may have fewer pots in their household assemblages than pottery-producing villages, such as Zuza and Guyla. This is in contrast to

other ethnoarchaeological studies that have found that stockpiling occurs in household assemblages where villages lack potters (Aronson et al. 1994:101; Nelson 1991:171; Tani 1994:56). Nelson (1991:171) states that the reasons people in the village of San Mateo Ixtatan, Guatemala, stockpile their pots are that markets are sporadic, cash is scarce, and pottery is made only seasonally. Although cash is limited among the Gamo, the market system in Gamo is consistent, and pottery is made throughout the year, even during the rainy season, by full-time specialists.

To strengthen the argument that the patron–client system affects pottery distribution, even if a Gamo household prefers pottery vessels made far away, most purchase local pottery. Hence, consumers are influenced more by proximity and socioeconomic relationships than by technological choices. Kalinga consumers, like the Gamo consumers, listed technological reasons rather than nontechnical reasons in deciding which pots to purchase. The Kalinga cited pottery strength and pot weight as their major reasons for purchasing particular vessels from Dangtalan and Dalupa villages, respectively (Aronson et al. 1994:98–102). The only predominant nontechnological reason given among Kalinga consumers who preferred a particular village water jar is that they were "nicely decorated" (Aronson et al. 1994:100). The Gamo consumers prefer pots because of their strength, so weight and decoration of the pot were never given as a concern. Although Gamo consumers emphasize technological aspects of pottery, they usually purchase a majority of their pots from local potters, indicating that proximity and social relationships take precedence.

The variation in an archaeological household's pottery assemblage may reflect the presence or absence of village potters. Villages without potters should have a wider range of pottery with different clays, forms, and decorations. Gamo non-pottery-producing villages have a wider variety of pottery from different areas than pottery-producing villages.

Although Gamo consumers may prefer pots manufactured from specific villages/regions, they are not always able to purchase pots they prefer. Gamo consumers purchase the majority of their pots from potters living in their village or from markets that are in close proximity to their village, rather than traveling to a distant market to purchase preferred pots.

A vessel's cost is another important element determining which pots people purchase, because the more preferred pots are the most expensive, and many consumers cannot always afford them. Hence, the higher-caste and wealthiest households purchase more expensive pots than lower-caste and poorer households.

Consumers living in villages with potters can use either the patron–client or the market systems to procure their household pottery vessels. Consumers living in villages without potters are able to obtain their household pots only from the weekly markets, causing their households to have smaller assemblages and a higher percentage of pots produced from different regions than consumer households that have potters living in their village. The next chapter further integrates the lifecycle of Gamo pots by focusing on the primary use of household pots at the scales of village, caste, and economic rank.

4

Pottery Primary Use

Previous research on primary-use pots has provided valuable information concerning variation in household assemblages, vessel function, and household activity areas (Deal 1998; Hally 1983; Longacre 1991; Skibo 1992). Primary-use pots are vessels that are not broken and are being used for their original purpose, which may include a number of different functions. The reasons people obtain and use specific vessel types are diverse and relate to conditions such as the proximity to potter households, a village's ecological location, and the household's social and economic position.

The Gamo cook, serve, and store foods mostly with earthenware pottery vessels (see the introduction). The goal of this chapter is to explain the reasons behind household and village ceramic variation based on the primary use of pots. The Gamo have four primary uses for household pottery—cooking, serving, storing, and transporting. This chapter combines aspects of the Gamo diet (chap. 1) and the different ceramic forms (chap. 2) through analyses of the primary use and functions of pots in preparing, serving, storing, and transporting foodstuffs (Table 4.1). Gamo vessels fall into two distinct use categories: (1) pots that are usually used for a specific function (e.g., a coffee pitcher only functions to boil coffee); and (2) types that have multiple functions as their primary use (e.g., a large jar may primarily function as a cooking pot, but it also may function to store and trans-

port water). Pots that are used specifically for either cooking or serving usually are not used later for a completely different function. For example, a cooking vessel is not secondarily used as a serving vessel, or vice versa. Four important factors, discussed in chapter 3, that affect which vessel types Gamo people use are (1) their village location, in terms of proximity to markets where potters sell their wares; (2) potters living in their village; (3) the types of vessels that are sold where consumers purchase their pots; and (4) the household's social and economic status. In addition to having a range of uses for the majority of vessel types, the types also range in size, which allows consumers to choose which vessels are best suited for their specific household needs (Table 4.1).

VILLAGE ANALYSIS
Industrial Types

The replacement of ceramics with industrial types among the Gamo people has not had the dramatic effects that have been witnessed in other parts of the world (Birmingham 1975:385; Sargent and Friedel 1986:192; Skibo 1994:117). Industrial types are more common in the villages of Zuza and Etello than they are in Guyla because Guyla is geographically more remote. The only type of industrial vessel that has completely replaced a Gamo ceramic form is the Chinese porcelain cup, which most of Ethiopia uses as a coffee cup. All of the inventoried Gamo households have replaced their ceramic coffee cups with

Table 4.1. Gamo Vessel Types and Their Corresponding Primary Use and Capacity

Emic Type	Primary Use	Mean Capacity (L)	Size Range (L)	S.D.
Coffee pitcher (*jebana*) (*n* = 60)	boil coffee	2.14	0.60–3.05	0.57
Wide-mouth medium jar (*diste*) (*n* = 61)	vegetable and grain cooking	8.40	0.90–65.42	8.93
Large jar (*otto*) (*n* = 188)	vegetable, grain, and beer cooking	12.63	3.88–50.94	6.04
Large jar (*otto*) (*n* = 80)	water storage	19.64	6.37–77.91	12.96
Large jar (*otto*) (*n* = 77)	water transport	14.10	4.85–36.07	6.41
Narrow-mouth medium jar (*tsaro*) (*n* = 159)	vegetable and grain cooking	4.59	0.26–10.30	1.97
Baking plate (*bache*) (*n* = 47)	roasting	4.56	0.78–7.91	1.42
Bowl (*shele*) (*n* = 182)	serving	11.73	0.06–87.07	12.76
Dish (*peele*) (*n* = 33)	serving	4.73	1.15–11.81	2.14
Narrow-mouth small jar (*tsua*) (*n* = 78)	serving	1.04	0.06–3.05	0.60
Beer jar (*batsa*) (*n* = 86)	storage and beer processing	64.96	20.57–195.33	30.73
Water pipe (*guya*) (*n* = 28)	smoking tobacco	1.44	0.90–2.14	0.26

Chinese porcelain cups, so no attempt was made to include them in the household inventory. Another common type of industrial container in use among the Gamo people is the plastic container people use to collect and transport water. Trucks from Kenya transport large quantities of these plastic water containers and distribute them into the Ethiopian hinterland. In the future, these plastic water containers may completely replace ceramic water jars. However, presently the Gamo use both ceramic water jars and plastic water containers to store and transport their water. Other types of industrial containers are small plastic bowls and drinking cups, as well as metal cooking pots, coffeepots, and baking plates.

In Zuza, a popular industrial type is the plastic water container, which is in use in 55 percent (*n* = 11) of the households inventoried. The use of the plastic water container makes it easier for people to transport water, especially the people who live in Zuza. Villagers with houses on the crest of the Ochollo Ridge, Zuza, must walk down a steep, rocky, 20- to 40-m ridge to a well, which is their closest water source. Only one Zuza house has a large assemblage of industrial vessels, predominantly metal cooking vessels. The adults in this household still use a ceramic jar to transport water, while the children use a plastic container. Another Zuza person stated that she uses plastic bowls instead of the ceramic serving bowls (i.e., *shele* and *peele*) because they last longer.

Etello uses more industrial vessels than either Zuza or Guyla, as Etello is located close to the town of Tuka (Chencha), which has many small stores that sell metal and plastic containers. In Etello, 85 percent (*n* = 17) of the households inventoried use some type of industrial container. Plastic water containers are the most common type used in Etello, but larger varieties of both metal and other plastic containers also are used. Two reasons why Etello households have more industrial

TABLE 4.2. Percentage of Primary-Use Vessel Types and Frequency of Primary-Use Vessel Types (Compared to Total Frequency of the Vessel Types) in the Entire Village Assemblage in Three Gamo Villages

EMIC TYPE	ZUZA		ETELLO		GUYLA	
	%	n	%	n	%	n
Coffee pitcher (*jebana*)	38.7	12 (30)	37.5	3 (8)	59.1	13 (22)
Wide-mouth medium jar (*diste*)	35.9	14 (39)	33.3	4 (12)	70.0	7 (10)
Large jar used for cooking, transporting and storing water (*otto*)	53.6	60 (112)	50.8	32 (63)	40.7	55 (135)
Narrow-mouth medium jar (*tsaro*)	27.6	13 (47)	45.4	15 (33)	49.4	39 (79)
Bowl (*shele*)	68.9	20 (29)	89.5	51 (57)	70.8	68 (96)
Baking plate (*bache*)	53.3	16 (30)	20.0	1 (5)	36.4	4 (11)
Narrow-mouth small jar (*tsua*)	62.5	10 (16)	76.5	13 (17)	75.0	33 (44)
Beer jar (*batsa*)	64.5	20 (31)	20.0	3 (15)	27.3	12 (44)
Water pipe (*guya*)	100	3 (3)	88.9	8 (9)	87.5	14 (16)
Dish (*peele*)	100	6 (6)	66.7	2 (3)	62.5	15 (24)
Foot-washing bowl (*gumgay*)	0	0 (0)	0	0 (0)	100	6 (6)
Single-handle jar (*kolay*)	50.0	1 (2)	0	0 (0)	0	0 (0)
Coffee cup (*sene*)	100	1 (1)	0	0 (0)	0	0 (0)
Wide-mouth small jar (*tayche*)	0	0 (0)	0	0 (0)	100	3 (3)

containers than either Zuza or Guyla are (1) there are no potters living in Etello and (2) their proximity to the town of Tuka. Etello consumers can travel to Tuka to purchase industrial containers, and there is nothing like the patron–client relationship between pottery producers and consumers that is evident in both Zuza and Guyla. Although Etello uses more industrial containers than Zuza or Guyla, Etello households still rely heavily on their household ceramic assemblages for everyday food processing.

Guyla has the least amount of industrial vessels of the three villages I studied, as plastic water containers, bowls, and cups are present in only 35 percent (*n* = 7) of Guyla households. Among the 20 Guyla households invento-

ried, no one reported using metal containers. People living in the least accessible areas of the Gamo region (e.g., Guyla) are slower to change from the ceramic vessels to the industrial containers. The cost of industrial types and their accessibility remain impediments to the technological change from ceramics to plastics and metals. In addition, the change to the industrial containers is hindered because people believe that food tastes better when it is cooked, served, and stored in ceramic vessels.

Frequency of Primary-Use Pottery
There are more Gamo pots representing the primary-use state compared to the later stages (i.e., reuse and discard; see Table 4.2), indicat-

TABLE 4.3. Percentage and Number of Primary-Use Vessel Types in Three Gamo Villages

EMIC TYPE	ZUZA (*n* = 176)		ETELLO (*n* = 132)		GUYLA (*n* = 269)	
	%	*n*	%	*n*	%	*n*
Coffee pitcher (*jebana*)	6.8	12	2.3	3	4.8	13
Wide-mouth medium jar (*diste*)	7.9	14	3.0	4	2.6	7
Large jar used for cooking, transporting and storing water (*otto*)	34.1	60	24.2	32	20.4	55
Narrow-mouth medium jar (*tsaro*)	7.4	13	11.4	15	14.5	39
Bowl (*shele*)	11.4	20	38.6	51	25.3	68
Baking plate (*bache*)	9.1	16	0.8	1	1.5	4
Narrow-mouth small jar (*tsua*)	5.7	10	9.8	13	12.3	33
Beer jar (*batsa*)	11.4	20	2.3	3	4.5	12
Water pipe (*guya*)	1.7	3	6.1	8	5.2	14
Dish (*peele*)	3.4	6	1.5	2	5.6	15
Foot-washing bowl (*gumgay*)	0	0	0	0	2.2	6
Single-handle jar (*kolay*)	0.6	1	0	0	0	0
Coffee cup (*sene*)	0.6	1	0	0	0	0
Wide-mouth small jar (*tayche*)	0	0	0	0	1.1	3
Comparison to entire assemblage	50.9	176 (*n* = 346)	59.4	132 (*n* = 222)	54.9	269 (*n* = 490)

ing that the vessel types in this stage provide a good indication of how a household uses its vessels on an everyday basis. Understanding the causes attributed to the variation witnessed in this stage will allow archaeologists to better interpret social and economic variation from their ceramic assemblages.

The differences between the three villages concerning the number of pots that people own in the primary-use stage correspond to the ecological zone where people live, the foods they are able to harvest and obtain from nearby markets, and the places where they purchase their pots. In Etello, households have smaller primary-use pottery inventories (*n* = 132) than the pottery-producing villages

of Zuza (*n* = 176) and Guyla (*n* = 269). Etello households have fewer pots because they do not have potters living within the village or in adjacent villages and consumers are reliant on the marketing of ceramic vessels rather than the patron–client system.

Etello has fewer pots than other villages, but a greater percentage of its assemblage is in the primary-use stage. For example, there are only 135 pots inventoried in Etello that are within the primary-use stage, compared to 176 in Zuza and 269 in Guyla. The number of vessels within each vessel type category is reduced among the Etello assemblages, except for four cases (see Table 4.3), compared to Zuza and Guyla. However, when comparing the percentage of primary-use pots to the total ceramic frequency in each village, Etello has a slightly higher percentage of primary-use vessels (59.4 percent) than Zuza (50.9 percent) and Guyla (54.9 percent). This suggests that the people in Etello are more careful with their wares because they have fewer reused and discarded pots. I expected that Etello households would be using their vessels with more care because there are no local potters to purchase pots from as there are in Zuza and Guyla. The lower frequency of pots within Etello assemblages is an important signature that a patron–client relationship does not exist and, thus, no potters live within the village.

Types of Primary-Use Pottery

A comparison of the three villages helps to elucidate why the Gamo use specific types of vessels. The vessel assemblages of the three Gamo villages of Zuza, Etello, and Guyla are distinct because of their different ecological locations, crops, diets, proximity to water and woodlands, population density, and cultural practices. Although there are numerous reasons why the Gamo choose to use specific types of pots, understanding the function of the different vessel types should aid archaeologists in explaining the variation between village and household pottery assemblages.

The village's ecological location is one factor that influences the types of foods people consume and therefore the types of pots they are more likely to use. Coffee pitchers are more common in the village of Zuza (Table 4.3), which is a reflection of Zuza's households' ability to grow their own coffee. In contrast, in Etello and Guyla, people are not able to grow coffee because of the high altitude, and consumers must purchase coffee at the weekly markets. Coffee beans are one of the more expensive crops, costing approximately 10 birr/kg (U.S.$1.40). Hence, where coffee is more readily affordable, there are more coffeepots in the assemblage. In addition, the types of drinking vessels that people use are influenced by their ecological location. The narrow-mouth small jars/tsuas, used for beer and water drinking, are less common in Zuza

(Table 4.3). Zuza people use gourds for drinking, rather than narrow-mouth small jars, because the area surrounding Zuza is conducive for growing gourds. There is a mean of 6.35 gourds per household among the Zuza households inventoried, whereas in Etello, the mean number of gourds is 2.85 gourds, and Guyla has a mean number of only 1.3 gourds.

There are also different types of cooking vessels in the three villages, which reflect their dietary habits. Wide-mouth medium jars/distes are more common in Zuza households than in Etello and Guyla (Table 4.3). Ninety-five percent of the wide-mouth medium jars present in Zuza households were produced either in Zuza or by neighboring Ochollo potters. Zuza's consumers eat more wat (a type of stew made with either lentils, chicken, or beef) than Etello and Guyla consumers, and the main function of distes is the preparation of wat.

Baking plates also are more common among Zuza households. The Zuza people eat more maize bread and roasted maize, which is cooked on baking plates. Maize, which cannot be grown in the high-altitude areas, is a major crop grown by Zuza farmers. The number of Zuza households that reported eating maize food is much higher ($n = 19$, 95 percent) than in the villages of Etello ($n = 6$, 30 percent) and Guyla ($n = 2$, 5 percent). Etello and Guyla households eat more barley and wheat, grown at higher altitudes. Although wheat and barley also are roasted, the majority is combined with other ingredients and cooked in narrow-mouth medium jars/tsaros and large jars/ottos (Table 4.3). The demand for baking plates and wide-mouth medium jars among Zuza and Ochollo households is the primary reason why Zuza potters specialize in the manufacture of these two vessel types. However, Guyla potters repeatedly stated that the types of clay mined by Guyla potters are not appropriate for manufacturing baking plates.

The location of villages in relation to local water sources, the availability of wood, and the population density of the surrounding area affect their ceramic assemblages. The majority of Zuza households are located on the ridge crest, and because water is difficult to transport, they use more large jars (34 percent; Table 4.3) for transporting and storing water than the other two villages, which are located adjacent to mountain streams.

Pottery serving vessels such as bowls, dishes, and narrow-mouth small jars occur with a much lower frequency within Zuza households than in Etello and Guyla households (Table 4.3). The land surrounding Zuza is less densely occupied than the higher elevations of Etello and Guyla and provides for an abundant supply of wood for the Zuza inhabitants. Thus, the majority of Zuza people use wooden bowls instead of pottery bowls and dishes for serving. Pottery dishes are more predominant in Guyla households, with the majority produced by Guyla potters (87.5 percent).

The water pipe is less common in Zuza than in Etello or Guyla (Table 4.3). A logical explanation for this would be that there might be more Protestants in Zuza. It is against their Protestant religion to indulge in smoking tobacco or drinking alcohol. However, there are only four inventoried Zuza Protestant households, compared to three in Etello and two in Guyla. Therefore, religion is not the reason for the lower frequency of water pipes in Zuza. While working in the three villages, I did not observe people gathering to smoke the water pipe everyday in Zuza, which I did witness in both Etello and especially Guyla. It is surprising that Zuza households do not smoke tobacco, for tobacco is more commonly grown in Zuza's ecological zone (*baso*) than in the *dega* zone of Etello and Guyla. Tobacco in Gamo is a mixture of cooked tobacco leaves and cow dung. Cattle in Zuza and Ochollo *dere* are not as common as they are in the central Gamo region, which may explain the low numbers of water pipes in Zuza households. Of the households inventoried there was only one cow reported in Zuza, but Etello and Guyla had 31 cows each. In addition, the central Gamo region around the town of Ezo is known for its high-quality tobacco. Thus, the smoking of tobacco in different Gamo regions seems to be a combination of economic, ecological, religious, and cultural factors.

There is a much larger proportion of beer jars in Zuza (11.4 percent) than in either Guy-la (4.5 percent) or Etello (2.3 percent). Etello and Guyla households had not replaced their broken beer jars. In addition, the low percentage of primary-use beer jars demonstrates that the majority of beer jars in both Guyla and Etello are in their reuse stage and function for storing crops and processing beer.

There is a direct relationship between the types of foods that people eat and the vessels that people use to prepare their food. This explains most of the ceramic assemblage variation among the three Gamo villages. The types of foods that people eat within a village have important implications because it is these consumers who push the potters to produce specific vessel forms. Gamo potters are influenced by consumers because of their acute poverty and the lack of farmland for the majority of potter families.

Spatial Analysis of Household Primary-Use Pottery

The layout of Gamo households varies depending on the region, social status, and economic wealth of the household (Figures 4.1–4.3). A wealthy household has several buildings that serve as the main house, the kitchen, and storage. This is especially true for the villages of Etello and Guyla. However, the village of Zuza is located on top of a narrow ridge, causing a shortage of land for the households. Therefore, Zuza households usually consist of only one house where all daily activities take place.

The interior of a wealthy house is divided into different sections. Vestibules are common in Etello and Guyla, but they are not built in Zuza. Usually two benches are placed on either side of the vestibule, where people can sit and sleep. Pots are sometimes stored underneath these benches. The central portion of the house is constructed for the hearth and the main gathering area. Benches and beds are placed along the central area, with bamboo walls separating this section from the partitioned areas for storage and keeping livestock. A wooden rack is constructed over the bamboo walls, where people keep large storage vessels. Other vessels are kept underneath the beds and benches and in the storage

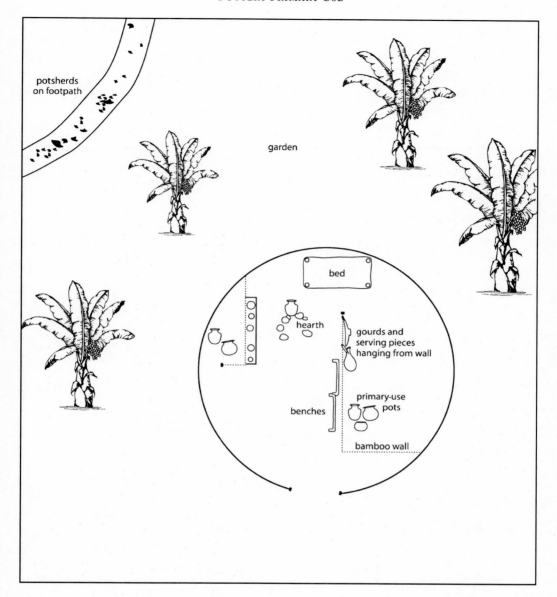

FIGURE 4.1. Generalized spatial pattern of the pottery primary-use stage in the village of Zuza and the low-caste and poor households of Etello and Guyla.

rooms, while serving vessels are hung from the bamboo walls for easy access. However, the majority of vessel types are informally stored in a variety of household areas, including well-defined storage areas. In addition, people stack smaller vessels on top of larger ones for lids and to have more floor area for other activities.

Poorer households have one structure containing only a bed and a few wooden chairs; such houses are found among the Zuza potters and the Etello hideworkers. Potter houses have wooden racks built over the hearth where they dry newly constructed vessels. The location of pots within the household context provides archaeologists with a key to under-

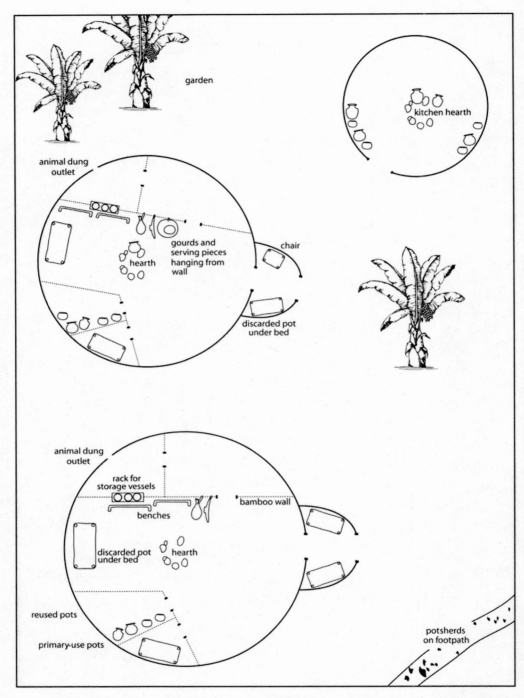

FIGURE 4.2. Generalized spatial pattern of the pottery primary-use stage in the villages of Etello and Guyla, including their high-caste and wealthy households.

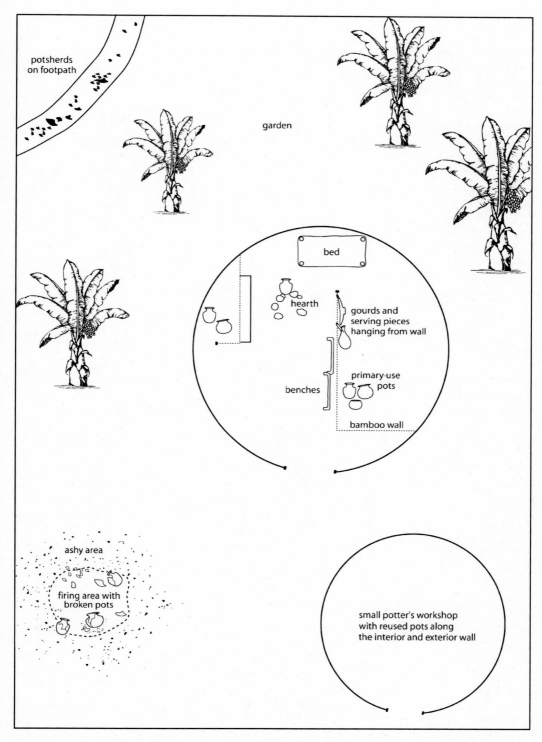

FIGURE 4.3. Generalized spatial pattern of the pottery primary-use stage in the potter households of Guyla.

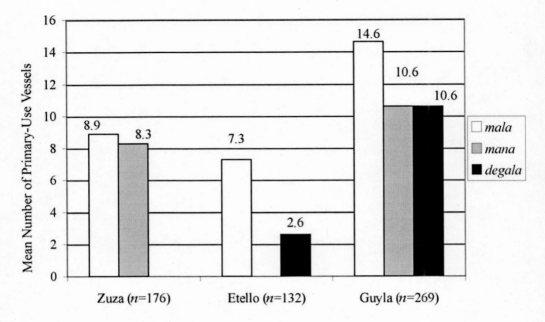

FIGURE 4.4. Mean number of primary-use vessels by caste and village.

standing pottery stages of use. In all villages, people keep the majority of their primary-use vessels stored within the main house. The second most common place to store primary-use vessels is in the kitchen, where people store them in clusters adjacent to the wall or surrounding the hearth.

Primary-use pots also are stored in clusters in the compound, adjacent to the house, and inside either the storehouse or the weaving house. Individual primary-use pots are rarely stored in the compound, garden, or adjacent to either the house or the kitchen. Only ten of the 60 households studied kept some of their primary-use vessels outside, adjacent to either the house or the kitchen. In addition, only six of the 60 households studied kept primary-use pots in either the garden or the compound, and five of these six houses store primary-use pots by themselves.

The spatial location of vessels is largely dependent on the vessels' stage in their lifecycle, providing archaeologists with a key to understanding stage of use. The Gamo exemplify this by placing their primary-use vessels near their hearths and within structures.

CASTE GROUP ANALYSIS

Archaeological pottery may provide clues in the interpretation of household social status. The analysis of ceramic use in association with the three Gamo caste groups, *mala* (predominately farmers and weavers), *mana* (potters), and *degala* (hideworkers), provides the social context concerning household pottery assemblages and caste groups. I expect that household pottery assemblages will reflect Gamo's rigid caste system regarding differences in frequency, typology, volume, and function.

Frequency of Primary-Use Pottery

The frequency of primary-use vessels among the different caste households is also an indication of the types of foods people are eating. Vessels used for pottery production are included in the analysis, except for wasters. The analyses indicate that there is a strong correlation between caste status and the frequency of household vessels. *Mala* households have more primary-use vessels in each of the three villages than both the *mana* and *degala* households (Figure 4.4).

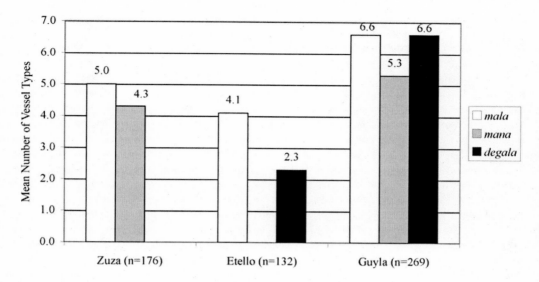

FIGURE 4.5. Mean number of primary-use vessel types by caste and village.

The *mala* households of Guyla have the highest average number of primary-use vessels per household, which is dramatically more than the average number of ceramic vessels from Zuza or Etello *mala* households. Guyla's *mala* households purchase a majority of their pots from Guyla potters. As discussed in chapter 3, there is a strong patron–client relationship in Guyla between the *mala* and *mana* households, as well as in Zuza. Etello's households have fewer numbers of vessels per household because there are no potters living there, and so the Etello consumers must travel to weekly markets to purchase their household vessels. In addition, Etello is located near Tuka, which sells industrial containers, thereby reducing their use of ceramic vessels.

There is a dramatic difference between Etello's and Guyla's *degala* hideworker households in the mean number of pottery vessels per household. The large difference in the number of vessels owned between the two hideworker groups demonstrates the variation in households belonging to the same caste. The ownership of land is a critical economic factor that is reflected in household pottery assemblages. Guyla's hideworker households need additional pottery vessels to process a more varied diet and also to store crops that they grow on their farmland, while Etello's *degala* hideworkers do not own farmland and use a majority of their pots only for cooking. The Etello hideworkers have a smaller number of pots because of their low status, lack of farmland, and the fact that their only livelihood comes from selling scraped cowhides.

In Zuza, the *mana* own slightly fewer pots than the *mala*. However, Zuza potters have large caches of wasters adjacent to their houses and scattered in parts of their compounds, and if wasters were included in the analysis, then potter households in Zuza would have more vessels per household than the Zuza *mala*. The large amount of wasters is one signature that indicates pottery production within Gamo society and clearly differentiates *mana* from non-*mana* households in Zuza. The differing frequencies of pots between the castes in Guyla clearly indicate the Gamo social hierarchy. The potter households in Guyla do not keep their wasters but, rather, deposit them in footpaths and gardens.

Types of Primary-Use Pottery
The number of primary-use vessel types in a household is not a strong indicator of social status in Gamo society (Figure 4.5). However,

the strict social status of Gamo society dictates that the three castes eat different types of foods, which ultimately affects the types of vessels they use.

Because potters can make their own household vessels, there is not a strong difference between *mana* and *mala* households in terms of the represented ceramic types. The *mala* in Zuza own only slightly more vessel types than the potters living in Zuza (Figure 4.5). The one vessel type that potters in Zuza do not own is the beer jar, because the potters do not have farmland and therefore do not need beer jars for storing excess crops, nor do they have enough grain to produce beer. Another difference is that the potters own over twice the amount of serving bowls (15.8 percent) than the *mala* households (7.5 percent). This indicates that the *mala* households eat more with wooden bowls compared to potters, who can easily produce their own serving bowls. Another example of Zuza potters producing their own wares instead of using another type of material is the difference in the frequency of narrow-mouth small jars. The Zuza *mana* own just less than twice the amount of narrow-mouth small jars (7.9 percent) compared to *mala* households (4.2 percent), which reflects the fact that the *mala* use gourds for drinking instead of pottery.

The Guyla *mana* use similar vessel types compared to the Guyla *mala*, except that they use vessel types such as the wide-mouth medium jar, baking plate, and coffee pitcher. Guyla *mala* are less likely to use these vessel types because they are more common in the lowland areas, such as Zuza. Two of the three Guyla potter households in which I conducted household inventories came from lowland areas, and one came from Zuza. This explains why the Guyla *mana* tend to use more lowland vessel types compared to the Guyla *mala*.

There is a strong difference in the number of vessel types found in *degala* and *mala* households in Etello (Zuza does not have a *degala* population). In Etello, hideworkers do not own coffee pitchers, baking plates, narrow-mouth small jars, beer jars, or serving dishes. Coffee pitchers, dishes, and baking plates are owned by less than 5 percent of *mala* households. Beer jars are not owned by hideworkers because they do not own land and thus generate no agricultural surplus for beer production or grain storage. Therefore, they have no need for large storage jars. Etello *degala* store food in smaller types such as wide-mouth medium jars and large jars. The lack of narrow-mouth small jars among the Etello hideworkers is related to one hideworker household owning plastic cups, which the two neighboring hideworker households borrow. Two types, large jars and narrow-mouth medium jars, predominate in pottery assemblages of the Etello hideworkers, as these two types function primarily for cooking. Coffee pitchers are not present in the hideworkers' household assemblage because it is expensive to purchase coffee. In both Guyla and Etello, the *degala* continue the trend of having more than twice the percentage of water pipes in their assemblage than the *mala*. Furthermore, the *degala* hideworkers use more foot-washing bowls, which may be a result of them trying to combat the idea on the part of the rest of Gamo society that they are "unclean." The narrow-mouth medium jar, used as a cooking vessel, is more common among the *degala* hideworkers of Guyla and Etello, indicating that these households rely on this vessel type for most of their cooking activities.

The status and wealth of a household can influence the ceramic types that are found within specific households. I would expect ritual-sacrificer households, which must redistribute their wealth through feasts, to have a larger number of gourds for drinking beer than non-ritual-sacrificer households. Again, Zuza ritual-sacrificer households confirm the hypothesis, with a mean of 20 gourds inventoried from two households, which compares to only 5.7 gourds for the remaining 15 Zuza *mala* households. Etello ritual-sacrificer households have a mean of seven gourds per household, compared to a mean of 3.2 gourds for the other 15 *mala* households. However, in the village of Guyla, where gourds are not commonly used, the ritual-sacrificer households have a mean of 1.5 gourds per household, compared to 1.7 gourds for the remaining 12 *mala* households.

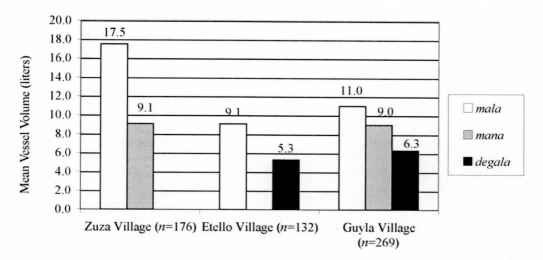

FIGURE 4.6. Mean vessel volume by caste and village.

Vessel Volume of Primary-Use Pottery

As with vessel frequency, the vessel volume of primary-use vessels directly reflects the caste hierarchy within Gamo society. The *mala* have larger vessels compared to the artisan castes because they can afford to purchase the large vessels that will be used to store crops and water, to ferment beer for daily consumption and for selling at weekly markets, and to conduct feasts for the induction of ritual sacrificers (Figure 4.6). The farmers of the *mala* caste have more farmland and can produce surplus grain for beer production.

Vessel volume is directly tied to the social status of a household and also to the redistributive feasting that is required by *mala* households that have high status and wealth. Wealthy members of the *mala* caste usually control feasts in Gamo society. However, in certain parts of the Gamo region, the artisan members have their own ritual sacrificers and produce their own feasts, though not on as grand a scale as the *mala* ritual sacrificers. The artisans usually request food and other items needed to hold a feast from their *mala* patron. There are no hideworker ritual sacrificers among the Etello and Guyla hideworkers, and Guyla and Zuza potters also do not conduct ritual-sacrificer ceremonies. Therefore, they are not required to have large vessels

to prepare the food and beer for these large feasts.

The *mala* ritual sacrificer provides two feasts, one at his household and the other in the village meeting place (*debusha*; see chap. 1 for details). He must have enough food and beer for his *dere*, and this entails having enough large ceramic containers to cook, serve, store for the fermentation of beer, and transport. The feast encompasses four days of providing wheat beer and Gamo foods. Processing the beer requires large vessels for the fermentation. The fermentation function of beer jars causes these vessels to have a short use-life, even though they are large jars, because the fermentation process breaks down the interior wall of the vessel, causing it to eventually crack (see chap. 5; Arthur 2002a, 2003). I did not expect the households that are led by a former ritual sacrificer to have a higher frequency of larger vessels than the non-ritual-sacrificer households. This is because all of the former ritual sacrificers gave feasts in the past, and their beer jars are old and, if used, are part of the reuse or discard stage (see chap. 5). Only in Zuza do the former ritual-sacrificer households have considerably more beer jars (an average of three per household) than the other 15 *mala* households (an average of 0.33 per household). The reason the Zuza ritual sacrificers have more beer jars than the other village ritual sacrificers is that they have recently purchased their pots and they are not yet broken. In addition, one of the ritual sacrificers produces beer to sell at the weekly market for extra income.

Spatial Analysis of Household Primary-Use Pottery

The spatial analysis of caste households indicates that the social status of a household can influence where people place their household ceramics. Caste households parallel the results discussed above concerning the spatial location of pots within each village. However, there is a larger range of household areas where *mala* villagers put their primary-use vessels. These areas include inside the house, kitchen, and storehouse; outside in the compound and garden; and adjacent to the house, kitchen, and weaving house. Artisan households have smaller plots of land and fewer structures, therefore they are restricted concerning where they store their primary-use pots, including inside the house and kitchen and adjacent to the house. Primary-use vessels are an important household tool, and so it is not surprising that all three castes in each village store the majority of their primary-use vessels inside their houses.

Household pottery assemblages reflect the strict social stratification that occurs within Gamo society. This is especially true in villages where artisans have not been given farmland and must engage in their full-time craft, such as in Etello and Zuza. The archaeological implications are that ceramics, as well as other types of material evidence, will provide an indication of household variation and differences based on the caste system. Given that some artisan households were given land during the Derg government, the ceramic assemblages of households occupied and abandoned before the Derg period potentially demonstrate the caste hierarchy more clearly.

ECONOMIC RANK ANALYSIS

The analysis of Gamo households indicates that the frequency and function of vessels used are strong indicators of economic wealth. The diversity of vessel types correlates more strongly with Gamo household economic wealth than with social status. As with analyses of pottery in caste households, the economic context refines the association between household wealth and household pottery assemblages. I expect that variation in household wealth influences diet and subsequently the frequency and spatial use of household pottery. The general pattern throughout indicates that household pottery can suggest differences in wealth given a larger population.

Frequency of Primary-Use Pottery

The frequency of vessels in terms of economically ranked households in Gamo indicates that the mean number of vessels is a strong indicator of economic wealth (Figure 4.7). The mean frequency of vessels indicates a strong correlation with household wealth. The general pattern suggests that household ceramic frequency in association with the household economic context may aid in the interpretation of household wealth. The economic ranks in each village mirror the differences in household wealth in Gamo society. Wealthier households can afford to have more vessels to meet their household needs.

Types of Primary-Use Pottery

The expectation is that primary-use vessels reflect a household's economic wealth because certain vessel types are directly associated with specific types of foods. The most dramatic difference between the different economic ranks occurs in the villages of Etello and Guyla (Figure 4.8). Here there is a disparity between the wealthier households and the medium-income and poorer households indicating that wealthier households eat a more varied diet. Households in Etello parallel the patterns found among caste households, as three of the four poorest households are *degala*. The different economic ranks in Zuza are similar, which is an outcome of most households engaging primarily in weaving, rather than farming.

The similarities among Gamo's wealthiest households indicate that their primary use of vessels reflects both their diet and their

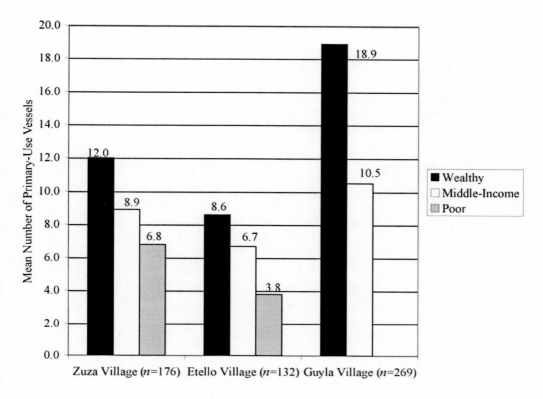

FIGURE 4.7. Mean number of vessels by economic rank and village.

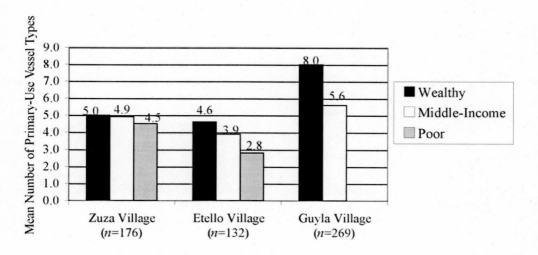

FIGURE 4.8. Mean number of vessel types by economic rank and village.

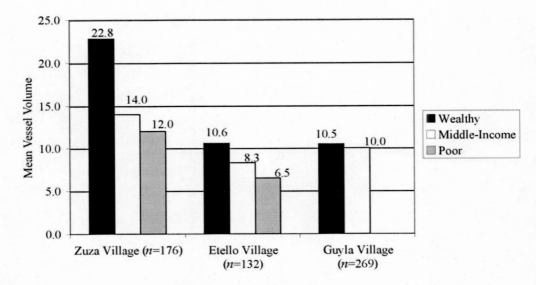

FIGURE 4.9. Mean vessel volume by economic rank and village.

wealth. For instance, the wealthiest households within each village rely more on their large jars and beer jars for the production of beer than the poorer households do, which is an indicator of wealth in Gamo society. The wealthiest households among the three villages studied use an average of 1.5 beer jars and 2.4 large jars per household for processing beer during the primary-use stage. This compares to an average of only 1.1 and 0.1 beer jars per household among the average and poorest households, respectively. In addition, the average and poorest households only use an average of 1.2 and 0.5 large jars per household for beer production during the primary-use stage.

Vessel Volume and Primary-Use Pottery
The mean vessel volumes for the ranked households in the three villages do correspond to their economic ranking (Figure 4.9). The large discrepancy between Zuza's wealthiest households and the other Gamo households in terms of vessel volume is the result of a higher frequency of large beer jars and water storage jars than in the other Gamo households. Zuza is located on a large ridge, and walking to the village wells requires a considerable amount of labor; therefore people tend to try to store

as much water in the houses as possible. In addition, the wealthier households throughout Gamo store more crops compared to the average and poorer households. Guyla is the only village with a similar range of vessel volumes between the two economic ranks. Vessel volume, along with vessel frequency and types, indicates that variation in economic wealth can be seen through household ceramic assemblages.

Spatial Analysis of
Household Primary-Use Pottery
The economic wealth of a household, especially the amount of structures per household, determines the spatial placement of pottery vessels throughout their lifecycle. Poorer households have less access to storage space, which affects where they store their ceramic pots during different lifecycle stages. However, the richer households have more structures and more area in which to store their pots (Figures 4.1–4.2).

During the primary-use stage of the ceramic lifecycle, the poorest households keep a majority of their primary-use vessels inside their houses. While the wealthier households also keep a majority of their primary-use vessels inside their houses, they also place vessels inside their kitchens. The number of buildings among the poorest households in Zuza and Etello averages only 1.1 and 1.0 per household, respectively. The wealthier households have an average of 2.0 and 4.6 buildings per household in Zuza and Etello, respectively. Therefore, the poorest households in Zuza and Etello are restricted to keeping their primary-use vessels inside their houses. Guyla has only two economic ranks, but with 2.1 buildings, the average-wealth rank has fewer buildings per compound, compared to 3.4 buildings per compound among the wealthiest Guyla households. This reflects where households place their primary-use vessels. A higher percentage of Guyla's first-ranked households keep their primary-use vessels in both their houses and their kitchens than do Guyla's second-ranked households.

GAMO PRIMARY-USE POTTERY IN CROSS-CULTURAL PERSPECTIVE

Patterns in pottery use among the Gamo indicate that archaeologists interested in accounting for pottery variation may find explanations through differences in use resulting from variations in village environment, diet, and socioeconomic status. Some relevant factors affecting the Gamo environmental setting, socioeconomic status, and the demand for and use of specific vessel types include (1) potential for crop production, (2) proximity to water sources, (3) household social status, (4) household economic wealth, and (5) social interaction between pottery-consuming and pottery-producing households.

Previous studies have shown that the ecology of a region does affect intervillage ceramic variation (Mohr Chávez 1992). In the southern Peruvian highlands, potters may specialize in specific vessel types; however, both food and pottery are distributed between the highland and lowland ecological zones, thereby creating a "vertical interdependency" (Mohr Chávez 1992:79). This "vertical interdependency" observed in the Peruvian highlands does not occur as strongly among the Gamo people. Although the Gamo distribute food and pottery between ecological zones, the location of Gamo villages in specific ecological zones affects the types of crops that people grow, which, in turn, influences their use of particular ceramic types. Coffee, an expensive crop to purchase, is grown in Zuza's household gardens, and so Zuza households have a higher frequency of coffee pitchers than do those of Etello or Guyla, where coffee does not grow because of the high altitude. In addition, Zuza's water sources are farther and more difficult to travel to, which encourages Zuza households to acquire and use more large water-transport vessels than Etello and Guyla households. Differences in food preparation do affect household assemblages, as demonstrated by the variability of food-processing techniques among the Tarahumara and the Maya of San Mateo Ixtatan (Nelson 1991). The San Mateo Ixtatan process maize by using different types of vessels to boil it, whereas the Tarahumara use only a single vessel form for steeping maize for food preparation (Robert J. Hard, personal communication, 1994). Furthermore, comparisons with the Gamo are difficult because the types of foods eaten contrast sharply to the foodstuffs in other subsistence patterns around the world. Further studies of societies that subsist on indigenous Ethiopian foods are needed to provide a more meaningful comparison for understanding how the subsistence regime affects household ceramic assemblages.

The location of the village and how humans have affected their ecological resources can have a substantial impact on the types of containers they use for food processing and serving. Ecological conditions provide Zuza households with more wooden serving vessels than either Etello or Guyla, because Zuza is located in a less densely inhabited region where there are abundant trees for producing serving vessels. In Guyla and Etello, where the land is densely occupied, there are only localized forests that are protected from cutting; thus Guyla and Etello have more ceramic serving vessels.

The study of the Gamo supports other ethnoarchaeological work that indicates that consumers' demand for specific types of pottery partly determines the vessel types that potters manufacture (see Crossland and Posnansky

1978; David and Hennig 1972; Dietler and Herbich 1989; Hodder 1979; Kramer 1997:165; Lathrap 1983). A direct association occurs between the types of foods consumers produce and eat and the vessel types that potters specialize in, which is then reflected in the village and household assemblages. In addition, where potters and consumers sell and purchase pots affects which types are found in particular villages and households. Because Zuza and Ochollo farmers grow maize and teff, Zuza consumers cook more *enjera* and Zuza potters manufacture more baking plates than Etello or Guyla households. Zuza consumers cook more stews (*wat*) in wide-mouth medium jars, and thus Zuza potters manufacture this type of cooking pot more than Guyla potters. In contrast, Etello and Guyla households have a higher frequency of bowls, narrow-mouth medium jars, and water pipes than Zuza households. Guyla consumers prefer dishes more than Zuza and Etello consumers, and hence Guyla potters specialize in the manufacturing of serving dishes.

Previous ethnoarchaeological research indicates that there are various associations between household pottery assemblages and social status (Deal 1998; Miller 1985). Deal's (1998:102–107, 168) ethnoarchaeological study of two Maya communities reveals a strong association between pottery diversity and social status. The strongest association occurs between social rank and the diversity of ritual vessel types rather than domestic types (Deal 1998:102–107). Miller's (1985:73) ethnoarchaeological study among 63 households in the village of Dangwara of Central India concludes that there is no association between caste hierarchy and household frequency of pots or specific types of water vessels. In addition, high castes have a higher frequency of metal vessels compared to the lower-caste households. The study also finds that caste hierarchy is related to specific types of cooking vessels based on color, indicating that cooking vessels transmit social power (Miller 1985:142–160, 773–774). My analyses of Gamo caste hierarchy and household pottery find strong associations between the average frequency of vessels, vessel types, the volume of vessels, and the spatial location of household pots and social status.

Ethnoarchaeological studies dealing with household wealth have indicated both positive and negative associations between pottery frequency and type with wealth. Deal's (1998:101–107, 168) ethnoarchaeological research among the Maya does not point toward a strong association between pottery diversity and economic wealth. Only when industrial types are included with the ceramic types does economic wealth become associated with ceramic diversity (Deal 1998:168). Trostel (1994:222–223) has found that vessel volume is a better indicator of wealth than the average number of pots (i.e., both ceramic and metal) per household. By contrast, Miller's (1985:73–74) study of wealth in India finds a strong association between the number of metal vessels and household economic wealth, with the wealthier households having a higher frequency of metal pots than the poorer households. The study concerning Indian wealth also demonstrates that wealthier families have a more diverse diet and eat more often than poorer households (Miller 1985:74). Concerning the correlation between household possessions and wealth, Smith (1987) hypothesizes that in an agrarian society, wealthier households would have a higher frequency of vessels, have more serving vessels, and use vessels for the processing of more elite items than poorer households would. Wealthier households in Gamo have more serving vessels than poorer households, corroborating Smith's (1987) theory that wealthier households would own more serving vessels than poorer households. Beer production is associated more with wealthy households because of the large amount of grain involved. Wealthier households in Gamo use more of their beer jars and large jars for beer production. In addition, during the primary-use stage, the beer jars are used to ferment the beer, which makes this the most expensive vessel type in the Gamo assemblage (see chap. 3).

The spatial analysis of household pots indicates that higher-caste and wealthier households have larger household areas and therefore store their primary-use vessels in different locales. Artisan and poorer households live in small areas and cannot afford to build different types of structures on their land; and thus, they store the majority of their primary-use pots within their houses or kitchens. The primary-use phase is the most important lifecycle stage for consumers, and therefore people store most of their pots within their houses to protect them from breaking.

This chapter provides archaeologists with a contextual perspective concerning the primary-use stage of pottery. Study of the primary use of pottery suggests that archaeologists should be able to decipher vessel function and household social and economic status. Primary-use vessels portray how people manipulate their household assemblages before pots are broken, mended, and/or discarded. The next chapter explores the multiple factors that affect the use-life of vessels.

5

Pottery Use-Life

This chapter explores the factors that affect the use-life of a vessel, its longevity. Numerous household social and economic conditions affect the use-life of vessels, including household size (Tani 1994), vessel size (Birmingham 1975:384; David and Hennig 1972; DeBoer 1985; de la Torre and Mudar 1982; Longacre 1985:340; Shott 1996), production methods (Arnold 1991:72; Bankes 1985:275–276; Deal 1983:155; Foster 1960; Okpoko 1987:452), and use (Bankes 1985:272; Foster 1960; Reid 1989; Tani 1994). Vessel use-life analysis indicates that consumer opinions of pottery correlate with a vessel's longevity. The analysis of vessel use-life has important implications for archaeologists trying to understand site function, population size, occupational duration, social status, and economic wealth. In addition, a vessel's use-life is determined by the production techniques and materials that potters use, as well as the pot's function, frequency of use, volume, and cost.

VILLAGE ANALYSIS
Production and Use-Life

Production techniques and materials may be factors that determine the use-life of vessels. Considering the range of techniques and materials used throughout the Gamo region, it is important to analyze the different pots that were produced in specific villages/regions to see if specific production methods affect the use-life of pots. In addition, Gamo consumers believe that certain villages/regions

produce the "best" pottery based on technological reasons (see chap. 3). Therefore, the use-life analysis will test whether potters who produce the "best" pottery actually produce pots with longer use-lives.

The consumers in Zuza prefer either the Zuza potters or a combination of potters from Ochollo *dere*, with the predominant reason that their pots are stronger and therefore last longer. When comparing the use-life of Zuza pots with the use-life of other Ochollo *dere* pots, the mean Zuza use-life is 2.1 years and the mean use-life for the Ochollo *dere* pots is 1.5 years. However, Zuza and Ochollo *dere* pots have a median use-life of one year. The number of households that prefer either Zuza or a combination of Ochollo potters is almost equal, with only four more households preferring Zuza pots than a combination of Ochollo pots. Therefore, it is interesting that the median use-life is the same, which reflects the opinions of households concerning pottery preference.

Etello consumers prefer Birbir pots, because they believe Birbir pots last longer than Guyla or Zada pots. The ten Birbir pots used in Etello, the majority (70 percent) of which are used for cooking, have a mean and median use-life of 2.7 and 1.8 years, respectively. The 40 Guyla and Zada pots, of which 68 percent were used only for cooking, have a mean and median use-life of 2.1 and 1.4 years, respectively. Therefore, the use-life data agree with the consumer opinions that Birbir pots do last

92

TABLE 5.1. Vessel Cost and Use-Life in Three Gamo Villages (Correlations in Bold Are Significant at the .05 Confidence Level)

VILLAGE	COST (BIRR)		USE-LIFE (YEARS)		CORRELATION: COST/USE-LIFE
	MEAN	MEDIAN	MEAN	MEDIAN	
Zuza	1.5	1	1.7	1	**0.24** ($n = 114$)
Guyla	4.4	2.5	2.9	1.7	**0.28** ($n = 141$)
Etello	3.6	2	2.8	2	0.05 ($n = 78$)

longer and are more durable than Zada or Guyla pots.

Guyla consumers also prefer Birbir pots to their own Guyla potters' pots, stating that they believe Birbir pots are stronger and last longer than Guyla pots. The use-life data also agree with Guyla consumers' opinions. Twenty-five of the 31 Birbir pots, used only for cooking, have a mean and median use-life of 2.8 and three years, respectively. This compares to the mean and median use-life of 2.1 and 1.7 years, respectively, for the 36 out of 123 Guyla pots used only for cooking. All three villages indicate that consumer opinions do parallel the use-life of pots, indicating the importance of the emic perspective concerning the technological and nontechnological aspects of pottery use.

Vessel Expenditure and Use-Life

The use-life of pots may influence the cost of the pots, for a cheaper price may reflect the quality of the pot and therefore its longevity. People who purchase more costly pots may be more careful than consumers who purchase less expensive pots. In Zuza, the cost of pots is less than in Guyla or Etello, and Zuza pots have a shorter use-life than pottery in the other two villages. This suggests that the more expensive the pot, the longer it will last.

In Zuza and Guyla, the cost of pots significantly correlates with use-life. The correlation is weak but significant in both villages (Table 5.1). However, in Etello, as discussed in chapter 3, consumers purchase their pots through the market. There is no correlation between the cost of pots and use-life in Etello, because Etello consumers get all of their vessels from weekly markets and these markets fluctuate

in their pricing of ceramic pots (Table 5.1). This fluctuation, caused by seasonal variations (e.g., higher market prices during Easter, Meskal, and Christmas) in the market price of pots, is the reason there is no correlation between the cost of Etello pots and use-life. The majority of consumers in Zuza and Guyla purchase their pots directly from the potter's household or from Zuza and Guyla potters at the weekly market, which may result in more consistent prices for the different vessel sizes and types.

Vessel Volume and Use-Life

Generally, the larger the vessel, the longer the vessel's use-life (DeBoer 1985; Longacre 1981:64; Shott 1989; Tani 1994:62), but the Gamo data do not support this trend (Tables 5.2–5.4). There is not a strong correlation between the use-lives and volumes of different vessel types. This suggests that factors other than size may be responsible for a vessel's use-life. Zuza's wide-mouth medium jars/distes have a significant correlation between vessel use-life and volume. All three villages use the wide-mouth medium jars for making wat, a type of stew, but this food is more common in Zuza, and so the Zuza wide-mouth medium jars have a shorter use-life than those in Guyla and Etello. The Zuza large jars/ottos also have a significant correlation between vessel use-life and volume. In Zuza, people primarily use large jars to store and transport water and beer, while in Etello and Guyla they are used for cooking. Therefore, these functional differences may explain why there is a significant correlation only in Zuza. However, beer jars/batsas, which people use for storing water and beer, do not demonstrate a corre-

TABLE 5.2. Zuza's Vessel Types and Their Use-Lives, Associated Volume Measurements, and the Correlations between Use-Life and Volume (Correlations in Bold Are Significant at the .05 Confidence Level)

VESSEL TYPE	n	USE-LIFE (YEARS)			VOLUME (L)			CORRELATION: USE-LIFE/ VOLUME
		MEAN	MEDIAN	S.D.	MEAN	MEDIAN	S.D.	
Coffee pitcher (*jebana*)	18	1.43	0.7	1.90	2.22	2.24	0.51	0.00
Wide-mouth medium jar (*diste*)	25	2.10	1	3.18	7.70	6.37	5.88	**0.53**
Large jar (*otto*)	47	10.28	1.8	22.47	17.48	14.77	11.39	**0.69**
Narrow-mouth medium jar (*tsaro*)	34	1.86	1	1.89	4.58	3.88	2.20	−0.09
Baking plate (*bache*)	14	2.41	1.4	3.53	4.36	4.14	1.53	0.22
Bowl (*shele*)	9	5.54	1	9.13	11.58	11.38	9.19	0.00
Narrow-mouth small jar (*tsua*)	5	7.88	1	15.17	0.95	0.9	0.41	−0.31
Beer jar (*batsa*)	1	2	2	–	64.50	64.50	0	–

TABLE 5.3. Guyla's Vessel Types and Their Use-Lives, Associated Volume Measurements, and the Correlations between Use-Life and Volume (Correlations in Bold Are Significant at the .05 Confidence Level)

VESSEL TYPE	n	USE-LIFE (YEARS)			VOLUME (L)			CORRELATION: USE-LIFE/ VOLUME
		MEAN	MEDIAN	S.D.	MEAN	MEDIAN	S.D.	
Coffee pitcher (*jebana*)	8	1.76	1.5	1.14	2.11	2.14	0.36	0.43
Wide-mouth medium jar (*diste*)	3	2.96	2.9	1	7.28	7.7	1.16	**−0.96**
Large jar (*otto*)	73	2.51	2	2.43	12.08	10.88	4.96	0.00
Narrow-mouth medium jar (*tsaro*)	41	1.97	1.9	1.85	5.25	5.57	1.88	−0.12
Baking plate (*bache*)	7	2.28	3	1.97	3.67	3.76	1.94	**0.59**
Bowl (*shele*)	29	2.09	1.9	2.15	21.25	12.11	20.37	0.25
Dish (*peele*)	9	2.3	2	2.35	5.41	4.42	2.76	0.00
Narrow-mouth small jar (*tsua*)	10	5.14	6	3.09	0.98	0.9	0.43	−0.08
Beer jar (*batsa*)	24	2.62	1.5	2.76	64.11	59.72	33.85	0.36
Water pipe (*guya*)	3	1.63	2	1.48	1.72	1.59	0.36	**−0.87**

TABLE 5.4. Etello's Vessel Types and Their Use-Lives, Associated Volume Measurements, and the Correlations between Use-Life and Volume (Correlations in Bold Are Significant at the .05 Confidence Level)

| VESSEL TYPE | n | USE-LIFE (YEARS) | | | VOLUME (L) | | | CORRELATION: USE-LIFE/ VOLUME |
		MEAN	MEDIAN	S.D.	MEAN	MEDIAN	S.D.	
Coffee pitcher (*jebana*)	5	1.34	0.2	1.87	2.2	2.35	0.37	0.20
Wide-mouth medium jar (*diste*)	8	1.81	1.7	1.26	7.85	7.23	2.7	0.21
Large jar (*otto*)	29	2.31	2	2.10	11.49	10.30	5.33	0.18
Narrow-mouth medium jar (*tsaro*)	17	1.47	1	1.18	4.55	4.19	1.78	−0.09
Baking plate (*bache*)	4	2.35	1.3	3.03	5.14	4.56	1.16	−0.51
Bowl (*shele*)	6	1.03	1	0.85	16.16	13.12	11.63	**0.96**
Dish (*peele*)	1	46	–	–	5.16	–	–	–
Narrow-mouth small jar (*tsua*)	4	3.02	3	2.54	1.19	1.24	0.58	**0.73**
Beer jar (*batsa*)	11	5.42	3	5.60	49.18	44.58	30.03	0.11
Water pipe (*guya*)	1	7.9	–	–	1.44	–	–	–

lation between use-life and volume. Because Gamo people use the majority of vessels for multiple activities, it is difficult to find a relationship between vessel type and use-life.

Vessel Typology and Use-Life

The function of a vessel is one of the most important determinations for how long a vessel will survive before it breaks (Tables 5.5–5.6). Vessels in Gamo have a large range of uses, with some pots functioning only as cooking pots, while other pots are used for cooking, storing, and transporting. Four functional categories were analyzed concerning their relationship to use-life: cooking, serving, storing, and transporting. The multifunctional vessels were considered in each of the functional categories.

The shortest use-life occurs among cooking vessels, which is not surprising because cooking pots continuously used in a hearth break from repeated thermal stress and shock. Serving vessels range in use-life among the three villages from 1.5 to two years (median)

and are broken because of their constant use within the household. Serving food is a communal activity in Gamo society, and therefore every member of a household handles serving vessels. Such widespread activity within the household provides a higher chance for serving vessels to break. In all three villages, storage vessels have the longest use-lives, and they are the largest pots by volume. Therefore, on a functional basis, larger pots do last longer than smaller pots. People usually break transport vessels by slipping on the footpaths, dropping the vessels, or hitting the pots on rocks while carrying the vessels on their backs (see chap. 6). Except for the use-life of storage vessels in Zuza, the range of median use-lives among the different functional categories is small.

CASTE GROUP ANALYSIS

The social status of a household and its use of ceramic vessels will have a direct relationship to vessel use-life. Gamo society, with its strict social hierarchy, provides an excellent

TABLE 5.5. Vessel Use-Life by Functional Type and Village

| VILLAGE | FUNCTIONAL TYPE | *n* | USE-LIFE (YEARS) | | | |
			MEAN	MEDIAN	RANGE	S.D.
Zuza	cooking	103	2.29	1	0.1–35.0	4.58
	serving	4	1.75	1.5	1.0–3.0	0.95
	storage	22	22.12	6	0.1–125.0	30.68
	transporting	25	2.80	1.9	0.2–20.0	4.04
Etello	cooking	60	2.04	1.9	0.1–10.0	1.91
	serving	9	6.57	2	0.2–46.0	14.82
	storage	18	4.28	2.5	0.6–19.7	4.69
	transporting	6	1.95	1.5	0.1–6.0	2.12
Guyla	cooking	118	2.39	2	0.1–9.0	1.78
	serving	34	2.95	2	0.1–9.0	2.65
	storage	48	3.56	2.5	0.1–14.0	3.09
	transporting	37	3.35	2	0.3–13.0	2.81

example for understanding the relationship between a household's status and vessel use-life.

Typology, Volume, and Use-Life

We would expect that because lower-caste households have fewer vessels than higher-caste households, the lower-caste households would have to use their vessels with more frequency, causing them to have shorter use-lives. With Zuza as the only exception, Etello and Guyla artisan households have vessels that have shorter use-lives than the *mala* households (Table 5.7). The lower-caste households use smaller vessels, but vessel frequency and repeated use seem to be more of a determinant factor concerning vessel use-life.

Vessel Expenditure and Use-Life

Lower-caste households use their vessels more often and purchase cheaper pots. Therefore, lower-caste pots have shorter use-lives than pots in higher-caste households (Table 5.8). In Guyla and Etello, the *mala* have more expensive pots than the *degala* households (see chap. 3). *Mana* households are not analyzed in Zuza and Guyla, because the *mana* households use pots that they have manufactured.

In addition, because Zuza has only *mala* and *mana* households, it is not possible to make a comparison. In Guyla and Etello, the *mala* spend more on their pots (which have longer use-lives) than the *degala* households.

Social status and how it reflects through the household ceramic assemblage have indicated that archaeologists may be able to explore status, household population, occupation span, and site function. Regarding how household population correlates to vessel use-life, the Gamo case indicates that differences do occur between caste households within one society. Therefore, social status cannot be explored by itself but, rather, must be placed in the proper context of where, who, and how pots are manufactured, distributed, and used in the society.

ECONOMIC RANK ANALYSIS

The economic wealth of a household can have a direct effect on vessel use-life. Poorer households have limited ceramic assemblages and therefore must use their vessels with more frequency than wealthier households. In addition, the relationship between the wealth of a household and the amount people spend on pots may have an effect on vessel use-life.

TABLE 5.6. Vessel Volume by Functional Type and Village

VILLAGE	FUNCTIONAL TYPE	n	VOLUME (L)			
			MEAN	MEDIAN	RANGE	S.D.
Zuza	cooking	103	5.50	4.08	0.52–24.42	4.58
	serving	4	7.10	6.92	0.45–14.13	5.64
	storage	22	27.16	19.79	5.96–113.04	25.48
	transporting	25	16.64	16.64	5.57–36.07	7.56
Etello	cooking	60	7.93	6.79	0.90–22.44	5.21
	serving	9	12.22	8.18	0.52–33.49	11.11
	storage	18	35.50	26.51	4.19–124.72	29.91
	transporting	6	3.44	3.89	0.90–5.57	1.84
Guyla	cooking	118	10.65	8.18	1.43–91.90	11.05
	serving	34	8.88	5.72	0.52–49.30	10.07
	storage	48	33.50	16.37	0.79–150.46	34.7
	transporting	37	6.87	6.37	0.79–22.44	4.56

TABLE 5.7. Vessel Use-Life and Volume by Functional Type and by Village and Caste

VILLAGE AND CASTE	FUNCTIONAL TYPE	n	USE-LIFE (YEARS)			VOLUME (L)		
			MEAN	MEDIAN	S.D.	MEAN	MEDIAN	S.D.
Zuza *mala*	cooking	96	2.29	1	4.70	5.60	4.14	4.68
	transporting	21	3.20	2	4.29	16.91	14.77	7.77
Zuza *mana*	cooking	6	2.65	1.95	2.67	4.36	3.05	2.95
	transporting	4	0.72	0.4	0.78	15.23	14.86	7.23
Etello *mala*	cooking	48	2.14	1.9	2.01	8.09	6.80	5.69
Etello *degala*	cooking	12	1.61	1.5	1.38	7.29	6.79	2.53
Guyla *mala*	cooking	90	2.66	2	1.89	10.83	8.18	11.28
	serving	26	3.21	2.5	2.78	9.39	5.49	11.30
	storage	35	4.02	3	3.25	37.02	22.44	38.12
	transporting	33	3.57	2.8	2.9	6.99	6.79	4.69
Guyla *mana*	cooking	10	1.64	1.25	1.15	6.95	6.59	4.21
	serving	6	2.16	0.95	2.53	5.68	5.50	2.92
	storage	8	2.88	2.3	2.78	25.46	11.31	24.92
	transporting	1	2	2	–	2.57	2.57	–
Guyla *degala*	cooking	17	1.5	1	0.85	11.97	7.70	12.80
	serving	2	1.95	1.95	0.07	11.78	11.78	5.38
	storage	5	1.46	2	0.74	21.66	15.59	17.21
	transporting	3	1.4	1.6	0.52	6.98	5.57	3.70

TABLE 5.8. Vessel Cost and Use-Life by Village and Caste (Correlations in Bold Are Significant at the .05 Confidence Level)

VILLAGE AND CASTE	COST (BIRR)		USE-LIFE (YEARS)		CORRELATION: COST/USE-LIFE
	MEAN	MEDIAN	MEAN	MEDIAN	
Guyla *mala*	4.6	2.7	3.0	2	**0.28** (*n* = 122)
Guyla *degala*	3.2	2	1.2	0.9	0.08 (*n* = 20)
Etello *mala*	3.7	2	3.0	1.9	0.04 (*n* = 71)
Etello *degala*	2.3	2	1	0.5	**0.43** (*n* = 7)

Typology, Volume, and Use-Life

Household economic wealth in association with vessel function, volume, or frequency of use affects the use-life of vessels. I would expect that storage vessels have longer use-lives in all of the economic ranks. This expectation tends to be true in all of the economic ranks from the three villages, with the only exception among the wealthiest households in Guyla, where serving and transporting vessels have longer use-lives than storage vessels (Table 5.9). Storage vessels also tend to be larger than most other vessels, which supports the view that larger vessels are used with less frequency and therefore have longer use-lives than smaller, more frequently used vessels (Table 5.9; Longacre 1985; Tani 1994).

Because the poorer castes have fewer pots per household (see chap. 4), I expected that vessels would be used more frequently and consequently would have shorter use-lives than those in the richer households. Thus, the vessel use-life in poorer households would be shorter than that in richer households. The vessels in poorer households do have shorter use-lives than those in richer households (Table 5.9). Therefore, (in)frequency of vessels per household, which causes vessels to be repeatedly used more often, has a direct effect on vessel use-life, which corresponds with a household's economic rank.

Vessel Expenditure and Use-Life

The purchase price of pots may have an effect on the use-life of vessels. The poorer households purchase cheaper pots than the wealthier households do, with the only exception occurring in Etello. Poorer households may be more careful with their pots, because they cannot afford to replace them. There are two contributing factors as to why poor households have shorter vessel use-lives. First, poorer households use their pots with more frequency because they have fewer pots to use (see chap. 4); and second, they purchase those of cheaper quality so their use-life is shortened. The wealthier households in both Etello and Guyla enjoy longer vessel use-life than the poorer households. However, in Zuza, the median use-life for all three economic ranks is the same, but the mean use-life is greater among the wealthier households. In addition, the correlation between the cost and the use-life of pots is significant in the majority of economic ranks, notably with Etello's average-wealth and poorest households and Guyla's average-wealth households (Table 5.10). Thus, the cost of pots in the context of a household's economic rank does influence the use-life of vessels.

GAMO CERAMIC USE-LIFE IN CROSS-CULTURAL PERSPECTIVE

The use-life of Gamo vessels is influenced by many factors, including manufacturing techniques and materials, vessel function, vessel size, frequency of use, household social status, household economic wealth, and vessel cost. Thus, the procurement, production, distribution, and use of ceramics, as well as the social and economic makeup of a household, influence the household's interaction with its ceramic assemblage and the longevity of pots.

TABLE 5.9. Vessel Use-Life and Volume by Functional Type and by Village and Economic Rank

VILLAGE AND RANK	FUNCTIONAL TYPE	n	USE-LIFE (YEARS)			VOLUME (L)		
			MEAN	MEDIAN	S.D.	MEAN	MEDIAN	S.D.
Zuza								
Wealthy	cooking	35	2.2	1	3.12	6.16	4.19	5.61
	serving	3	2	2	1.00	7.49	7.89	6.84
	storage	9	22.3	2	41.73	29.76	24.42	21.01
	transporting	10	4.2	2	5.79	14.98	13.76	7.98
Average	cooking	31	2.8	1.8	6.15	6.23	4.85	4.41
	storage	7	26.7	20	20.98	30.09	17.15	37.24
	transporting	6	0.9	0.9	0.62	14.04	14.45	1.64
Poor	cooking	37	2.0	1	4.3	4.26	3.31	3.33
	serving	1	1	1	–	1	1	–
	storage	6	16.5	4.4	23.87	19.84	12.75	16.36
	transporting	9	2.5	1.9	2.36	20.21	22.43	8.69
Etello								
Wealthy	cooking	13	2.3	1.9	1.60	8.64	5.57	7.16
	serving	4	13	2.5	22.04	7.30	6.66	5.24
	storage	3	7.9	3	10.26	31.83	26.51	11.08
	transporting	2	4	4	2.82	3.58	3.58	2.81
Average	cooking	33	2	1.9	2.04	8.15	7.23	5.18
	serving	5	1.4	2	0.81	16.16	12.11	13.52
	storage	15	3.5	2	2.88	36.24	26.51	32.64
	transporting	4	0.9	0.8	0.80	3.38	3.89	1.73
Poor	cooking	14	1.9	1.5	1.94	6.75	6.58	2.72
Guyla								
Wealthy	cooking	45	3.2	2.4	2.16	12.29	9.20	13.27
	serving	11	4.5	3	3.17	10.28	8.89	8.89
	storage	22	3.9	2.5	14.20	42.16	26.74	39.36
	transporting	19	4.4	3	3.24	7.78	7.23	4.30
Average	cooking	73	1.9	1.9	1.32	9.64	7.23	9.38
	serving	23	2.2	1	4.25	8.21	4.51	10.72
	storage	26	3.2	2.5	5.80	26.16	11.86	28.98
	transporting	18	2.2	1.9	1.71	5.91	5.21	4.76

TABLE 5.10. Vessel Cost and Use-Life by Village and Economic Rank (Correlations in Bold Are Significant at the .05 Confidence Level)

VILLAGE AND RANK	COST (BIRR)		USE-LIFE (YEARS)		CORRELATION: COST/USE-LIFE
	MEAN	MEDIAN	MEAN	MEDIAN	
Zuza					
Wealthy	1.9	1.5	2	1	0.25 (*n* = 45)
Average	1.1	1	1.5	1	−0.08 (*n* = 27)
Poor	1.2	1	1.6	1	0.24 (*n* = 42)
Etello					
Wealthy	2.3	1	6	1.9	−0.19 (*n* = 16)
Average	4.2	2.2	2.2	1.9	0.39 (*n* = 53)
Poor	2.5	2	1.5	0.5	**0.85 (*n* = 9)**
Guyla					
Wealthy	5.2	3	3.6	3	0.21 (*n* = 73)
Average	3.5	2	3.5	1.9	0.39 (*n* = 69)

Understanding the use-life of pottery vessels is important to archaeologists attempting to decipher site function, population size, occupational duration, social status, and economic wealth. Use-life research has been conducted by a number of researchers, who have indicated that a vessel's longevity is related to production techniques and materials, frequency of use, vessel function and size, and replacement costs (Bankes 1985; Birmingham 1975; David 1972; David and Hennig 1972; Deal 1998; DeBoer 1974; Foster 1960; Kramer 1985; Longacre 1985; Nelson 1991; Okpoko 1987; Pastron 1974; Rice 1987; Shott 1996; Stanislawski 1978; Tani 1994). Two important contributions that have been established from cross-cultural studies regarding ceramic use-life are that cooking pots have shorter use-lives than noncooking pots and that larger vessels have longer use-lives than smaller pots (P. Arnold 2000:115). Among the Kalinga (Longacre 1981), the Shipibo-Conibo (DeBoer 1985), and the Fulani (David 1972; David and Hennig 1972) societies, use-life studies have shown that larger vessels have longer use-lives. However, frequency of use also contributes to a vessel's use-life (Longacre 1981:64), and "frequency of use is related

to vessel size" (Tani 1994:62). In addition, the type of use will affect a vessel's use-life according to its size. Thus, larger vessels used for cooking will have a shorter use-life than smaller vessels because of thermal fatigue (Tani 1994:62). This is reported by Nelson (1985:327), who has found that large cooking vessels have a high rate of breakage after only being used less than a half dozen times.

Gamo cooking pots usually do have a shorter use-life compared to other pots used in functions that do not require heating. In addition, the Gamo analysis indicates that when vessel function is associated with vessel size, larger vessels used for storage do have longer use-lives than other vessels. Shott (1996) has found that vessel height and volume are good indicators of use-life. However, the Gamo vessel types do not follow a predictable trend concerning vessel size and use-life, because each village and household uses many of its vessel types for multiple functions. This indicates the importance for archaeologists of attempting to understand the actual uses of each vessel by its household context and morphological and use-alteration attributes.

The Gamo use-life analysis also indicates that consumers are knowledgeable about their society's ceramic production methods. Gamo consumers' opinions concerning which villages and/or regions manufacture the strongest vessels correlate with the vessel use-life analysis. Therefore, the manufacturing and materials that potters use seem to be an important component concerning a vessel's longevity.

The social and economic analyses of Gamo vessel use-life suggest that because the lower-status and poorer households have fewer pots, they must use them with more frequency, causing a reduced use-life compared to that in higher-status and wealthier households. In addition, the cost of the vessel influences its use-life, with higher-caste and wealthier households purchasing more expensive vessels, which last longer than those of lower-caste and poorer households. This may be related to lower-caste and poorer households either using their vessels more often or purchasing cheaper vessels, which causes them to break faster than those in the households of high status and wealth.

6

Pottery Mending and Reuse

This chapter explores how and why pots are mended, reused, and stored during their reuse stage. The study of vessel reuse provides beneficial insights into the interpretation of formation processes, activity areas, and socio-economic status (Deal and Hagstrum 1995). The reuse of vessels, which is reportedly common in the ethnoarchaeological literature (Atherton 1983:93; Calder 1972; David and Hennig 1972:21; Deal 1998:107–114; De-Boer and Lathrap 1979:111, 125, 127; London 1989:221; Rye and Evans 1976:123; Solheim 1965:259, 1984:100; Stanislawski 1969, 1978:221–222; Sterner 1989:458; Tschopik 1950:209; Weigand 1969:23–24) can cause confusion among archaeologists when attempting to interpret functional categories for specific vessels (Deal and Hagstrum 1995:122). Hence, understanding the variation concerning how reused vessels are used, as well as their spatial patterning, should help archaeologists interpret the role of formation processes and activity areas within archaeological sites.

Historically, reuse is the "use of an object in a secondary context when it can no longer serve its original function" (Deal and Hagstrum 1995:111). Thus, the pot's function is different during the reuse stage than during its primary-use or original-function stage. Poor and low-caste households may reuse their pots for the same function as before they broke. By contrast, wealthy and high-caste households may replace the broken pot with a new pot or reuse the broken pot for a secondary function. This chapter will explore reuse under its original definition but also contributes an additional line of reasoning by discussing how pots may be reused for the same function as before they broke.

The goal of this chapter is not only to document how pots move though the lifecycle but to explain why there is ceramic variation with relation to the village context and a household's social and economic level. Explaining the variation with regard to the frequency of vessels and vessel types, vessel volume, and the spatial location of where vessels are stored in the reuse stage should add to our understanding of archaeological interpretations of ceramic assemblages.

THE REASONS VESSELS BREAK

The primary reason that vessels are placed in discard or secondarily reused is breakage. How vessels break in households is a reflection of their use, movement, random acts, and production problems. The majority of cases involve the use and movement of vessels. Specifically, cooking is the most common cause of vessel breakage, with the base as the most likely place where pots crack from thermal stress and shock. Because cooking vessels usually break at the base, they are not able to be reused for cooking or functions that require holding liquids because they will leak. Dropping the vessel on a stone is a common explanation for the breakage of transport vessels especially in Zuza, where the footpaths are usually slippery and lined with rock outcrops. In terms of the production process, firing pots causes the majority of them to break. Then there are a number of other reasons given that range from use (e.g., making butter), to transport (Figures 6.1–6.2; e.g., bringing home from the market), to various other factors that cause vessels to break. The process of beer fermentation erodes the interior vessel wall, and when the beer is cooked and the hot liquid is poured into the vessel, the vessel wall cannot withstand the thermal shock, causing the vessel to crack (Arthur 2002a, 2003). This is one of the reasons why large beer fermentation jars have a short use-life (see chap. 5). The production of butter involves rocking the large jar back and forth on its side for hours while the milk changes to butter. This rocking motion sometimes causes vessels to break (Table 6.1).

Some vessel types such as bowls, dishes, baking plates, and narrow-mouth small jars may only crack during use, and therefore people then will continue to reuse them for the same primary function. Baking plates might

FIGURE 6.1. Women using jars to collect and transport water from a well in Zuza.

FIGURE 6.2. A woman collecting and transporting water from a stream in Guyla.

TABLE 6.1. Reasons Why Vessels Break, with Their Corresponding Frequency and Percentage (*n* = 380)

REASONS WHY VESSELS BREAK	*n*	%
Cooking	202	53.1
Dropping	59	15.5
Firing the vessel	32	8.4
Hitting a stone	26	6.8
Pouring beer into a pot	18	4.7
Use for a long time	12	3.1
Falling from storage area	3	0.8
Dog stepping on vessel	3	0.8
Broke when bringing home from market	3	0.8
Making butter	3	0.8
Picked up with one hand and it broke	2	0.5
Cooking with salt	1	0.3
Store milk and just broke	1	0.3
Drilling two holes in the vessel for bee house	1	0.3
Sitting on vessel	1	0.3
Child threw a stone	1	0.3
Hit her leg and broke	1	0.3
Storing *farso* (beer)	1	0.3
Hitting with stick	1	0.3
Hit on another pot	1	0.3
Cleaning the interior	1	0.3
When someone was pounding the crops in the wooden grinder	1	0.3
Continuous use	1	0.3
Cow broke while drinking water	1	0.3
Broke during wedding ceremony	1	0.3
By moving pot	1	0.3
Bought it broken	1	0.3
Cracked during production	1	0.3

crack from continuous cooking, but because baking plates function for only roasting or baking and not to hold liquids, they can continue to function for cooking for an extended period of time. Serving vessels such as bowls and dishes might crack from the rim to the base but continue to function for serving until the vessel eventually forms a large break. The narrow-mouth small jars used as drinking vessels also have a low percentage of discard among the three villages. Thin cracks usually form along the rim, which does not hinder its ability to hold liquids for drinking.

VILLAGE ANALYSIS
Mending

The Gamo mend vessels with a variety of materials (Table 6.2). The enset plant is the most common material for mending pots. The different enset parts used for mending pots

TABLE 6.2. Absolute and Relative Frequencies of Materials Used for Mending Pots

TYPE OF MENDING MATERIAL	n	%
Inner part of enset leaves	2	9.5
Etema	2	9.5
Shona (wheat and enset porridge)	2	9.5
Enset rope	2	9.5
Dung	1	4.8
Cow dung and enset rope	1	4.8
Cow dung and soil	1	4.8
Cow dung and cloth	1	4.8
Burlap	1	4.8
Honeycomb	1	4.8
Frankincense	1	4.8
Nora (white clay)	1	4.8
Cloth	1	4.8
Cloth tied around neck to hold neck and rim together	1	4.8
Concrete	1	4.8
Tar	1	4.8
Plastic	1	4.8

include *etema* juice, rope (*gola*) made from its leaves, and the inner part of the enset leaves, which are stuffed into holes (Figures 6.3–6.4). Another common mending material is cow dung, usually used by itself or in combination with soil, cloth, or enset rope.

Among the 60 households inventoried, the percentage of broken vessels that are mended is 4.3 percent (N = 487, n = 21), indicating that a small percentage of the vessels reused are mended. It would be expected that Etello would have mended more pots than Zuza and Guyla, because Etello has no potters living within the village and it is more difficult for consumers to obtain pots. Etello's assemblage indeed contains the highest percentage of mended pots (Table 6.3). The age range of all the mended vessels from the three villages is from one month to 50 years. Locally made pots were repaired as often as pots obtained from distant sources. Most mended pots are transport or storage pots, particularly large jars.

Although the Gamo mend pottery pur-chased from distant markets, they more fre-quently mend locally made pots. All three of the pots mended in Guyla came from Guyla potters, and the majority of pots mended in Zuza were produced by local potters. In Etello, where there are no local potters, five of the mended pots came from the Birbir region, four from Zada, one from Gema, and one the owner was uncertain about its manufactured location. Clearly, distance to the ceramic source/market does not affect the decision to mend a vessel. The pots that were mended in the three villages were more expensive than the pots that were not mended (Table 6.3). This indicates that the cost of the pot is an important factor in the curation of pottery vessels.

Although the number of reuse pots is small compared to the larger village assemblage, mending vessels does indicate the importance that the reuse stage has in the overall house-hold ceramic assemblage. The average cost of the mended vessels indicates that mending/ reuse has an economic value to the household.

FIGURE 6.3. A large jar mended with enset leaves.

FIGURE 6.4. A large jar mended with enset rope.

The mending of vessels consists of a transformation between the primary-use and reuse stages, with curation prolonging the household use and value of the vessel.

Frequency of Reused Pottery

Whether a vessel is mended or not, once a vessel breaks the household has to decide to either discard the pot, reuse it for the same function as before, or give it a new secondary use. I gathered information to see how people reuse vessels after they break, noting whether they reused for the same function as before the vessel broke or they changed the vessel's function. Among the households inventoried in Zuza, Etello, and Guyla, the Gamo reuse 19 percent of their vessels after they break for a secondary function and 14 percent of the vessels for the same function as before they broke; therefore, combined, 33 percent of the entire assemblage is reused for either the same function or a different function. The comparison between whether ves-

sels are reused for the same function or for a different function should be a result of the household's social and economic status within Gamo society.

In the reuse analysis, I assumed that because Etello does not have potters, its households would reuse their vessels more than those of Zuza and Guyla, where potters live. However, Etello households only reuse 23.0 percent of their assemblage, compared to 32.1 percent for Zuza and 37.1 percent for Guyla households (Tables 6.4–6.6). Although Etello households mend more vessels than in the other two villages, they also discard more jars (i.e., large jars, narrow-mouth medium jars, and beer jars), rather than reusing them. Although no inventory was conducted, one possibility is that Etello households use more bamboo baskets to store grains and other foods rather than ceramic vessels. As with the other villages, most of the mending is to continue cooking with the vessel, rather than to store foods (see Table 6.3). However, it still

TABLE 6.3. Types, Functions, Frequencies, Percentages, and Costs of Mended Vessels by Village, Illustrating That the Nonpotter Village (Etello) Has a Higher Frequency of Mended Pots

VILLAGE	VESSEL TYPE AND FUNCTION	NUMBER OF MENDED VESSELS	% MENDED VESSELS	AVERAGE COST (BIRR)
Zuza	large jar (transport water and store crops)	5	71.4	2.90
	beer jar (store beer)	1	14.3	16.50
	coffee pitcher (boil coffee)	1	14.3	2.00
	total mended vessels	7	2.3	9.00 (U.S.$1.50)
	total cost all vessels			1.84 (U.S.$0.31)
Etello	large jar (cook and store butter)	4	36.4	1.87
	beer jar (store beer)	3	33.3	15.00
	narrow-mouth small jar (drink beer and cook)	2	18.2	0.40
	narrow-mouth medium jar (transport water and cooking)	1	9.1	1.20
	bowl (serving and as lid)	1	9.1	.50
	total mended vessels	11	12.3	3.63 (U.S.$0.60)
	total cost all vessels			2.77 (U.S.$0.46)
Guyla	large jar (store water and as a wind protector when firing pots)	2	66.7	not available
	bowl (serve and store beer)	1	27.3	7.00
	total mended vessels	3	1.3	7.00 (U.S.$1.20)
	total cost all vessels			3.71 (U.S.$0.62)

TABLE 6.4. Percentage and Frequency of Broken Zuza Vessel Types Reused for Secondary Functions, the Same Function as before They Broke, and All Functions ($n = 346$)

EMIC TYPES	SECONDARY FUNCTION		SAME FUNCTION		ALL FUNCTIONS	
	%	n	%	n	%	n
Coffee pitcher (*jebana*)	0	0	13.3	10	9.0	10
Wide-mouth medium jar (*diste*)	16.7	6	9.3	7	11.7	13
Large jar (*otto*)	36.1	13	32.0	24	33.3	37
Narrow-mouth medium jar (*tsaro*)	22.2	8	9.3	7	13.5	15
Bowl (*shele*)	5.6	2	6.7	5	6.3	7
Baking plate (*bache*)	0	0	17.3	13	11.7	13
Narrow-mouth small jar (*tsua*)	11.1	4	1.4	1	4.5	5
Beer jar (*batsa*)	8.3	3	9.3	7	9.0	10
Water pipe (*guya*)	0	0	0	0	0	0
Dish (*peele*)	0	0	0	0	0	0
Single-handle jar (*kolay*)	0	0	1.4	1	0.9	1
Comparison to entire assemblage	10.4	36	21.7	75	32.1	111

TABLE 6.5. Percentage and Frequency of Broken Etello Vessel Types Reused for Secondary Functions, the Same Function as before They Broke, and All Functions (*n* = 222)

EMIC TYPE	SECONDARY FUNCTION		SAME FUNCTION		ALL FUNCTIONS	
	%	*n*	%	*n*	%	*n*
Coffee pitcher (*jebana*)	0	0	5.9	2	3.9	2
Wide-mouth medium jar (*diste*)	11.9	2	2.9	1	5.9	3
Large jar (*otto*)	58.6	10	23.5	8	35.3	18
Narrow-mouth medium jar (*tsaro*)	17.7	3	11.8	4	13.7	7
Bowl (*shele*)	5.9	1	11.8	4	9.8	5
Baking plate (*bache*)	0	0	11.8	4	7.8	4
Narrow-mouth small jar (*tsua*)	0	0	11.8	4	7.8	4
Beer jar (*batsa*)	5.9	1	14.7	5	11.8	6
Water pipe (*guya*)	0	0	2.9	1	2.0	1
Dish (*peele*)	0	0	2.9	1	2.0	1
Comparison to entire assemblage	7.6	17	15.3	34	23.0	51

TABLE 6.6. Percentage and Frequency of Broken Guyla Vessel Types Reused for Secondary Functions, the Same Function as before They Broke, and All Functions (*n* = 490)

EMIC TYPE	SECONDARY FUNCTION		SAME FUNCTION		ALL FUNCTIONS	
	%	*n*	%	*n*	%	*n*
Coffee pitcher (*jebana*)	1.8	2	2.8	2	2.2	4
Large jar (*otto*)	48.7	54	19.7	14	37.4	68
Narrow-mouth medium jar (*tsaro*)	21.6	24	11.3	8	17.6	32
Bowl (*shele*)	5.4	6	25.4	18	13.2	24
Baking plate (*bache*)	0	0	8.4	6	3.3	6
Narrow-mouth small jar (*tsua*)	6.3	7	4.2	3	5.5	10
Beer jar (*batsa*)	15.3	17	15.5	11	15.4	28
Water pipe (*guya*)	0	0	2.8	2	1.1	2
Dish (*peele*)	0.9	1	9.9	7	4.4	8
Comparison to entire assemblage	22.6	111	14.5	71	37.1	182

is surprising that Etello has the lowest reuse percentage.

Typology and Reused Pottery

The village socioeconomic and ecological setting influences the types of vessels that are reused, similar to the result discussed in chapter 4 on primary use. All of the villages reuse more large jars compared to any other vessel type, which is not surprising because this vessel form is most suitable for storing crops and other household items. This is especially true in the villages of Etello and Guyla, where agricultural production is much more common than in the heavily weaving-based economy of Zuza. Other vessel forms that the Gamo use throughout the region are the narrow-mouth medium jar and the beer jar, also used for storing items after the vessel has cracked.

Different villages reuse certain vessel types more so than other villages. Potters produce specific ceramic types based on consumer demands that are driven by the types of foods they eat. For example, Zuza is located within the coffee-growing altitude; hence they more frequently reuse their broken coffee pitchers to boil coffee by turning them on their side. In addition, Zuza potters produce both the wide-mouth medium jar and the baking plate, whereas in the more central part of the Gamo region, where the Etello and Guyla consumers live, these two vessel forms are not as common. The wide-mouth medium jar functions primarily to make *wat*, which is an Amhara food, and the Zuza people seem to have adopted this type of food more so than other Gamo regions. This form is reused for storing materials and crops when it can no longer be used for the same function during its primary use. In addition, the baking plates are popular in the lowland areas of Gamo because teff is grown in this region and people tend to also use their baking plates for roasting coffee and other food crops. All of the Zuza baking plates are reused for the same function, which is not surprising, given their form as flat trays with a small rim. They are only suitable for roasting or making bread. With regard to the reuse of these two vessel forms, the Zuza people reuse them for secondary functions and the same function as before they broke.

Another example of village variation is with the reuse of bowls in Zuza, which is relatively rare compared to the case in Etello. This is a result of the lush woodlands adjacent to Zuza, where people are able to use wooden bowls instead of the ceramic bowls more readily produced by potters living in highland areas of Gamo. However, at the time of my household ceramic census, it seems that the Etello bowls were also relatively new and had not had the time to reach their next stage of life. Thus, the socioeconomic and ecological context influences the variation of ceramic reuse that is found within the Gamo region.

The reuse of a vessel depends on its pri-

FIGURE 6.5. A large jar reused to store water in a Zuza household.

mary use and form, with a majority of the reused pots being large, expensive noncooking vessels. Differences occur among the three villages in the range of types that are the most and least commonly reused. The large jar used for transporting and storing water and the narrow-mouth medium jar are generally the most common reused vessel types. The reason these two vessel types have a high reuse percentage is that they are useful for secondary functions such as storing excess crops and, in the case of Zuza, continuing to store water (for the well is difficult to get to, especially for elderly widow women living in Zuza; Figure 6.5). In addition, we would assume that because Etello does not have potters, its households would reuse their vessels more than those of Zuza and Guyla, where potters live. However, the Etello vessel assemblage has only 23 percent reused broken vessels, which is 9.1 and 14.1 percent less than Zuza and Guyla, respectively (Table 6.5).

Cooking vessels vary in their reuse among the three villages. The large jar used just for cooking is one of the least reused vessels in Zuza (6.4 percent) and Guyla (6.3 percent) but has a high reuse rate in Etello (15.4 percent). Coffee pitchers also are rarely reused in the three villages: Zuza, 9.0 percent; Guyla, 2.2 percent; and Etello, 3.9 percent (Tables 6.4–6.6). When coffee pitchers are reused after they break, they are turned on their side and placed on the hearth to boil coffee or are reused for storing crops, especially in Guyla. However, coffee pitchers and wide-mouth medium jars are rarely reused for storing crops because both vessel types are predominately used for cooking, which causes large cracks on the base of the vessel, making it hazardous to store valuable seed crops within. Coffee pitchers and wide-mouth medium jars are usually discarded or placed into provisional discard, until there is a need for a large sherd or to function as lids for larger storage jars (Figure 6.6). Large sherds and necks of jars are sometimes reused to make beehives in the villages of Guyla and Zuza, respectively (Figures 6.7–6.8). The narrow-mouth medium jar, another type of cooking vessel, has a high reuse rate in Zuza (13.5 percent), Guyla (17.6 percent), and Etello (13.7 percent). People reuse narrow-mouth medium jars by turning them on their side for cooking or to store crops.

Spatial Analysis of Household Reused Pottery

The village spatial analysis demonstrates that after pots break, Gamo people begin to gradually shift their storage location from inside the house or kitchen to outside, adjacent to either the kitchen or the house (Figure 6.9). However, as with the primary pots, the majority of reuse pots continue to be stored in clusters of two or more within the house or kitchen. The spatial use of household compounds affects where pots will be stored during different stages of the lifecycle.

During the reuse stage, larger numbers of households in both Etello and Guyla store pots individually or in association with each other in their kitchens. Zuza has fewer households with separate kitchen structures ($n = 6$), compared to Etello ($n = 19$) and Guyla ($n = 20$). Zuza's location on top of the Ochollo Ridge restricts the size of household compounds, resulting in a smaller number of

structures. In Guyla, they store reused pots in a larger number of different household areas. For example, a broken reused pot might be in storage in an abandoned adjacent house, and the storage of vessels in groups might occur in firing areas and adjacent to a workhouse.

CASTE GROUP ANALYSIS

The reuse stage should be an important indicator of social status, for the social hierarchy may determine who decides to reuse the vessel for the same or a secondary function or to discard the vessel altogether. Given that the Gamo caste hierarchy is fully entrenched in their cultural fabric, I would expect that the artisan households, especially the *degala* households, would reuse more frequently and reuse more vessel types because of a lack of economic capital to replace their broken pots. Furthermore, it is likely that the *degala* and *mana* would store their reuse vessels in different areas than the *mala*.

Frequency of Reused Pottery

In Zuza, Guyla, and Etello, the *mala* caste reuse more of their vessels, either for a secondary or the same function, than the *mana* and *degala* households. This difference between caste groups is a result of *mala* households having more vessels per household on average compared to the artisan castes.

There is also a clear pattern of the low frequency of reuse among *degala* households compared to the *mana* and *mala* in both Guyla and Etello (Table 6.7). The Guyla *mala* and *mana* reuse their vessels with more frequency in all categories compared to the Guyla *degala*. Yet the frequency of reused vessels among the Guyla *degala* is similar to that among the Zuza *mala* and far exceeds the numbers found within Etello *degala* households. The Guyla *degala* have been granted farmland by the *mala* caste and therefore can afford to purchase more household pots than the poorer artisan and *mala* households in other villages. Therefore, the reuse of vessels among caste groups mirrors the economic variation that occurs among villages.

Generally, more *mala* reuse vessels for a secondary use than the *mana* or *degala*. How-

Figure 6.6. A large sherd and a jar reused as lids.

Figure 6.7. Large sherds being used to form a beehive in the village of Guyla.

Figure 6.8. Jar necks being reused to make openings for a beehive in the village of Zuza.

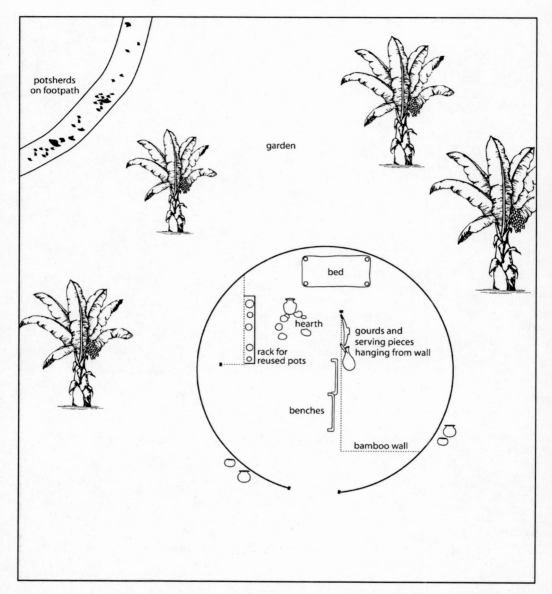

FIGURE 6.9. Generalized spatial pattern of the pottery reuse stage in the village of Zuza and the low-caste and poor households of Etello and Guyla.

ever, in Etello, the *degala* reuse more of their vessels for secondary uses than the *mala*. It seems that the Etello *mala* are more likely to reuse their broken vessels for the same function than to reuse them for a different function. The reason this is so is that Etello people cannot replace their vessels as easily as Zuza and Guyla consumers, because it is more dif-

ficult to travel to markets. Thus, Etello consumers continue to reuse their broken vessels as long as they can before they are forced to travel to a market and purchase a new vessel. Furthermore, the Guyla *mala* and *mana* reuse their household wares for secondary functions at a similar frequency. In contrast to the Etello consumers, it is easy for Guyla consum-

TABLE 6.7. Average Number of Vessels per Household Reused for Secondary Functions, the Same Function as before They Broke, and All Functions by Village and Caste

FUNCTION	ZUZA		ETELLO		GUYLA		
	MALA	MANA	MALA	DEGALA	MALA	MANA	DEGALA
Secondary function	2.3	0.3	0.8	1.3	5.6	5.3	3.6
Same function	3.5	3.3	1.9	0.6	4.0	4.7	2.3
All functions	5.9	3.6	2.6	2.0	9.6	10.0	6.0

TABLE 6.8. Average Number of Vessel Types per Household Reused for Secondary Functions, the Same Function as before They Broke, and All Functions by Village and Caste

FUNCTION	ZUZA		ETELLO		GUYLA		
	MALA	MANA	MALA	DEGALA	MALA	MANA	DEGALA
Secondary function	1.7	0.3	0.7	1.3	2.1	3.0	2.3
Same function	2.2	3.3	1.5	0.3	2.1	2.0	1.7
All functions	3.9	3.3	2.2	1.6	4.2	5.0	4.0

ers and potters to replace a broken vessel with a new vessel and then use the broken pot for a secondary function.

Types of Reused Pottery
The average number of vessel types is not a good indicator of the overall caste status in Gamo society because of the behavioral variation that occurs within each village. The *mala* in Zuza tend to reuse more than other caste groups. The Zuza *mala* are engaged in weaving and farming, and therefore when a vessel breaks they attempt to reuse the vessel for a secondary function, such as the storage of grain or some household item such as cotton or other weaving materials. These vessel types are mostly jars such as beer jars, large jars, and narrow-mouth medium jars (Table 6.8). In addition, sometimes a *mala* household will engage in honey production to supplement its income, as witnessed in Zuza and Guyla households, where they use the necks of large jars to form the openings of the beehive or use large sherds to form the hive. As with the Zuza *mala*, the Etello *mala* households more frequently reuse their vessels for storing crops, but surprisingly the average number of vessel types per household used for a secondary function is smaller than the number in

the hideworker households. Guyla *mala* are divided in reusing their pots for either a secondary or the same function, but as with the Etello and Zuza *mala*, they do reuse jars.

The Zuza *mana* do not have the opportunity to use vessels for storing grain because they are subsisting from day to day. In fact, they reuse only one vessel type to store grain (i.e., large jars); all the other broken vessels are used for the same function, mostly for cooking or transporting water. In Guyla, the *mana* have a surprisingly high number of reused vessel types, which are used for a secondary function or the same function as before the vessel broke (Table 6.8). This differs considerably from the Zuza *mana*. The Guyla *mana* use their broken household pots for pottery production activities such as to store and mix the clay (i.e., large jars, bowls, and beer jars), to store water (i.e., large jars), or for protecting the vessels during the firing process. These vessel types are large jars, bowls, and beer jars. Instead of reusing pots, the Zuza *mana* have a large amount of wasters directly adjacent to their houses, which far exceeds the amount of wasters found in Guyla households. After firing, the Zuza *mana* pull pots out of the fire and use the vessels that they feel are not acceptable for sale for pottery production activities. This

TABLE 6.9. Average Vessel Volume (l) per Household of Vessels Reused for Secondary Functions, the Same Function as before They Broke, and All Functions by Village and Caste

| | ZUZA | | ETELLO | | GUYLA | | |
FUNCTION	MALA	MANA	MALA	DEGALA	MALA	MANA	DEGALA
Secondary function	17.1	15.6	14.7	8.3	19.1	18.3	13.0
Same function	16.4	7.8	12.5	9.5	24.9	11.7	17.8
All functions	16.7	8.5	12.8	8.7	21.5	15.2	14.9

explains the variation that we see between the Zuza and Guyla potter households regarding how they reuse their vessels.

The *degala* in Etello use their broken pots to store different types of food. Of the six reused pots (i.e., two wide-mouth medium jars, three large jars, and one narrow-mouth medium jar), the *degala* families use four of the vessels for storing food. The Etello *degala* own very few pots, and their overall number of reused vessel types per household is lower compared to Etello *mala* households (Table 6.8). *Degala* use sherds to heat and produce the mastic for their scraping handles outside the household and also to scrape off excess butter when they soften hides. *Mala* and *degala* households in Guyla are similar regarding how many vessel types they reuse because the Guyla *degala* have obtained farmland from the *mala*, which has elevated their economic status.

Volume of Reused Pottery

A study of the average volume of reused vessels clearly indicates that the Gamo *mala* have larger vessels compared to the artisan castes (Table 6.9). Higher-caste households purchased larger vessels that eventually reached the reuse cycle. These vessels are more expensive than smaller pots, and the *mala* have more economic advantage, on average, than the poorer artisan castes, who have little or no farmland. The larger vessel types such as large jars and narrow-mouth medium jars provide ample volume to store crops and other materials and help to protect these items from rodents and moisture.

For potters in Zuza and Guyla, most of the high-volume pots reused for a secondary function are for pottery production activities such as storing and mixing clay, storing water, and making a wind barrier during firing. These vessels are larger than the vessels that are reused for their original function, which are usually for cooking.

The volume of the Etello and Guyla *degala* pots is a good material example of the variation within a caste group. The Guyla *degala* were granted land, and this has contributed to an overall increase in their economic prosperity compared to the Etello *degala*. Although the Guyla *degala* have larger vessels and more economic opportunities, the *mala* still consider them socially inferior. The disparity in vessel volume between the Guyla *mala* and the Zuza and Etello *mala* households is also striking and parallels the differences observed among the *degala* households. Guyla *mala* are able to reuse much larger vessels because of their ability to originally purchase larger vessels compared to the Etello and Zuza *mala*. Etello consumers do not have the opportunity to buy large vessels at the weekly markets because potters rarely carry these types to the market. Zuza consumers purchase a majority of their pots from the Zuza *mana*, who do not form large jars compared to the Guyla *mana*, who are known throughout the Gamo region for specializing in making the beer jar and large jar vessel types.

*Spatial Analysis of
Household Reused Pottery*

Mala households continue to place their individual reused vessels in more household areas compared to artisan households. Artisan households store their broken vessels in more household areas than they do their primary-use vessels, with the majority of ves-

TABLE 6.10. Average Number of Vessels per Household Reused for Secondary Functions, the Same Function as before They Broke, and All Functions by Village and Economic Rank

FUNCTION	ZUZA			ETELLO			GUYLA	
	WEALTHY	AVERAGE	POOR	WEALTHY	AVERAGE	POOR	WEALTHY	AVERAGE
Secondary function	1.8	1.6	2.5	0.8	0.8	1.0	6.3	4.7
Same function	5.4	3.0	2.9	2.2	1.7	1.0	3.6	4.0
All functions	7.2	4.6	5.4	3.0	2.5	2.0	9.8	8.7

sels stored inside houses, but not to the extent that they are during the primary-use stage (Figure 6.10).

There are differences in reuse locations between the *mana* households of Zuza and Guyla. The Zuza *mana* use vessels for pottery production that were not accepted as quality vessels to sell to Gamo consumers. The Guyla *mana* use broken household vessels for pottery production. This difference in the types of vessels used for pottery production affects where broken reuse vessels are stored. Two-thirds of the Zuza potter households store their vessels in groups of two or more inside their houses. However, the Guyla potters store vessels in clusters of two or more either in the compound or adjacent to the workhouse or pottery firing area as wind protectors (Figure 6.11).

Although the higher- and lower-caste households parallel the results in the village spatial analysis, the context of different caste households demonstrates that differences do occur. Because *mala* households have more structures than the artisan households, they are able to place pots in more locations than the lower castes can. The spatial analysis of pots may help to identify the social status of a household, as the locations of reuse vessels grouped together among Guyla potter households (e.g., groups of vessels in the firing area) demonstrate ceramic production areas.

ECONOMIC RANK ANALYSIS

The reuse of vessels within households provides a valuable measure of household wealth. The economic wealth of a household measures its potential to replace vessels after they break. I first thought that wealthier households would not be reusing many pots, but considering that they have more farmland and need more containers for storing excess crops, it is clear that storing crops is a perfect reuse function for an old cracked cooking jar. In addition, wealthier households have more reused vessels compared to poorer households because they have a larger household assemblage. Furthermore, at the same time that wealthier households reuse their broken pots to store food, they are not as reliant on their broken vessels as the poorer households, which are economically less prosperous and have difficulty purchasing a new vessel for a specific function.

Frequency of Reused Pottery

Surprisingly, in all the villages the wealthier households reuse more of their vessels than the poorer households (Table 6.10). In addition, wealthier households in Zuza and Etello reuse more vessels for the same function than the poorer households. In Guyla, which is more economically prosperous than the other two villages, the middle-income households reuse their vessels for the same original function only slightly more than the wealthy households.

Poorer households tend to reuse their vessels for a secondary function more often than wealthy households. Perhaps this reflects the fact that wealthier households can afford to purchase new and functionally specific wares and do not need to use their broken vessels for secondary use as much as poorer households, which have difficulty affording a new pot. In Zuza and Etello, poorer households reuse

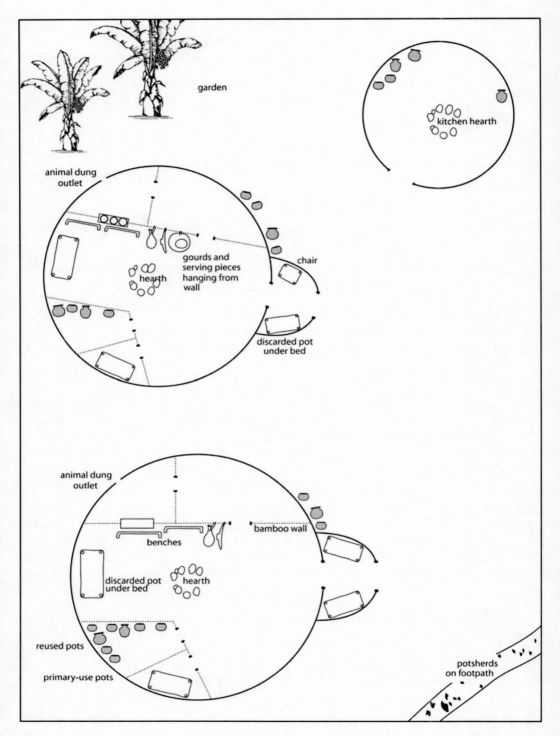

FIGURE 6.10. Generalized spatial pattern of the pottery reuse stage in the villages of Etello and Guyla, including their high-caste and wealthy households.

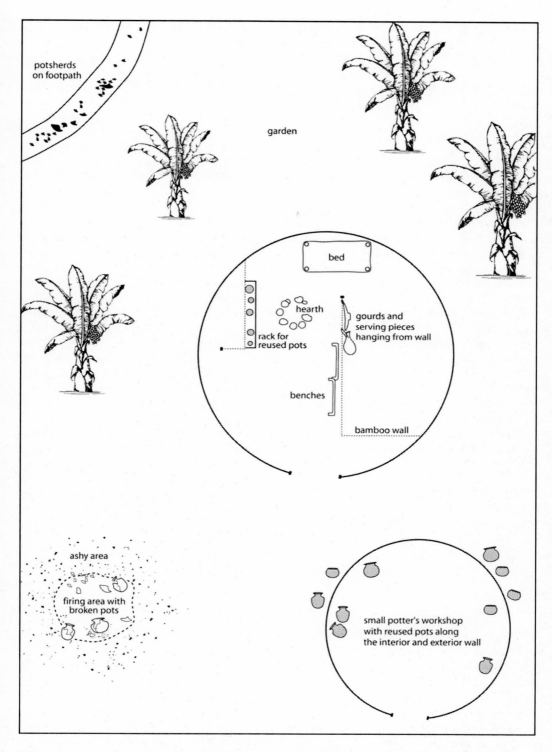

FIGURE 6.11. Generalized spatial pattern of the pottery reuse stage in the potter households of Guyla.

TABLE 6.11. Average Number of Vessel Types per Household Reused for Secondary Functions, the Same Function as before They Broke, and All Functions by Village and Economic Rank

	ZUZA			ETELLO			GUYLA	
FUNCTION	WEALTHY	AVERAGE	POOR	WEALTHY	AVERAGE	POOR	WEALTHY	AVERAGE
Secondary function	1.8	1.1	1.4	0.6	0.6	1.0	2.1	2.4
Same function	2.8	2.1	2.4	2.2	1.7	0.7	1.7	2.2
All functions	4.6	3.3	3.7	2.8	2.0	1.7	3.8	4.6

slightly more of their vessels for storing food and materials, that is, for secondary functions, compared to the middle-income and wealthier households. In Zuza, the poorer households reuse these pots for lids and for storing cotton and clothing. In Etello, the *degala* represent 75 percent of the poorer households, and as stated in the caste section, they reuse their vessels to store foods such as peppers and barley. Gamo *degala* also use broken pots to apply and scrape off butter when softening the hides they are preparing. In addition, they use broken pots to prepare the mastic, which they use to hold scrapers in their wooden handles. Again, this is surprising given that we would expect wealthier households to more often reuse these vessels for storing their surplus food.

The average frequency of reused vessels is lower than in the primary-use stage for economic ranks. However, the high frequency of vessel reuse still indicates that this is an important stage that may affect the frequency of vessels and types in the archaeological record.

Types of Reused Pottery

In general, the wealthiest economically ranked households reuse more types of vessels than the lower ranks (Table 6.11). However, there is not great disparity concerning the average number of vessel types among the different economically ranked households. This sharply contrasts with the average number of vessel types within the primary-use stage among wealthier and poorer households. The number of reused vessel types tends to be reduced

by almost half compared to the number of types in the primary-use stage. Etello provides an interesting example, in that during the primary-use stage the difference in the average number of vessel types in the wealthier and poorer households is dramatic (see Figure 4.8). However, in the reuse stage, this disparity is lessened because households tend to be able to only reuse jars, which have an adequate form for storing items in the reuse stage. For example, vessel types such as the coffee pitcher, which has a small mouth and long, narrow neck, are not reusable and tend to go from primary use directly to the discard stage. Thus, wealthier households may have more houses, land, livestock, wives, and occupations, but their average reuse of vessel types does not differentiate them based on their economic well-being. Among the Gamo the different economic ranks reuse similar vessel types such as large jars and narrow-mouth medium jars because many vessel types simply are not suitable for reuse.

Volume of Reused Pottery

Volume is the best indicator of economic variation among the ranks, with the wealthier ranks reusing larger vessels compared to the middle-income and poorer households (Table 6.12). Wealthier households are able to afford larger vessels such as the large jars for fermenting beer, and poorer households tend to buy vessels that are smaller and thus monetarily cheaper. There is a large contrast between the primary-use and reuse stages, with the average volume of reused pots being much larger than that of primary-use pots. This un-

TABLE 6.12. Average Vessel Volume (l) per Household of Vessels Reused for Secondary Functions, the Same Function as before They Broke, and All Functions by Village and Economic Rank

FUNCTION	ZUZA			ETELLO			GUYLA	
	WEALTHY	AVERAGE	POOR	WEALTHY	AVERAGE	POOR	WEALTHY	AVERAGE
Secondary function	25.6	9.9	17.2	17.4	11.9	8.3	15.6	20.1
Same function	13.7	32.9	15.1	13.3	12.9	6.7	37.9	12.3
All functions	16.6	14.7	16.0	14.4	12.6	7.4	23.7	17.5

derscores that jars are being reused and that smaller vessels such as coffee pitchers, bowls, and dishes are not being reused but, rather, discarded.

Spatial Analysis of Household Reused Pottery

The size of the land and the number of houses within the household tend to define where reused pots are stored (Figures 6.9–6.11). Zuza households and Etello's poorest households have, in general, only one house each, and so reused vessels are stored individually and in groups within the house. People also store reused pots adjacent to their houses (Figure 6.10). The wealthier households in Etello and Guyla store their reused pots within their different structures (i.e., main houses and kitchens). This compares to the middle-income households, which tend to store their reused pots clustered together outside between houses or within the household. The storage of reuse vessels clustered together follows the general pattern found in the storage of primary-use vessels. The only exception is that more of Guyla's middle-income households now store reused pots in the firing areas because they belong to the potter caste. All three villages' economic ranks generally follow the village trend, with reuse vessels associated less within houses and kitchens than during the primary-use stage. As with the caste analysis, the village landscape and the wealth of the household determine where people are able to store their pots. Poorer households, such as in Etello, that have only one house are confined to storing their reused pots with the house. Wealthier households are able to store their reused vessels in a number of structures, such as in houses, kitchens, storehouses, and weaving workshops.

GAMO POTTERY REUSE IN CROSS-CULTURAL PERSPECTIVE

Archaeologists have recognized for some time that once a vessel is broken it may be discarded or reused (Deal 1998; Deal and Hagstrum 1995; Stanislawski 1969, 1978). This study duplicates results from other studies, namely, that the reuse of vessels is a common occurrence (Deal 1998:168). The study of the Gamo indicates the process of mending is most common in the nonpotter village of Etello. Etello, as expected, because of its lack of potters, has the highest percentage of mended pots (12.3 percent), which is far greater than the 4 percent and 1.3 percent for Zuza and Guyla, respectively. Therefore, the low frequency of mending in an archaeological assemblage may suggest that potters live within the village or surrounding area.

Senior (1995:97–98) has found in her analysis of Mexican Rarámuri pots that large vessels are most often mended. Similarly among the Gamo, large vessels such as large jars and beer jars are the most common types of vessels that Gamo households repair. These two vessel types are most commonly used after they are mended for the storage of surplus agricultural crops. Furthermore, the mending of specific types of pots may indicate particular economic activities such as farming because these large pots are used to store surplus crops.

Deal's (1998) ethnoarchaeological study

conducted among the Tzeltal Maya of Mexico indicates that reused vessels, which he categorizes as used for a secondary function, made up on average 21 percent of the household inventories. The Maya example is similar to the Gamo inventory, where 19 percent of the vessels are reused for a secondary function. When vessels break among the Gamo, 14 percent are reused for the same original function; therefore, 33 percent of the Gamo household assemblages are broken reused pots. Among the Wanka of Peru's central highlands (Deal and Hagstrum 1995), as in the studies of the Maya and Gamo, similar results have been found regarding reuse. The potter households in the Tzeltal Maya region had an average of twice the amount of reused vessels than nonpottery households (Deal 1998:109, 167). Differences between the Gamo *mala* and *mana* tend to indicate more village variation. The *mala* do tend to reuse larger vessels than potter households. Although the Gamo examples indicate regional variation, vessel reuse can provide information concerning the social and economic context of households, which has rarely been investigated.

The spatial analysis indicates that the landscape of the village and household compound can have a direct effect concerning where reused vessels are stored. Villages such as Etello and Guyla, which are able to have large household compounds, are more likely to spread their reused vessels to outside the houses and within special activity houses such as kitchens and storage houses.

Caste groups are not a good indicator of who will more likely reuse vessels because of the variation in behavior among castes in each of the three villages. The best indicator is that higher-caste households more frequently reuse larger jars than the artisan groups because they can afford these vessels in the first place and may need to reuse them for storing foods. The archaeological implications are that higher-caste households may have larger vessels in their household assemblages: they can afford these vessels, they use them for storage, and they use them for longer periods of time.

The economic rank analysis mirrors the caste analysis regarding the difficulty in interpreting the amount of reused vessels and types within a specific economic rank. Again, the average volume of vessels is the best indicator of wealth, with the wealthier households reusing large vessels. Once vessels break, most Gamo people reuse jars because their morphology best suits them for food storage. The middle-income and poorer households use their reused vessels for storing foods, a secondary function, more so than the wealthier households. This indicates that wealthier households can afford to purchase new vessels to replace the pots that are broken. Thus, the reuse analysis does indicate specific economic and social characteristics of the household, and if archaeologists are also using other signatures of wealth such as household frequency and size and botanical and faunal remains, then they may be able to distinguish social and economic differences. Pottery reuse remains an important cycle given that one-fifth to one-third of the household inventory falls within the reuse stage of the lifecycle. Discerning ceramic reuse and spatial patterning are critical to accurately inferring activity areas.

7

Pottery Discard

This chapter explores the final stage of a vessel's lifecycle, discard. Provisionally discarded vessels, in this analysis, represent pots that informants stated were broken and had no further function but might be used again in the future (Deal 1985:253, 1998:118–119; Hayden and Cannon 1983:131–138). Based on previous ethnoarchaeological analysis of discard from agrarian-based societies (Deal 1998:118–119; Hayden and Cannon 1983: 131–138; Lindahl and Matenga 1995:106; Reina and Hill 1978:247; Weigand 1969:23), there are similar patterns of refuse, providing a more complete model for archaeologists in their interpretation of household ceramics. This chapter indicates that the function of the vessel and the caste and economic rank of a household will determine which vessels are discarded and where they will be stored within the household.

VILLAGE ANALYSIS
Frequency of Discarded Pottery
In the Gamo villages, 12.9 percent of the 1,058 vessels inventoried are considered in the discard stage. The percentage of discarded vessels within each of the three villages is consistent except for Guyla, which has only 7.9 percent of the household assemblage being discarded. This compares to Zuza and Etello, which have 17.1 and 17.6 percent, respectively. There is a higher frequency of wealthier households in Guyla than in Zuza and Etello,

and these households use their broken pots for storage of excess crops.

Types of Discarded Pottery
The Gamo make decisions on whether to reuse or discard their broken vessels. The most common use for broken sherds, which occur from all vessel types, is to use them to carry fire to the hearth or from one household to another to light a water pipe. In addition, all types may be used as lids for larger pots or beehives.

The vessel types most frequently discarded in all three villages are the narrow-mouth medium jars (Zuza, 32.2 percent; Etello, 28.2 percent; and Guyla, 20.5 percent) and the large jars (Zuza, 25.4 percent; Etello, 30.8 percent; and Guyla, 30.8 percent; Table 7.1). Although these two vessel types are commonly reused because they are used for cooking, the vessels sometimes succumb to large cracks on the base caused by repeated exposure to the hearth. The severity of these cracks causes people to discard the vessel rather than reuse it as a container. All of the vessel types that have a high rate of discard are used for cooking (i.e., coffee pitcher, wide-mouth medium jar, large jar, and narrow-mouth medium jar) and cannot be reused if a large enough break occurs on the vessel's wall (Figure 7.1). The number and percentage of discarded vessel types mirror what is found in other stages of the lifecycle, especially with regard to the wide-mouth medium jar and the coffee

FIGURE 7.1. A coffeepot sitting on a cooking hearth; after it breaks it usually cannot be reused and is immediately discarded.

TABLE 7.1. Percentage of Discarded Vessel Types in Three Gamo Villages

EMIC TYPES	ZUZA (n = 59) %	ZUZA (n = 59) n	ETELLO (n = 39) %	ETELLO (n = 39) n	GUYLA (n = 39) %	GUYLA (n = 39) n
Coffee pitcher (*jebana*)	13.6	8	7.7	3	10.5	4
Wide-mouth medium jar (*diste*)	20.3	12	12.8	5	7.9	3
Large jar (*otto*)	25.4	15	30.8	12	30.8	12
Narrow-mouth medium jar (*tsaro*)	32.2	19	28.2	11	20.5	8
Bowl (*shele*)	3.4	2	2.6	1	10.2	4
Baking plate (*bache*)	3.4	2	0	0	2.6	1
Narrow-mouth small jar (*tsua*)	1.7	1	0	0	2.6	1
Beer jar (*batsa*)	0	0	17.9	7	10.2	4
Water pipe (*guya*)	0	0	0	0	0	0
Dish (*peele*)	0	0	0	0	2.6	1
Foot-washing bowl (*gumgay*)	0	0	0	0	0	0
Single-handle jar (*kolay*)	0	0	0	0	0	0
Coffee cup (*sene*)	0	0	0	0	0	0
Wide-mouth small jar (*tayche*)	0	0	0	0	0	0
Comparison to entire assemblage	17.1	59 (n = 346)	17.6	39 (n = 222)	7.9	39 (n = 490)

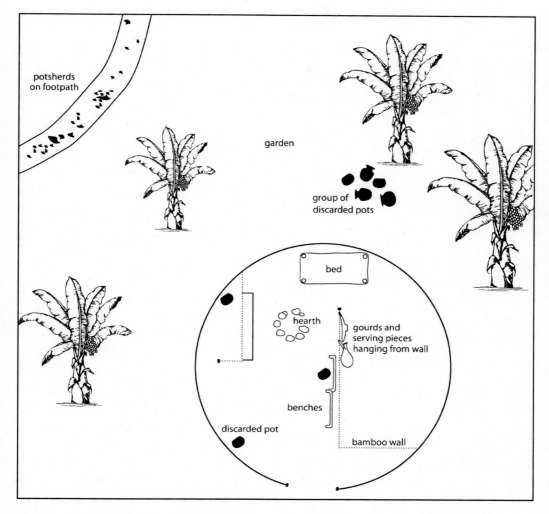

FIGURE 7.2. Generalized spatial pattern of the pottery discard stage in the village of Zuza and the low-caste and poor households of Etello and Guyla.

pitcher, which are more popular types found in Zuza (Table 7.1).

Spatial Analysis of Household Discarded Pottery

The Gamo dispose of broken and discarded pots, many of which are eventually lost, in storage rooms, on racks, and under benches and beds. Clusters of pots are found adjacent to the exterior walls of structures and are either used for water storage or kept for future use. Both types could be wrongly interpreted as representing different activities in the archaeological record.

Although there is a gradual change in the spatial storage of vessels from the primary-use to the broken/reuse stage, the spatial location of pots in their discard stage is dramatic compared to the two previous stages. The village landscape and the future potential of a vessel's function determine where people store their discarded pots. Zuza inhabitants place pots that they believe might be used in the future in their houses, in contrast to people living in Guyla and Etello, who store these vessels inside their kitchens (Figures 7.2–7.3). Pots that are thought to have little future potential are usually stored in gardens; adjacent to the

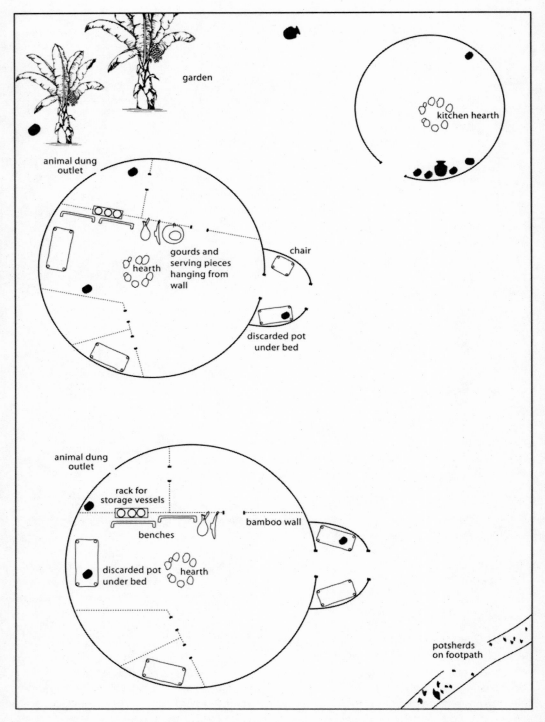

garden

kitchen hearth

animal dung outlet

gourds and serving pieces hanging from wall

hearth

chair

discarded pot under bed

animal dung outlet

rack for storage vessels

benches

bamboo wall

discarded pot under bed

hearth

potsherds on footpath

FIGURE 7.3. Generalized spatial pattern of the pottery discard stage in the villages of Etello and Guyla, including their high-caste and wealthy households.

FIGURE 7.4. View of pots being provisionally discarded in the household garden.

house or weaving house, compound, or garden; or inside the storehouse (Figures 7.4–7.5). Although the pots are in the discard stage, the household may decide to reuse them to fulfill some function, break and use the sherds, or toss the vessels into the household garden or village footpath.

Once a vessel has broken into sherds, people throw the sherds into either the household garden or the footpaths, depending on the household. Women sweep the compound clean at frequent intervals, and so I rarely witnessed the accumulation of sherds. However, imbedded sherds are a common sight along the footpaths of all villages. The sherds are repeatedly walked over and become part of the pathway. This accumulation of sherds in the footpaths provides people with traction during the rainy season (Figure 7.6). This type of formational process is especially noticeable in Zuza and Ochollo *deres*, where water from pumps run down the ridge into the footpaths, making them slippery even during the dry season. Therefore, women carrying water jars on their backs may slip and fall and break their

vessels. Potsherds are also visible along the footpaths adjacent to the Guyla potter households. Archaeologically the study of household ceramic spatial patterning throughout the different lifecycle stages is important to help archaeologists decipher vessel function, household abandonment, activity areas, and the social and economic variation among different households.

CASTE GROUP ANALYSIS
Frequency of Discarded Pottery

The *mala* households discard a higher percentage of their vessels compared to the artisan households (Figure 7.7). Guyla *mala* discard a smaller percentage of vessels than either the Zuza or Etello *mala*. The livelihoods of many Zuza *mala* are dependent on weaving (52.9 percent of households), and so storing excess amounts of crops in large vessels is not as common as it is among the Guyla *mala*. In addition, widows occupy a large percentage (47 percent) of the Zuza *mala* households, and so farming is not an economic option, making discard more common than the reuse

FIGURE 7.5. View of provisionally discarded pots being stored adjacent to the house at a *halaka* household in Zuza.

of broken vessels for storage. The Etello *mala* have more discarded vessels (41.2 percent) than the *mala* in the two other villages. And the Etello *mala* discard a larger percentage of their beer jars than the Zuza and Guyla *mala*. As discussed above, it is surprising that a village without potters would discard a higher percentage of vessels than villages that have potters and therefore easier access to new pots.

Types of Discarded Pottery

The potters in both Zuza and Guyla discard only 15.4 percent and 23.1 percent of their vessels, respectively. The Zuza potters commonly discard only two types (wide-mouth medium jars and narrow-mouth medium jars), but the Guyla potters discard six different types of vessels (i.e., wide-mouth medium jars, narrow-mouth medium jars, bowls, dishes, baking plates, and beer jars; Figure 7.8). In addition, Zuza *mana* have fewer broken vessels (34.2 percent) in their household assemblages compared to the Guyla potters

FIGURE 7.6. View of a typical Gamo village footpath where discarded sherds are often thrown.

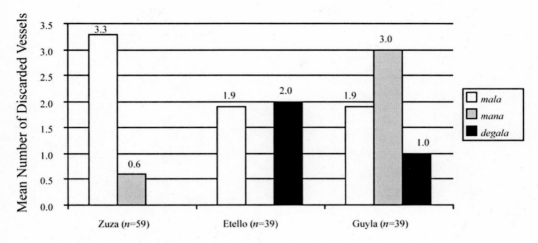

FIGURE 7.7. Mean number of discarded vessels by caste and village.

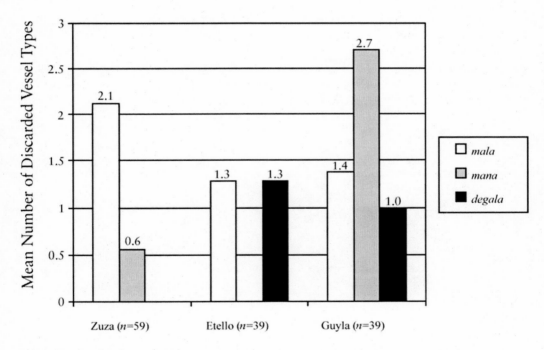

FIGURE 7.8. Mean number of discarded vessel types by caste and village.

(54.9 percent). The reason the Guyla *mana* discard a greater number of types and have a higher discard rate is that they manufacture more types—when those types break during production, they keep these vessels for possible future use. Zuza *mana* use some of their broken vessels for pottery production, but the majority are discarded as wasters and are eventually ground up as grog.

The Etello *degala* have half of their broken vessels in discard, compared to only 15 percent for the Guyla *degala*. Although the Etello *degala* have 35 percent more vessels in discard than the Guyla *degala*, they only have three

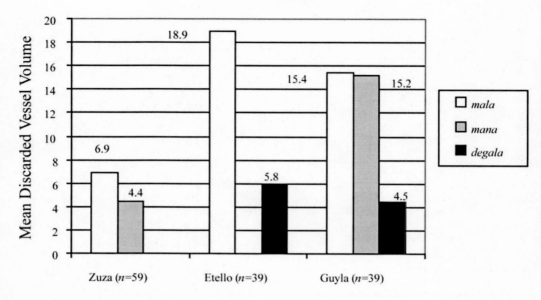

FIGURE 7.9. Mean volume of discarded vessels by caste and village.

vessel types in the broken lifecycle stage, compared to six types among the Guyla *degala*. Furthermore, 60 percent of the Etello *degala*'s assemblage is in the broken lifecycle stage, compared to only 37.7 percent for the Guyla *degala*'s assemblage. Finally, the Etello *degala* primarily use their vessels for cooking, which is an important component to their high discard rate. Cooking vessels usually crack on the base when they break and therefore cannot be used to store liquids such as water or beer but only dry goods. Because the Etello *degala* do not have farmland, they do not have the need to store a seasonal harvest; and although they do store food in their broken pots, they do not have the amount of storable food that the Guyla *degala* have.

Volume of Discarded Pottery
The volume of discarded vessels among the different caste groups mirrors the distribution of vessel volume in the primary-use and reuse stages (Figure 7.9). This is promising because it is these vessels that would most likely be left behind if a family abandoned a household. In addition, vessel volume provides an indication of the caste hierarchy that is prevalent in Gamo society. The average vessel volume for *mala* households is more than the average

volume found in artisan households. However, in Zuza, Etello, and Guyla, *mala* ceramics have volumes similar to those found among the *mana* households. The low vessel volume found in the Guyla *degala* households is surprising because they have been granted land by the *mala* caste. Here the *degala* discard smaller vessel types such as a coffee pitcher, a wide-mouth medium jar, and a narrow-mouth medium jar. The higher *mala* caste households discard larger vessels because they are able to afford a larger assemblage, but also they use large vessels for cooking and fermenting beer that eventually break and can no longer be used for cooking or a secondary function.

Spatial Analysis of Household Discarded Pottery
Different castes may place their discarded vessels in distinct locations, thereby providing clues in identifying a household's social status. Zuza and Etello *mala* store vessels in different areas of the household compound. All *mala* households deposit the majority of their discarded vessels in either their houses or their kitchens (see Figure 7.3). However, the lack of space requires Gamo artisans to place discarded pots in clusters within their gardens (see Figure 7.2). In addition, the Zuza *mala*

store more of their discarded vessels outside in the compound compared to the farmers from either Etello or Guyla. This is possibly a result of having an average of 1.5 buildings per Zuza *mala* household, compared to 2.8 and 2.7 buildings per *mala* household for Etello and Guyla, respectively. Thus, Zuza *mala* have fewer buildings, and they must place discarded vessels outside either adjacent to buildings or in the garden or compound areas. However, Guyla potters tend to place their discarded pots in clusters in household gardens or individually in the compound or in the main living house (Figure 7.10).

ECONOMIC RANK ANALYSIS

The economic wealth of a household in Gamo society may affect the frequency, type, and volume of discarded vessels within a household. In addition, the analysis of vessel use-life and its relationship with household wealth furthers our understanding of the connection between household ceramic assemblages and the economic component of society.

Frequency of Discarded Pottery

The wealthier households in Zuza and middle-income households in Etello and Guyla discard more vessels, on average, than the other economic ranks (Figure 7.11). This is a result of these households processing more beer and cooking with vessels with more frequency. In general, the households that have a higher frequency of discarded vessels have more vessels with shorter use-lives than the other economic ranks (see Table 7.1). Using cooking vessels with more frequency wears down the resistance of the vessel wall against thermal stress, causing these vessels to break sooner. The poorer economic rank in Etello comprises three-fourths of the hideworker households, which constantly reuse their broken cooking vessels because they cannot afford to purchase new pots. The wealthier Zuza households have a higher discard rate than the other ranked households because of their high number of coffee pitchers, which are repeatedly used every day to brew coffee and have no secondary function. Therefore the functions of the vessels, which affect their

use-lives, are an important factor in why certain economically ranked households have either a lower or a higher average rate of discarded vessels.

Typology of Discarded Pottery

As with the frequency of discarded vessels, Zuza's wealthiest households and Etello's and Guyla's middle-income households discard a higher average of vessel types than the other ranks (Figure 7.12). This can be explained by analyzing the types of vessels and their primary-use function. The wealthiest households in Zuza discard a large number of coffee pitchers that have broken during the process of boiling coffee. Coffee pitchers cannot be reused for any secondary function, so people put them in provisional discard. The average-wealth households in Etello and Guyla discard a high number of large vessels that have been used in the processing of beer and for cooking. These two types of activities will break a vessel so that a household cannot mend it or reuse it for a secondary function.

Volume of Discarded Pottery

An interesting pattern appears with the middle-income group discarding larger vessels compared to both the wealthier and the poorer households (Figure 7.13). This is a change from previous stages when vessel volume corresponded to the economic ranks, with wealthier households using larger vessels. It is also quite distinct from how the wealthier caste groups discard more vessels. These middle-income households in Gamo use fewer cooking vessels with more frequency and use large vessels for processing beer. As mentioned in the above section, these types of food-processing activities will shorten the use-life of vessels and cause such damage that households will not be able to reuse them in the future.

Spatial Analysis of Household Discarded Pottery

Once pots have completed the reuse stage, households begin to place an increasing number of discarded pots in outside areas, usually adjacent to buildings or in the compound

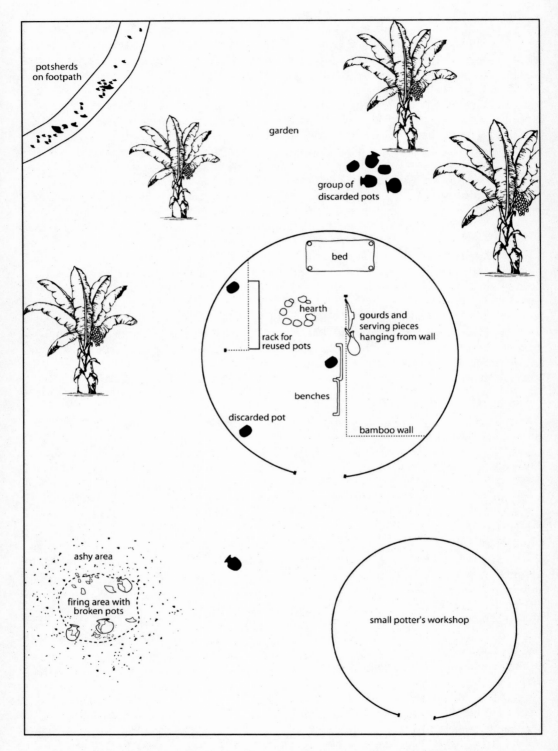

potsherds
on footpath

garden

group of
discarded pots

bed

hearth

rack for
reused pots

gourds and
serving pieces
hanging from wall

benches

discarded pot

bamboo wall

ashy area

firing area with
broken pots

small potter's workshop

FIGURE 7.10. Generalized spatial pattern of the pottery discard stage in the potter households of Guyla.

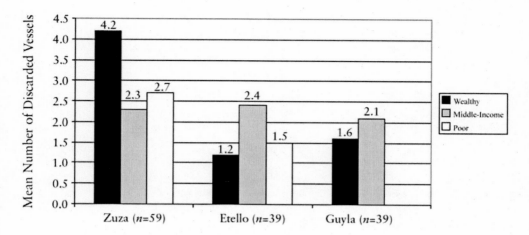

FIGURE 7.11. Mean number of discarded vessels by economic rank and village.

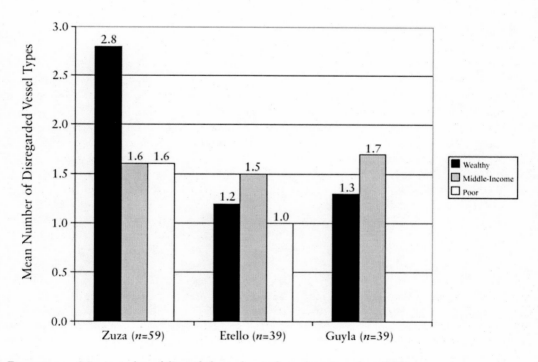

FIGURE 7.12. Mean number of discarded vessel types by economic rank and village.

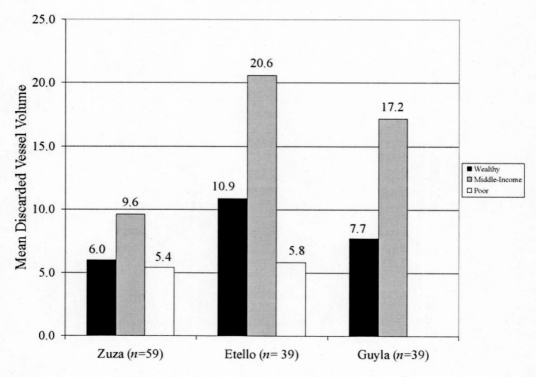

FIGURE 7.13. Mean volume of discarded vessels by economic rank and village.

or garden. This occurs in all economic ranks among the three villages. Both Zuza's and Etello's poorest households store all of their provisionally discarded pots in clusters in the garden area (see Figure 7.2). This is possibly related to their lack of storage space, because all of these households, except for one, have only one structure in their compound.

The spatial placement of vessels within households of the different economic ranks depends on the vessels' particular lifecycle stage. Primary-use and reuse vessels are usually stored in the house or kitchen for all economic ranks, and then, as vessels reach the discard stage, people begin to store discarded vessels in different outdoor areas of the compound. The economic ranks among the different villages vary in the number of buildings per household, with the poorer households having fewer buildings compared to the wealthier ones, and this influences the placement of vessels. The wealthier households have a larger number of buildings, so vessels can be stored

in more diversified areas of the compound. The poorer households usually only have one building. Therefore, the economic wealth of a household determines the spatial organization of the household pottery assemblage.

GAMO CERAMIC DISCARD IN CROSS-CULTURAL PERSPECTIVE

I have defined discarded vessels among the Gamo as pots that have no function but are still kept within the household. Nelson (1991:171) terms provisional vessel discard as "dead storage," which he observed among the Maya. In addition, Deal (1985:253, 1998:118–123) and Lindahl and Matenga (1995:106) describe broken vessels being stored in provisional discard among the Maya of Mexico and the Shona of Zimbabwe, respectively.

Other ethnoarchaeological studies of discard have only focused on spatial distribution. Thus, this study of the Gamo is unique because it considers the social and economic aspects related to discard. For instance, among the Gamo it is demonstrated that in wealthier agrarian villages, such as Guyla, people tend not to discard as many pots because they reuse the broken vessels for storing crops. Cooking pots are the vessels most likely to be placed in provisional discard because they form such large breaks that the Gamo are unable to reuse them.

In the less wealthy villages of Zuza and Etello, the artisan households tend to discard less than the *mala* caste group. Surprisingly, Etello *mala* discard a high percentage of their vessels, which one would not expect considering it is more of a challenge for them to purchase a new vessel than it is for a consumer living among potters. There is also variation within caste group concerning the frequency of vessels that are discarded. This is because of the recent political changes, whereby some artisan households have obtained land from the majority *mala* caste and are able to become economically wealthier than artisan households that have not been granted farmland. In addition, differences among potter households are a result of whether they reuse the pots for pottery production, to store water, as clay, for firebricks during firing, or simply grind up the discarded pots for grog. Discarded vessel volume among the three caste groups generally mirrors the social hierarchy, with the higher-caste households discarding larger vessels because they can afford them compared to the lower artisan households.

The economically ranked households (i.e., wealthy households in Zuza and middle-income households in Etello and Guyla) that use more of their vessels for brewing beer and cooking have more discarded vessels. The complexity concerning whether a household has a high discard rate of its household assemblage is partly based on the types of vessels they use (e.g., coffee pitchers and beer jars) and their economic status. The biggest change from previous lifecycle stages occurs with the volume of discarded pottery. In the previous stages, vessel volume corresponded with economic rank in each of the three villages. In the discard stage, the average-ranked households discard larger vessels in all of the three villages. These average-ranked households use a higher number of beer vessels and use cooking vessels with more frequency, all of which causes a short use-life.

The spatial studies of Gamo discard support other ethnoarchaeological studies. Once the vessel breaks into many sherds, the Gamo throw the fragments into their agricultural fields or footpaths. In Zuza, it is common to find footpaths littered with sherds where people either have fallen because of the slippery paths or have thrown their broken pots to help with traction. Longacre (1981:63) has also found that among the Kalinga, a higher breakage rate of pottery occurs during the rainy season because people slip on the wet footpaths.

Discarded vessel storage among the Tzeltal Maya represent two distinct types of household placement (Deal 1998:118–122). One is the isolated storage of ceramic vessels in out-of-the-way areas, where vessels are often lost. The placement of these vessels indicates little value to the household, and it is expected that they would be left behind when the people abandon their houses. The second type of spatial placement is a cluster of pots that are in continuous use (Deal 1998:118–122). These clusters of pots are found along the outer areas of structures. Among the Shona, broken discarded vessels are stored in association with unbroken, rarely used vessels, under the raised floors of granaries, protecting the vessels from further destruction by livestock (Lindahl and Matenga 1995:106).

My analysis of the discarding of pots by the Gamo parallels other important studies mentioned above. The Gamo discard pots adjacent to the outside of the house and within kitchens or storehouses. Individual pots are placed under beds in the house vestibule, within the house, and on rafters between where people gather and animals are confined. The discard stage may be the most important stage for archaeologists, and the clustering of these discarded vessels within specific areas may provide an important context for understanding social and economic conditions within specific households. Tomka and Stevenson (1993:191) indicate that there are cross-cultural patterns concerning abandonment but that each specific culture has unique aspects concerning how people abandon their homes. Therefore, as indicated, the discard pattern of ceramic vessels among the Gamo is similar to those in other societies. However, the Gamo's cultural uniqueness is evident in their strict social hierarchy, which determines where specific families place their discarded vessels. The poorer and low-caste households usually have only one house, and so they must place their discarded vessels within a restricted area. This contrasts with the wealthier and high-caste households that can afford more land and more houses and therefore store their pots in different contexts such as kitchens and storehouses. Thus, the Gamo example indicates what Tomka and Stevenson (1993) stress, that archaeologists have to excavate in a large area to find patterns to recognize the specific cultural pattern of abandonment. If large horizontal areas are excavated within abandoned Gamo areas, then the patterning of the social and economic hierarchy found within Gamo society should be discerned.

8

Gamo Pottery
and its Implications for
Ethnoarchaeology and Archaeology

This study of the Gamo importantly illustrates the need for archaeologists to examine pottery in terms of its lifecycle. Ceramic ethnoarchaeology provides valuable information from which archaeologists can gain better insights into the multiple factors, such as socioeconomic stratification, diet, household space, and the village ecology, that affect variation in household ceramic assemblages. In particular, I focused on how the pottery lifecycle (e.g., procurement, production, distribution, use, use-life, mending, reuse, and discard) reveals past socioeconomic systems to form the basis for understanding human behavior from the archaeological record.

PRODUCTION AND MICROTRADITIONS
Among the Gamo, ceramic production is a female craft performed by a landless, submerged caste group and learned through two microtraditions. Full-time craft specialists procure, produce, and distribute pottery in Gamo society. Gamo potters are part of an artisan caste group, the *mana*, which is considered low status compared to the majority *mala* caste. Potters in many different cultural settings also have a low status (Behura 1978:32–36; Blurton 1997; David and Kramer 2001:215–216; Foster 1965; Frank 1993; Gelbert 1999; Gupta 1969:21; Herbert 1993; LaViolette 2000:91; London 2000:105; Mitchell 1979; Sillar 1997:7; Stark 1995; Thompson 1974:121, 123, 130). The Gamo potters produce and distribute their pots in

order to provide household income for their families because many potter households do not own land. Thus, the Gamo potters produce pottery even during the rainy season, when procuring clays and drying and firing vessels become difficult.

Gamo potters produce 14 different ceramic forms used primarily for processing, cooking, serving, storing, and transporting food and drink. These vessel types are produced using a variety of techniques including hand-building, coil-and-scrape, and paddle-and-anvil. The potters learn these techniques through two microtraditions, one within their natal villages and one when the women marry and move to their husbands' villages. Among the Gamo, daughters usually learn from their mothers, which is similar to what is found among Maya potters during recent times (Deal 1998:29–30). However, in the past, Maya daughters married at such an early age that they learned pottery production skills from their mothers-in-law. This also is found among the Luo of Kenya, where women marry young and learn from their mothers-in-law (Herbich 1987:200). Producing pottery in Gamo is first learned through informal instruction. Eventually Gamo girls begin to make their own pots and are engaged in more formal learning from their mothers or mothers-in-law. Although Gamo potters learn pottery production in their natal villages, once they marry their husbands and move to their new households and villages, they must learn new production techniques such as acquiring local clays, decoration motifs, and how to distribute their pots. This resocialization of the potter's production techniques is dictated by what the consumers prefer when they are purchasing their pots either in the market or through the patron–client system within the potter's village. The potter must conform because she is competing with other potters for the consumers' attention, and if she does not produce pottery based on the local tradition, the consumers will choose another potter's work.

PROCUREMENT: PROXIMITY, SOCIAL RELATIONS, AND TECHNICAL FACTORS

The study of Gamo procurement strategies reflects other ethnoarchaeological studies that stress the importance of socioeconomic position, geological conditions, and proximity to resources for potters' access to clays and tempers (Arnold 1991:23; Aronson et al. 1994:88; Davison and Hosford 1978; Haaland 1978:49; Handler 1963:315–316; Lauer 1974:143–144; Rye and Evans 1976:126; Van de Velde and Van de Velde 1939:22). Specifically, Neupert (2000) has found among the potters in Paradijon in southern Luzon, Philippines, that political factionalism affects where potters mine their clays and indicates the importance of social and political networks in pottery production. Stark et al. (2000) have found that when Kalinga potters are deciding on which clays to mine, kin relations between potters and the landowners where clays are mined are just as important as performance characteristics in production and use. Gamo potters have to rely on the *mala* for access to clays and tempers; because many potters do not own farmland, they also are dependent on social and political relationships to obtain their clay.

D. Arnold (2000) argues that because of the geological, social, and behavioral variables affecting clay procurement, it is difficult to determine production organization. However, he (2000:370) does suggest that mineralogical and chemical analyses of pastes can help to indicate how pots are distributed and changes that occur over time. Thus, mineralogical and chemical analyses of Gamo clays found in pottery-producing and non-pottery-producing villages should indicate more heterogeneity of the clays in the non-pottery-producing villages, such as Etello, because pots are bought from potters living throughout the Gamo region.

Once the Gamo potters receive permission to mine for clays, they try to find multiple clay sources that contain clays with the specific qualities conducive to successful production. Notably for archaeologists, the Gamo potters use multiple clay sources to produce all of their vessel forms. Therefore, archaeologists should not assume that the clays came from one source. Yet the study of Gamo potters supports previous research that clay and temper sources are usually found within a 7-km radius of the potter's village (Arnold 1985: 39–52).

Kalinga potters also are concerned with the technical qualities of the clays during production rather than during distribution or use (Aronson et al. 1994:89–90). The Gamo prefer clays that are elastic, do not crack during firing, and prevent breakage during the firing process. Most Gamo potters do not need to mine for temper because it naturally occurs in the clays. However, the Guyla potters do mine a volcanic ash (i.e., *ano*) that provides multiple benefits during the production process (i.e., it provides elasticity and strength, particularly during the firing). Aronson et al. (1994:90) have found that plasticity and lack of stones are the two most important clay selection criteria among the Kalinga villages of Dalupa and Dangtalan. Zuza potters among the Gamo use grog in their clays but do not need to add additional tempers to their clays. Although Gamo potters are reliant on a myriad of social conditions for procuring their materials, they have a sophisticated set of conditions that they require to make the production process successful.

PROXIMITY AND SOCIAL OBLIGATIONS: CONSUMER PREFERENCE IN POTTERY-PRODUCING VILLAGES

Although the Gamo list technical qualities as foremost in the selection of specific wares, in reality they most often succumb to social obligations and purchase locally made pots. Consumers consider the technical qualities of pottery to be the most important criteria when considering which pottery-producing region makes the highest-quality pots. The descriptions given by consumers for the best pottery include that it is strong and lasts a long time, the quality of the clay, the quality of the potter's work, the use of specific types of fuelwoods, and the potter dried or fired the pot for a long time. Consumers also stated nontechnological reasons related to pottery preference, in particular that the proximity of where the pot was sold was important. In addition, exchanging food for pots is another important nontechnological motivation in pottery selection. It is the nontechnological reasons that have precedence when purchasing locally available vessels, for a majority of pots come from within the village of Zuza or Guyla or from nearby markets in the case of Etello. The strong patron–client system in Gamo society results in a majority of consumers obtaining their pots from within their village. Although Guyla and Etello consumers prefer Birbir pots, the Guyla consumers are tied to purchasing their pots through the local patron–client system because of the presence of potters living within their village. Zuza consumers also are tied to the patron–client system because they live in a pottery-producing village and region. In Etello, the majority of consumers purchase pots from markets located near Etello. The Gamo example indicates that people will more likely obtain pots from neighboring households because of the patron–client system and that, in non-pottery-producing villages, consumers will obtain pots from potters selling in nearby markets. Thus, social obligations and the proximity to markets affect the types of pots found within each village.

SCARCITY IN VILLAGES
WITHOUT POTTERS

The Gamo represent an anomaly in cross-cultural studies of non-pottery-producing versus pottery-producing villages (Aronson et al. 1994:101; Nelson 1991:171; Tani 1994:56). The village of Etello (a non-pottery-producing village) has far fewer pots per household and pots of more diverse origins than the pottery-producing villages of Zuza and Guyla. Gamo consumers living without potters purchase and use only what is absolutely necessary to meet their household needs. Variability in the clays, tempers, vessel morphology, and stylistic attributes within an archaeological site should suggest whether consumers engaged in a patron–client relationship with potters living within the village or obtained their household pots from a range of potters in markets outside of the village.

Previous ethnoarchaeological research indicates that because of the inadequate distribution of pottery vessels, non-pottery-producing villages stockpile vessels, whereas pottery-producing villages do not (Aronson et al. 1994:101; Nelson 1991:171; Tani 1994:56). The reason Etello, a non-pottery-producing village, has fewer pots per household is that there is not a strong patron–client relationship, as there is in Zuza and Guyla, where potters live and are dependent on village consumers to trade for or purchase their pots.

POTTERY USE:
ENVIRONMENT, DIET, AND STATUS

The Gamo demonstrate that village environment, diet, and socioeconomic status determine the types of pots people use in their household assemblages. Gamo people sometimes purchase from potters selling their wares in markets who live in different ecological zones, but the types of crops grown and the social interactions (i.e., patron–client system) occurring within a village have a strong influence on the types of pots people use. Thus, the types of crops people grow and eat have a strong influence on the types of pots potters specialize in to sell within their village or at the market. Previous researchers working in a number of different societies around the world also have documented the importance of consumer demand and its influence on household assemblages (Crossland and Posnansky 1978; David and Hennig 1972; Dietler and Herbich 1989; Hodder 1979; Kramer 1997:165; Lathrap 1983).

Previous researchers reveal that types of

foods and the technology required to process them significantly affect household vessel frequencies and types (Arnold 1985:127–144; Arnold 1991:64–65; Nelson 1985:324–328). The Gamo live in both highland and lowland environments. In the highland region, people rely predominately on enset, barley, wheat, and potatoes; corn, sorghum, teff, and coffee are grown in lowland regions. Therefore the types of crops people grow and eat influence the frequency of vessel types that households use. A household in a village like Zuza, which is situated within the lowland area of the Gamo region, is able to grow coffee in its gardens and therefore has more coffeepots than households in highland villages such as Etello and Guyla. Furthermore, people in Zuza use more wooden vessels, which reduces the number of ceramic bowls used for serving food, and because Zuza is situated on top of the steep ridge of Ochollo, people use a higher frequency of water-transport vessels than in Etello and Guyla. Zuza consumers cook more stews (*wat*) and make *enjera* in wide-mouth medium jars and baking plates, respectively, and this influences Zuza potters to specialize in the production of these two vessel types.

The type of environment and the use of other types of mediums for containers also influence ceramic use. For instance, in the lowland Gamo regions there are more woodlands. Thus, the village of Zuza uses a lot of wooden bowls for serving, while the villages of Guyla and Etello have a higher percentage of ceramic serving vessels (bowls, plates, and narrow-mouth small jars). The lack of woodland areas in the highland districts limits their use of wooden implements for food processing. Presently, we do not have a good understanding of when the highland forests were cleared, and so this difference between the villages in the types of ceramic serving vessels may be an important indication of past changes in the environment and landscape use.

Researchers have discussed the important role household pottery plays in distinguishing social status and economic wealth (Deal 1998:101–107; Longacre 1985:337; Miller 1985:74; Otto 1977, 1984; Smith 1987; Trostel 1994:223; Wilson 1994:55). My study has found that vessel quality, frequency, size, type, and function all correspond to the strict social and economic hierarchy of the Gamo. Lower artisan castes and economic ranks purchase and use less expensive pots than the higher-caste and wealthier households. Lower castes and economic ranks have, on average, fewer vessels, fewer vessel types, and smaller pots than the higher caste and the wealthy households. These findings concerning the relation of pottery and the socioeconomic context can make a significant contribution to how archaeologists interpret the social status and economic wealth systems of past societies. Hence, archaeologists should examine the quality and frequency of household ceramics to interpret socioeconomic status.

USE-LIFE AND FUNCTION

Pottery use-life estimates for utilitarian vessels remain a central component for determining past population estimates, occupation span, site function, social status, and economic wealth (Foster 1960; Longacre 1985; Rice 1987:300; Shott 1996; Tani 1994). The median and mean use-lives of Gamo vessels for the different functional classes fall within the median and mean use-life ranges given by other researchers working among a number of cultures throughout the world. The use-life of Gamo vessels in the village, caste, and economic rank analyses is determined by function, size, frequency of use, production, and cost. The analysis of vessel function vis-à-vis use-life is the most important determinant regarding how long the vessel will be in use. Cooking pots have the shortest use-life because of the continued thermal stress and shock, and more vessels break from cooking than from any other type of activity (Arthur 2002a). Contrary to cooking, storage vessels have the longest use-life because of their lack of movement, and it is the storage vessels that are the largest vessels. Therefore, larger pots do have longer use-lives than smaller vessels. However, vessel size only influences use-life when controlling for vessel function, indicating the importance of understanding vessel function in the archaeological record. Production materials and methods seem to influence vessel longevity, which is in agreement with Gamo consumer opinions concerning which potters make the most durable pots. Vessel use-life influences the cost of pots, except for the villages that are dependent on weekly markets, which are more severely affected by seasonal fluctuations in market prices. My analysis of vessel use-life specifically finds that households of lower social status and economic wealth use fewer vessels, causing a higher rate of use and therefore shorter use-lives than are found in high-caste and wealthier households. Furthermore, the correlation between cost and socioeconomic levels is manifested in the use-life of vessels, for the longevity of cheaper pots is less than that of well-produced expensive vessels.

MENDING, REUSE, AND DISCARD

Several ethnoarchaeologists have provided evidence that mending and reusing vessels are important components in the life history of pots (Deal 1998:107–111, 169; Deal and Hagstrum 1995; Stanislawski 1969). My findings suggest that once a vessel breaks, people either try to mend it using a combination of materials, reuse the vessel for the storage of crops and as lids, or discard the vessel. As expected, the largest and most expensive vessels are mended because of their economic value. In addition, Etello (a non-pottery-producing village) mends more vessels than Zuza or Guyla because it is more difficult in terms of time and energy for Etello consumers to obtain a new vessel.

This study looked at two different methods for reusing pottery, either reusing the vessel for a new function after it broke or using the vessel for the same function as before it broke. The purpose of this analysis is to see if pots are reused differently based on the social and economic conditions of the household. The Gamo reuse 19 percent of their vessels for a different function after they break, which is exceptionally similar to case among the Tzeltal Maya, where Deal (1998) has found that they reuse 21 percent of their vessels. However, the Gamo reuse 14 percent of their vessels for the same function as before they broke. Thus, when combining both types of

reuse, one-third of the Gamo vessels inventoried are in the reuse stage, indicating that the reuse of vessels is an important component of this lifecycle stage.

The presence of other material containers, such as woven baskets and wood serving bowls, can affect reuse. For instance, Etello households reuse a lower percentage of their assemblage than either Zuza or Guyla households, which was not expected but is related to the using of bamboo baskets rather than pots to store food. Guyla reuses a higher percentage of their broken vessels than Zuza, predominantly for the storage of surplus grain. In addition, I expected that the lower-caste and economically poorer households would mend and reuse more of their vessels. Instead, the higher castes and wealthier households mend and reuse a higher percentage of their vessels. The reason for this is that they need their reused pots to store their surplus grain. The only exception is that Etello *mala* reuse more of their vessels for the same function, predominantly for cooking, rather than using them for storing grain, because it is difficult to obtain pots and they tend to using bamboo baskets for storing food. Last, the form and function of the vessel are important determinants concerning whether the vessel will be reused or discarded. If a vessel has a small orifice (i.e., *jebana* [coffeepot]) or a cooking vessel has severe breaks or cracks, then it is less likely to be reused and is immediately discarded.

One of the most important lifecycle stages is discard, as it is assumed that the majority of discarded pots are left after the abandonment of living areas. The function of the vessel is an important determinant concerning whether it will be discarded or reused. Among the Gamo, narrow-mouth medium jars are the most discarded vessel type because people use this vessel type for cooking, which after continuous use will cause large cracks on the base—or the vessel will fall apart, thereby rendering it useless for reuse. All vessel types used for cooking have a higher rate of discard than vessel types used for serving, transport, or storage. I expected that higher-caste and wealthier households would discard a higher percentage of their assemblages, which has been reported in the archaeological literature (Garrow 1987; Henry 1987; King and Miller 1987:46–47; McBride and McBride 1987; Moran 1976; Otto 1977; Spencer-Wood 1987). However, higher-caste and wealthier households discard a smaller percentage of their household assemblages because of the need to reuse vessels for the storage of surplus crops and foods. For archaeologists, understanding vessel function may lead to a better interpretation of household occupation as well as a society's social and economic conditions.

SPATIAL ANALYSIS

Archaeologists often use spatial analysis of material remains to distinguish storage from disposal units, as well as the social, economic, and political relations of a past society (Arnold 1991; Binford 1978; Deal 1998:86–89, 115–140; Hayden and Cannon 1984; Kent 1999; Schiffer 1972; Sinopoli 1999). The ceramic spatial arrangements of the Gamo village and household are directly associated with how vessels are stored as they move through each stage of the lifecycle. The most significant finding regarding the different lifecycle stages and their storage patterns is the difference between primary use and reuse in the storage of discarded pots. Once pots reach the discard stage, people in each of the three villages store these pots informally throughout the household property. As reported in other ethnographic contexts (Deal 1998:118–122; Lindahl and Matenga 1995:106; Nelson 1991:171), Gamo households keep their broken and discarded pots in their houses and kitchens, and increasing numbers of these pots are stored within the compound and adjacent to buildings. This "dead storage" indicates that vessels may eventually be used for some function in the future, even though the owner considers the vessels as providing no use (Nelson 1991:171). When vessels break into many different pieces, the Gamo keep some sherds to transport fire from household to household or to light a smoking pipe that farmers use while farming. If the pottery vessel fragments are not used, then the Gamo throw them onto the footpaths to add traction during the rainy season or throw the sherds into the adjacent agricultural fields.

Another aspect of the spatial study reflects the location of the village landscape, which affects the number and types of buildings found in each household. Households in Zuza, a hilltop village that has a limited amount of land to build on, store their vessels within specific localities. This is in contrast to the villages of Etello and Guyla, which have access to large amounts of land. Lower social and economic households store their vessels in restricted areas, because they have smaller household properties, usually containing only one building. However, the higher social and economically ranked households have several buildings, and as vessels move through the lifecycle they become more dispersed across the household landscape. For an archaeologist, the spatial analysis of sites and their associated material remains is an integral component in the interpretation of site use. Thus, the spatial change from primary use to discard is significant when trying to interpret activity areas, village organization, and socioeconomic status.

CLOSING THOUGHTS

This ethnoarchaeological study among the Gamo of southwestern Ethiopia suggests that pottery is a complex technology that significantly contributes to an understanding of regional, political, social, and economic aspects of a society. By controlling for the interaction among procurement, production, distribution, use, reuse, and discard, archaeologists can examine material remains for a better understanding of historic and prehistoric behavior in future archaeological endeavors. It is my hope that these regional, caste, and wealth analyses, in combination with a life history approach to ceramic vessels, have removed some of the interpretive filters that plague archaeologists and will allow for a richer, contextualized interpretation concerning the interaction between people and their pots.

References

Abélès, M.

1978   Pouvoir et Societe Chez les Ochollo d'Ethiopie Meridionale. *Cahiers d'Etudes Africaines* 18:293–310.

1979   Religion, Traditional Beliefs: Interaction and Changes in a Southern Ethiopian Society: Ochollo (Gamu-Gofa). In *Society and History in Ethiopia: The Southern Periphery from the 1880s to 1974*, pp. 184–195. African Studies Centre, University of Cambridge, Cambridge.

1981   In Search of the Monarch: Introduction of the State among the Gamo of Ethiopia. In *Modes of Production in Africa: The Precolonial Era*, edited by D. Crummey and C. Steward, pp. 35–67. Sage Publications, Beverly Hills.

Arnold, D. E.

1978   Ethnography of Pottery Making in the Valley of Guatemala. In *The Ceramics of Kaminaljuyu*, edited by R. K. Wetherington, pp. 327–400. Pennsylvania State University Press, University Park.

1985   *Ceramic Theory and Cultural Process.* Cambridge University Press, Cambridge.

1993   *Ecology of Ceramic Production in an Andean Community.* Cambridge University Press, Cambridge.

1999   Advantages and Disadvantages of Vertical-Half Molding Technology: Implications for Production Organization. In *Pottery and People: A Dynamic Interaction*, edited by J. M. Skibo and G. M. Feinman, pp. 59–80. University of Utah Press, Salt Lake City.

2000   Does the Standardization of Ceramic Pastes Really Mean Specialization? *Journal of Archaeological Method and Theory* 7:333–375.

Arnold, P. J., III

1991   *Domestic Ceramic Production and Spatial Organization: A Mexican Caste Study in Ethnoarchaeology.* Cambridge University Press, Cambridge.

2000   Working without a Net: Recent Trends in Ceramic Ethnoarchaeology. *Journal of Archaeological Research* 8:105–133.

Aronson, M., J. M. Skibo, and M. T. Stark

1994   Production and Use Technologies in Kalinga Pottery. In *Kalinga Ethnoarchaeology: Expanding Archaeological Method and Theory*, edited by W. A. Longacre and J. M. Skibo, pp. 83–112. Smithsonian Institution Press, Washington, D.C.

Arthur, J. W.

1997   Producers and Consumers: The Ethno-Archaeology of Gamo Pottery Production and Use. In *Ethiopia in Broader Perspective: Papers of the 13th International Conference of Ethiopian Studies*, vols. 1–3, edited by K. Fukui, E. Kurimoto, and M. Shigeta, pp. 284–298. Shokado Book Sellers, Kyoto.

2001   A Functional Analysis of Early Pithouse Ceramics. In *Early Pithouse Villages of the Mimbres Valley and Beyond: The McAnally and Thompson Sites in Their Cultural and Ecological Contexts*, edited by M. W. Diehl and S. LeBlanc, pp. 69–76. Peabody Museum of Archaeology and Ethnology, Harvard University Press, Cambridge, Massachusetts.

2002a   Pottery Use-Alteration as an Indicator of Socioeconomic Status: An Ethnoarchaeological Study of the Gamo of Ethiopia. *Journal of Archaeological Method and Theory* 9:331–355.

2002b   The Social and Economic Conditions of Ceramic Production: An Ethnoarchaeological Perspective. Paper presented at the 67th Annual Meeting of the Society for American Archaeology, Denver, March.

2003   Brewing Beer: Status, Wealth, and Ceramic Use-Alteration among the Gamo of South-Western Ethiopia. *World Archaeology* 34:516–528.

Arthur, J. W., and K. J. Weedman
2005   Ethnoarchaeology. In *Handbook of Archaeological Methods*, edited by H. D. G. Machner and C. Chinppendale, pp. 216–267. AltaMira Press, Walnut Creek, California.

Atherton, J.
1983   Ethnoarchaeology in Africa. *African Archaeological Review* 1:75–104.

Bankes, G.
1985   The Manufacture and Circulation of Paddle and Anvil Pottery on the North Coast of Peru. *World Archaeology* 17: 269–277.

Behura, N. K.
1978   *Peasant Potters of Orissa*. Sterling Publications, Delhi.

Binford, L. R.
1978   Dimensional Analysis of Behavior and Site Structure: Learning from an Eskimo Hunting Stand. *American Antiquity* 43:330–361.

Birmingham, J.
1975   Traditional Potters of the Kathmandu Valley: An Ethnoarchaeological Study. *Man* 10:370–386.

Blurton, T. R.
1997   Terracotta Figurines of Eastern Gujarat. In *Pottery in the Making*, edited by I. Freestone and D. Gaimster, pp. 170–175. Smithsonian Institution Press, Washington, D.C.

Bowser, B. J.
2000   From Pottery to Politics: An Ethnoarchaeological Study of Political Factionalism, Ethnicity, and Domestic Pottery Style in the Ecuadorian Amazon. *Journal of Archaeological Method and Theory* 7:219–248.

Brandt, S. A.
1984   New Perspectives on the Origins of Food Production in Ethiopia. In *From Hunters to Farmers: The Causes and Consequences of Food Production in Africa*, edited by J. D. Clark and S. A. Brandt, pp. 173–190. University of California Press, Berkeley.

1997   The Evolution of Enset Farming. In *Ethiopia in Broader Perspective: Papers of the 13th International Conference of Ethiopian Studies*, vols. 1–3, edited by K. Fukui, E. Kurimoto, M. Shigeta, pp. 843–852. Shokado Book Sellers, Kyoto.

Brandt, S. A., and R. Fattovich
1990   Late Quaternary Archaeological Research in the Horn of Africa. In *A History of African Archaeology*, edited by P. Robertshaw, pp. 95–108. Curry, London.

Brandt, S. A., A. Spring, C. Hiebsch, J. T. McCabe, E. Tabogie, M. Diro, G. Wolde-Michael, G. Yntiso, M. Shigeta, and S. Tesfaye
1997   *"The Tree against Hunger": Enset-Based Agricultural Systems in Ethiopia.* American Association for the Advancement of Science, New York.

Braun, D.
1980   Experimental Interpretation of Ceramic Vessel Use on the Basis of Rim and Neck Formal Attributes. In *The Navajo Project: Archaeological Investigations Page to Phoenix 500 KV Southern Transmission Line*, edited by D. C. Fiero, R. W. Munson, M. T. McClain, S. M. Wilson, and A. H. Zier, pp. 171–231. Museum of Northern Arizona, Research Paper 11. Flagstaff.

1983   Pots as Tools. In *Archaeological Hammers and Theories*, edited by J. Moore and A. Keene, pp. 107–134. Academic Press, New York.

Brumbach, H. J., and R. Jarvenpa
1990   Archeologist–Ethnographer–Informant Relations: The Dynamics of Ethnoarchaeology in the Field. In *Powers of Observation: Alternative Views in Archaeology*, edited by S. M. Nelson and A. B. Kehoe, pp. 39–46. Archaeological Papers of the American Anthropological Association 2. Washington, D.C.

Bureau, J.
1978   Etude Diachronique de Deux Titres Gamo. *Cahiers d'Etudes Africaines* 18: 279–291.

1981   *Les Gamo d'Ethiopie: Etude du Syteme Politique*. Societe d'Ethnographie, Paris.

Calder, A. M.
1972   Cracked Pots and Rubbish Tips: An Ethnoarchaeological Investigation of Vessel and Sherd Distribution in a Thai-Lao Village. M.A. thesis, Department

of Anthropology, University of Otago, Dunedin, New Zealand.

Cartledge, D.
1995   Taming the Mountain: Human Ecology, Indigenous Knowledge, and Sustainable Resource Management in the Doko Gamo Society of Ethiopia. Unpublished Ph.D. dissertation, University of Florida, Gainesville.

Castro, A., N. Hakansson, and D. Brokensha
1981   Indicators of Rural Inequality. *World Development* 9:401–427.

Cerulli, E.
1956   *Peoples of South-West Ethiopia and Its Borderland.* International African Institute, London.

Chávez, K. M.
1992   The Organization of Production and Distribution of Traditional Pottery in South Highland Peru. In *Ceramic Production and Distribution: An Integrated Approach*, edited by G. J. Bey III and C. Pool, pp. 49–92. Westview Press, Boulder.

Cowgill, G. L., J. H. Altschul, and R. S. Sload
1984   Spatial Analysis of Teotihuacan, a Mesoamerican Metropolis. In *Intrasite Spatial Analysis in Archaeology*, edited by H. J. Hietala, pp. 154–195. Cambridge University Press, New York.

Crossland, L. B., and M. Posnansky
1978   Pottery, People, and Trade at Begho, Ghana. In *The Spatial Organisation of Culture*, edited by I. Hodder, pp. 77–89. University of Pittsburgh Press, Pittsburgh.

Curtis, F.
1962   The Utility Pottery Industry of Bailén, Southern Spain. *American Anthropologist* 64:486–503.

Cushing, F. H.
1886   A Study of Pueblo Pottery as Illustrative of Zuni Culture Growth. *Washington Bureau of American Ethnology Annual Report* 4:457–521.

David, N.
1972   On the Life Span of Pottery, Type Frequencies, and Archaeological Inference. *American Antiquity* 37:141–142.

David, N., and H. Hennig
1972   *The Ethnography of Pottery: A Fulani Case Seen in Archaeological Perspective.* Addison-Wesley, Reading, Massachusetts.

David, N., and C. Kramer
2001   *Ethnoarchaeology in Action.* Cambridge University Press, Cambridge.

Davison, P., and J. Hosford
1978   Lobedu Pottery. *Annals of the South African Museum* 75:291–319.

Deal, M.
1983   Pottery Ethnoarchaeology among the Tzeltal Maya. Unpublished Ph.D. dissertation, Department of Archaeology, Simon Fraser University, Burnaby, B. C.
1985   Household Pottery Disposal in the Maya Highlands: An Ethnoarchaeological Interpretation. *Journal of Anthropological Archaeology* 4:243–291.
1998   *Pottery Ethnoarchaeology in the Central Maya Highlands.* University of Utah Press, Salt Lake City.

Deal, M., and M. B. Hagstrum
1995   Ceramic Reuse Behavior among the Maya and Wanka: Implications for Archaeology. In *Expanding Archaeology*, edited by J. M. Skibo, W. H. Walker, and A. E. Nielsen, pp. 111–125. University of Utah Press, Salt Lake City.

DeBoer, W. R.
1974   Ceramic Longevity and Archaeological Interpretation: An Example from the Upper Ucayali, Peru. *American Antiquity* 39:335–343.
1985   Pots and Pans Do Not Speak, Nor Do They Lie: The Case of Occasional Reductionism. In *Decoding Prehistoric Ceramics*, edited by B. Nelson, pp. 347–357. Southern Illinois University Press, Carbondale.

DeBoer, W. R., and D. W. Lathrap
1979   The Making and Breaking of Shipibo-Conibo Ceramics. In *Ethnoarchaeology: Implications of Ethnography for Archaeology*, edited by C. Kramer, pp. 102–128. Columbia University Press, New York.

Deetz, J.
1968   Cultural Patterning of Behavior as Reflected by Archaeological Materials. In *Settlement Archaeology*, edited by Kwang-chih Chang, pp. 31–42. National Press Books, Palo Alto, California.

de la Torre, A., and K. M. Mudar
1982   The Becino Site: An Exercise in Ethnoarchaeology. In *Houses Built on Scattered Poles: Prehistory and Ecology in Negros Oriental, Philippines*, edited

by K. Hutterer and W. MacDonald, pp. 117–146. San Carlos University, Cebu City, Philippines.

DeWalt, K. M.
1983   *Nutritional Strategies and Agricultural Change in a Mexican Community.* UMI Research Press, Ann Arbor.

Dietler, M., and I. Herbich
1989   *Tich Matek*: The Technology of Luo Pottery Production and the Definition of Ceramic Style. *World Archaeology* 21:148–164.

Dumont, L.
1957   For a Sociology in India. In *Contributions in Indian Sociology*, edited by L. Dumont and D. Pocock, pp. 7–22. Mouton and Co., The Hague.

Foster, G. M.
1960   Life-Expectancy of Utilitarian Pottery in Tzintzuntzan, Michoacán, Mexico. *American Antiquity* 25:606–609.
1965   The Sociology of Pottery: Questions and Hypotheses Arising from Contemporary Mexican Work. In *Ceramics and Man*, edited by F. R. Matson, pp. 43–61. Aldine, Chicago.

Frank, B. E.
1993   Reconstructing the History of an African Ceramic Tradition: Technology, Slavery and Agency in the Region of Kadiolo (Mali). *Cahiers d'Etudes Africaines* 33:381–401.

Freeman, D.
1997   Images of Fertility: The Indigenous Concept of Power in Doko Masho, Southwest Ethiopia. In *XIII International Conference of Ethiopian Studies*, vols. 1–3, edited by K. Fukui, E. Kurimoto, and M. Shigeta, pp. 342–357. Shokado Book Sellers, Kyoto.

Garrow, P. H.
1987   The Use of Converging Lines of Evidence for Determining Socioeconomic Status. In *Consumer Choice in Historical Archaeology*, edited by S. Spencer-Wood, pp. 217–231. Plenum Press, New York.

Gelbert, A.
1999   Technological and Stylistic Borrowings between Ceramic Traditions: A Case Study from Northeastern Senegal. In *Ethno-Analogy and the Reconstruction of Prehistoric Artefact Use and Production*, edited by L. R. Owen and M. Porr, pp. 207–224. Urgeschichtliche Materialhefte 14. Mo Vince Verlag, Tübingen.

Goody, J.
1982   *Cooking, Cuisine and Class: A Study in Comparative Sociology.* Cambridge University Press, New York.

Gosselain, O.
1992   Technology and Style: Potters and Pottery among the Bafia of Cameroon. *Man* 27:559–586.
1998   Social and Technical Identity in a Clay Crystal Ball. In *The Archaeology of Social Boundaries*, edited by M. T. Stark, pp. 79–105. Smithsonian Institution Press, Washington, D.C.
2000   Materializing Identities: An African Perspective. *Journal of Archaeological Method and Theory* 7:187–217.

Gould, R. A.
1971   The Archaeologist as Ethnographer: A Case from the Western Desert of Australia. *World Archaeology* 3:143–177.

Gupta, S. P.
1969   Sociology of Pottery: Chirag Dilli, a Case Study. In *Potteries in Ancient India*, edited by B. P. Sinha, pp. 15–24. Department of Ancient Indian History and Archaeology, Patna, India.

Haaland, R.
1978   Ethnographical Observations of Pottery-Making in Darfur, Western Sudan, with Some Reflections on Archaeological Interpretation. In *New Directions in Scandinavian Archaeology*, edited by K. Kristiansen and C. Paludan-Muller, pp. 47–61. Studies in Scandinavian Prehistory and Early History, Vol. 1. National Museum of Denmark, Copenhagen.

Haberland, E.
1984   Caste and Hierarchy among the Dizi (Southwest Ethiopia). In *Proceedings of the Seventh International Conference of Ethiopian Studies*, edited by S. Rubenson, pp. 447–450. University of Lund, Lund, Sweden.

Hally, D. J.
1983   The Interpretive Potential of Pottery from Domestic Contexts. *Midcontinental Journal of Archaeology* 8:163–196.

Halperin, R., and J. Olmstead
1976   To Catch a Feastgiver: Redistribution among the Dorze of Ethiopia. *Africa* 46:146–165.

Hamer, J.
1987   *Humane Development: Participation*

and Change among the Sadama of Ethiopia. University of Alabama Press, Tuscaloosa.

Handler, J.

1963   Pottery Making in Rural Barbados. *Southwestern Journal of Anthropology* 19:314–333.

Harlan, J. R.

1969   Ethiopia: A Center of Diversity. *Economic Botany* 23:309–314.

1992   Indigenous African Agriculture. In *The Origins of Agriculture: An International Perspective*, edited by C. W. Cowan and P. J. Watson, pp. 59–70. Smithsonian Institution Press, Washington, D.C.

Hasen, A.

1996   *The 1994 Population and Housing Census of Ethiopia Results for Southern Nations Nationalities and Peoples' Region*. Office of Population and Housing Census Commission Central Statistical Authority, Addis Ababa.

Hayden, B., and A. Cannon

1983   Where the Garbage Goes: Refuse Disposal in the Maya Highlands. *Journal of Anthropological Archaeology* 2: 117–163.

1984   *The Structure of Material Systems: Ethnoarchaeology in the Maya Highlands.* Paper No. 3. Society for American Archaeology, Washington, D.C.

Hendry, J. C.

1992   *Atxompa: A Pottery Producing Village of Southern Mexico in the Mid-1950's.* Vanderbilt University Press, Nashville.

Henry, S. L.

1987   Factors Influencing Consumer Behavior in Turn-of-the-Century Phoenix, Arizona. In *Consumer Choice in Historical Archaeology*, edited by S. Spencer-Wood, pp. 359–382. Plenum Press, New York.

Herbert, I.

1993   *Iron, Gender, and Power: Rituals of Transformation in African Societies.* Indiana University Press, Bloomington.

Herbich, I.

1987   Learning Patterns, Potter Interaction and Ceramic Style among the Luo of Kenya. *African Archaeological Review* 5:193–204.

Hill, J. N.

1970   Prehistoric Social Organization in the American Southwest: Theory and Method. In *Reconstructing Prehistoric Pueblo Societies*, edited by W. A. Longacre, pp. 11–58. University of New Mexico Press, Albuquerque.

Hocart, A. M.

1950   *Caste: A Comparative Study.* Methuen and Co. Ltd., London.

Hodder, I.

1979   Pottery Distribution: Service and Tribal Areas. In *Pottery and the Archaeologist*, edited by M. Millett, pp. 7–23. Institute of Archaeology Occasional Publication 4. University of London, England.

Huffnagel, H. P.

1961   *Agriculture in Ethiopia.* Food and Agriculture Organization, Rome.

Hutton, J. H.

1963   *Caste in India: Its Nature, Function, and*
[1946] *Origins.* Oxford University Press, Oxford.

Jackson, R. T.

1971   *Land Use and Settlement in Gamu Gofa, Ethiopia.* Department of Geography, Makerere University Occasional Paper No. 17. Kampala, Uganda.

Kakubayashi, F.

1978   A Study on the Pottery-Making and Its Economic Function around Madang, Papua New Guinea. *Minzokugaku Kenkyu* (Japanese Journal of Ethnology) 43:138–155.

Kent, S.

1999   The Archaeological Visibility of Storage: Delineating Storage from Trash Areas. *American Antiquity* 64:79–94.

King, J. A., and H. M. Miller

1987   The View from the Midden: An Analysis of Midden Distribution and Composition at the van Sweringen Site, St. Mary's City, Maryland. *Historical Archaeology* 21:37–59.

Kramer, C.

1985   Ceramic Ethnoarchaeology. *Annual Review in Anthropology* 14:77–102.

1997   *Pottery in Rajasthan: Ethnoarchaeology in Two Indian Cities.* Smithsonian Institution Press, Washington, D.C.

Lackey, L.

1981   *The Pottery of Acatlán: A Changing Mexican Tradition.* University of Oklahoma Press, Norman.

Lathrap, D.

1983   Recent Shipibo-Conibo Ceramics and Their Implications for Archaeological Interpretation. In *Structure and Cognition in Art*, edited by D. K. Washburn, pp. 25–39. Cambridge University Press, Cambridge.

Lauer, P. K.

1974   *Pottery Traditions in the D'Entrecasteaux Islands of Southeastern Papua.* Occasional Papers in Anthropology 3. Anthropology Museum, University of Queensland, Queensland, Victoria, Australia.

LaViolette, A. J.

2000   *Ethno-Archaeology in Jenne, Mali: Craft and Status among Smiths, Potters, and Masons.* British Archaeological Reports, International Series 838. Archaeopress, Oxford.

Leach, E. R.

1962   Introduction: What Should We Mean by
[1960]   Caste? In *Aspects of Caste*, edited by E. R. Leach, pp. 1–10. Cambridge University Press, Cambridge.

Levine, D. N.

1974   *Greater Ethiopia: The Evolution of a Multiethnic Society.* University of Chicago Press, Chicago.

Lewis, H. S.

1970   Wealth, Influence, and Prestige among the Shoa Galla. In *Social Stratification in Africa*, edited by A. Tuden and L. Plotnicov, pp. 177–185. Collier-McMillian Ltd., New York.

Lewis, O.

1951   *Life in a Mexican Village: Tepoztlan Restudied.* University of Illinois Press, Urbana.

Lindahl, A., and E. Matenga

1995   *Present and Past: Ceramics and Homesteads: An Ethnoarchaeological Project in the Buhera District, Zimbabwe.* Studies in African Archaeology 11. Department of Archaeology, Uppsala University, Uppsala, Sweden.

Linton, R.

1944   North American Cooking Pots. *American Antiquity* 9:369–380.

London, G. A.

1989   *Traditional Pottery in Cyprus.* Philipp von Zabern, Mainz, Germany.

2000   Continuity and Change in Cypriot Pottery Production. *Near Eastern Archaeology* 63:102–110.

Longacre, W. A.

1981   Kalinga Pottery: An Ethnoarchaeological Study. In *Pattern in the Past*, edited by I. Hodder, G. Isaac, and N. Hammond, pp. 49–66. Cambridge University Press, Cambridge.

1985   Pottery Use Life among the Kalinga, Northern Luzon, the Philippines. In *Decoding Prehistoric Ceramics*, edited by B. Nelson, pp. 334–346. Southern Illinois University Press, Carbondale.

1991   Sources of Ceramic Variability among the Kalinga of Northern Luzon. In *Ceramic Ethnoarchaeology*, edited by W. A. Longacre, pp. 95–111. University of Arizona Press, Tucson.

Longacre, W. A., and M. T. Stark

1992   Ceramics, Kinship, and Space: A Kalinga Example. *Journal of Anthropological Archaeology* 11:125–136.

Longacre, W. A., J. Xia, and T. Yang

2000   I Want to Buy a Black Pot. *Journal of Archaeological Method and Theory* 7: 273–293.

Maquet, J.

1970   Rwanda Castes. In *Social Stratification in Africa*, edited by A. Tuden and L. Plotnicov, pp. 93–124. Free Press, New York.

Matson, F. R.

1965   Ceramic Ecology: An Approach to the Study of the Early Cultures of the Near East. In *Ceramics and Man*, edited by F. R. Matson, pp. 202–217. Viking Fund Publications in Anthropology No. 41. Wenner-Gren Foundation, New York.

McBride, W. S., and K. A. McBride

1987   Socioeconomic Variation in a Late Antebellum Southern Town: The View from Archaeological and Documentary Sources. In *Consumer Choice in Historical Archaeology*, edited by S. Spencer-Wood, pp. 143–161. Plenum Press, New York.

Miller, D.

1985   *Artefacts as Categories: A Study of Ceramic Variability in Central India.* Cambridge University Press, Cambridge.

Mitchell, W. P.

1979   Inconsistencia de Status Social y Dimensiones de Rango en los Andes Centrales del Perú. *Estudios Andinos* 15:21–31.

Mohr Chávez, K. L.

1992   The Organization of Production and Distribution of Traditional Pottery in South Highland Peru. In *Ceramic Production and Distribution: An Integrated Approach*, edited by G. J. Bey III and

C. A. Pool, pp. 49–92. Westview Press, Boulder.

Moran, G. P.

1976 Trash Pits and Natural Rights in the Revolutionary Era: Excavations at the Narbonne House in Salem, Massachusetts. *Archaeology* 29:178–185.

Nelson, B. A.

1981 Ethnoarchaeology and Paleodemography: A Test of Turner and Lofgren's Hypothesis. *Journal of Anthropological Research* 37:107–129.

1985 Reconstructing Ceramic Vessels and Their Systemic Contexts. In *Decoding Prehistoric Ceramics*, edited by B. Nelson, pp. 310–329. Southern Illinois University Press, Carbondale.

1991 Ceramic Frequency and Use-Life: A Highland Mayan Case in Cross-Cultural Perspective. In *Ceramic Ethnoarchaeology*, edited by W. A. Longacre, pp. 162–181. University of Arizona Press, Tucson.

Nelson, B. A., and S. LeBlanc

1986 *Short-Term Sedentism in the American Southwest: The Mimbres Valley Salado.* Maxwell Museum of Anthropology and University of New Mexico Press, Albuquerque.

Neupert, M. A.

2000 Clays of Contention: An Ethnoarchaeological Study of Factionalism and Clay Composition. *Journal of Archaeological Method and Theory* 7:249–272.

Nicholson, P. T., and H. L. Patterson

1992 The Ballas Pottery Project: Ethnoarchaeology in Upper Egypt. In *Ceramic Production and Distribution: An Integrated Approach*, edited by G. J. Bey III and C. A. Pool, pp. 25–48. Westview Press, Boulder.

Okpoko, A. I.

1987 Pottery-Making in Igboland, Eastern Nigeria: An Ethno Archaeological Study. *Proceedings of the Prehistoric Society* 53:445–455.

Otto, J. S.

1977 Artifacts and Status Differences: A Comparison of Ceramics from Planter, Overseer and Slave Sites on an Antebellum Plantation. In *Research Strategies in Historical Archaeology*, edited by S. South, pp. 91–118. Academic Press, New York.

1984 *Cannon's Point Plantation, 1794–1860: Living Conditions and Status Patterns in the Old South.* Academic Press, New York.

Pankhurst, A.

1999 Caste in Africa: The Evidence from Southwestern Ethiopia Reconsidered. *Africa* 69:485–509.

2001 Introduction: Dimensions and Conceptions of Marginalisation. In *Living on the Edge: Marginalised Minorities of Craftworkers and Hunters in Southern Ethiopia*, edited by D. Freeman and A. Pankhurst, pp. 1–22. Department of Sociology and Social Administration, Addis Ababa University, Addis Ababa.

Papousek, D. A.

1981 *The Peasant Potters of Los Pueblos.* Van Gorcum, Assen, the Netherlands.

Pastron, A. G.

1974 Preliminary Ethnoarchaeological Investigations among the Tarahumara. In *Ethnoarchaeology*, edited by C. Donnan and C. Clewlow, pp. 93–114. UCLA Institute of Archaeology Monograph 4. University of California, Los Angeles.

Plog, S.

1980 *Stylistic Variation in Prehistoric Ceramics: Design Analysis in the American Southwest.* Cambridge University Press, Cambridge.

Reid, K. C.

1989 A Materials Science Perspective on Hunter-Gatherer Pottery. In *Pottery Technology: Ideas and Approaches*, edited by G. Bronitsky, pp. 167–180. Westview Press, Boulder.

Reina, R. E., and R. M. Hill II

1978 *The Traditional Pottery of Guatemala.* University of Texas Press, Austin.

Rice, P.

1987 *Pottery Analysis: A Sourcebook.* University of Chicago Press, Chicago.

1996 Recent Ceramic Analysis: Composition, Production, and Theory. *Journal of Archaeological Research* 4:165–202.

Rye, O., and C. Evans

1976 *Traditional Pottery Techniques of Pakistan: Field and Laboratory Studies.* Smithsonian Contributions to Anthropology 21. Smithsonian Institution Press, Washington, D.C.

Sargent, C. F., and D. A. Friedel

1986 From Clay to Metal: Culture Change

and Container Usage among the Bariba of Northern Benin, West Africa. *African Archaeological Review* 4:177–195.

Sassaman, K. E.
1993   *Early Pottery in the Southeast: Tradition and Innovation in Cooking Technology.* University of Alabama Press, Tuscaloosa.

Sauer, C. O.
1952   *Agricultural Origins and Dispersals.* American Geographical Society, New York.

Schiffer, M. B.
1972   Archaeological Context and Systemic Context. *American Antiquity* 37:156–165.
1983   Toward the Identification of Formation Processes. *American Antiquity* 48:675–706.
1987   *Formation Processes of the Archaeological Record.* University of New Mexico Press, Albuquerque.

Schiffer, M. B., and J. M. Skibo
1987   Theory and Experiment in the Study of Technological Change. *Current Anthropology* 28:595–622.
1997   The Explanation of Artifact Variability. *American Antiquity* 62:27–50.

Senior, L. M.
1995   The Estimation of Prehistoric Values: Cracked Pot Ideas in Archaeology. In *Expanding Archaeology*, edited by J. M. Skibo, W. H. Walker, and A. E. Nielsen, pp. 92–110. University of Utah Press, Salt Lake City.

Shack, W. A.
1963   Some Aspects of Ecology and Social Structure in the Ensete Complex in South-West Ethiopia. *Journal of Royal Anthropological Institute* 93:72–79.
1964   Notes on Occupational Castes among the Gurage of South-West Ethiopia. *Man* 54:50–52.
1966   *The Gurage: A People of the Ensete Culture.* Oxford University Press, London.

Shepard, A.
1956   *Ceramics for the Archaeologist.* Carnegie Institution of Washington, Publication No. 609. Washington, D.C.

Shott, M. J.
1989   On Tool Class Use Lives and the Formation of Archaeological Assemblages. *American Antiquity* 54:9–30.
1996   Mortal Pots: On Use Life and Vessel Size in the Formation of Ceramic Assemblages. *American Antiquity* 61:463–482.

Shutler, M. E.
1968   Pottery Making at Wusi, New Hebrides. *South Pacific Bulletin* 18:15–18.

Sillar, B.
1997   Reputable Pots and Disreputable Potters: Individual and Community Choices in Present-Day Pottery Productions and Exchanges in the Andes. In *Not So Much a Pot, More a Way of Life*, edited by C. C. Cumberpatch and P. W. Blinkhorn, pp. 1–20. Oxbow Books, Oxford.

Silverman, R. A.
1994   Contemporary Pottery Production in Woayta (Ethiopia). In *Clay and Fire: Pottery in Africa*, edited by C. D. Roy, pp. 168–183. Iowa Studies in African Art: The Stanley Conferences at the University of Iowa, School of Art and Art History. University of Iowa, Iowa City.

Simmons, F.
1960   *Northwest Ethiopia: Peoples and Economy.* University of Wisconsin Press, Madison.

Sinopoli, C. M.
1999   Levels of Complexity: Ceramic Variability at Vijayanagara. In *Pottery and People: A Dynamic Interaction*, edited by J. M. Skibo and G. M. Feinman, pp. 115–136. University of Utah Press, Salt Lake City.

Skibo, J. M.
1992   *Pottery Function: A Use-Alteration Perspective.* Plenum Press, New York.
1994   The Kalinga Cooking Pot: An Ethnoarchaeological and Experimental Study of Technological Change. In *Kalinga Ethnoarchaeology: Expanding Archaeological Method and Theory*, edited by W. A. Longacre and J. M. Skibo, pp. 113–126. Smithsonian Institution Press, Washington, D.C.
1999   Pottery and People. In *Pottery and People: A Dynamic Interaction*, edited by J. M. Skibo and G. M. Feinman, pp. 1–8. University of Utah Press, Salt Lake City.

Smith, J.
1967   The Potter of Yabob. *Australian Territories* 7:9–13.

Smith, M. F.
1987   Household Possessions and Wealth in Agrarian States: Implications for Ar-

chaeology. *Journal of Anthropological Archaeology* 6:297–335.

Solheim, W.

1965   The Functions of Pottery in Southeast Asia: From the Present to the Past. In *Ceramics and Man*, edited by F. R. Matson, pp. 154–273. Viking Fund Publications in Anthropology 41. Wenner-Gren Foundation, New York.

1984   Pottery and the Prehistory of Northeastern Thailand. In *Pots and Potters: Current Approaches in Ceramic Archaeology*, edited by P. Rice, pp. 95–106. Archaeological Survey Monograph 24. Institute of Archaeology, University of California, Los Angeles.

Spencer-Wood, S. M.

1987   Miller's Indices and Consumer-Choice Profiles: Status-Related Behaviors and White Ceramics. In *Consumer Choice in Historical Archaeology*, edited by S. M. Spencer-Wood, pp. 321–358. Plenum Press, New York.

Sperber, D.

1974   *Rethinking Symbolism*. Translated by A. L. Morton. Cambridge University Press, Cambridge.

1975   Paradoxes of Seniority among the Dorze. In *Proceedings of the First U.S. Conference on Ethiopian Studies, 1973*, edited by H. G. Marcus, pp. 209–222. Michigan State University Press, East Lansing.

Stanislawski, M. B.

1969   What Good Is a Broken Pot? An Experiment in Hopi-Tewa Ethnoarchaeology. *Southwestern Lore* 35:11–18.

1978   If Pots Were Mortal. In *Explorations in Ethnoarchaeology*, edited by Richard A. Gould, pp. 201–227. University of New Mexico Press, Albuquerque.

Stanislawski, M. B., and B. B. Stanislawski

1978   Hopi and Hopi-Tewa Ceramic Tradition Networks. In *The Spatial Organization of Culture*, edited by I. Hodder, pp. 61–76. Duckworth, London.

Stark, M. T.

1992   From Sibling to Suki: Social Relations and Spatial Proximity in Kalinga Pottery Exchange. *Journal of Anthropological Archaeology* 11:125–136.

1994   Pottery Exchange and the Regional System: A Dalupa Case Study. In *Kalinga Ethnoarchaeology: Expanding Archaeological Method and Theory*, edited

by W. A. Longacre and J. M. Skibo, pp. 169–198. Smithsonian Institution Press, Washington, D.C.

1995   Economic Intensification and Ceramic Specialization in the Philippines: A View from Kalinga. *Research in Economic Anthropology* 16:179–226.

Stark, M. T., R. L. Bishop, and E. Miksa

2000   Ceramic Technology and Social Boundaries: Cultural Practices in Kalinga Clay Selection and Use. *Journal of Archaeological Method and Theory* 7:295–331.

Stark, M. T., and W. A. Longacre

1993   Kalinga Ceramics and New Technologies: Social and Cultural Contexts of Ceramic Change. In *Ceramics and Civilization*, vol. 6, edited by W. D. Kingery, pp. 1–32. American Ceramics Society, Waterville, Ohio.

Steponaitis, V. P.

1983   *Ceramics, Chronology, and Community Patterns*. Academic Press, New York.

Sterner, J.

1989   Who Is Signaling Whom? Ceramic Style, Ethnicity, and Taphonomy among the Sirak Bulahay. *Antiquity* 63:451–459.

Sterner, J., and N. David

1991   Gender and Caste in the Mandara Highlands: Northeastern Nigeria and Northern Cameroon. *Ethnology* 30:355–369.

Tani, M.

1994   Why Should More Pots Break in Larger Households? Mechanisms Underlying Population Estimates from Ceramics. In *Kalinga Ethnoarchaeology: Expanding Archaeological Method and Theory*, edited by W. A. Longacre and J. M. Skibo, pp. 51–70. Smithsonian Institution Press, Washington, D.C.

Thompson, R. A.

1974   *The Winds of Tomorrow: Social Change in a Maya Town*. University of Chicago Press, Chicago.

Todd, D.

1978a   Aspects of Chiefship in Diman, South-West Ethiopia. *Cahiers d'Études Africaines* 18:311–332.

1978b   The Origins of Outcastes in Ethiopia: Reflections on an Evolutionary Theory. *Abbay* 9:145–158.

Tomka, S. A., and M. G. Stevenson

1993   Understanding Abandonment Processes: Summary and Remaining Concerns. In *Abandonment of Settlements and Regions: Ethnoarchaeological and Archaeological Approaches*, edited by C. M. Cameron and S. A. Tomka, pp. 191–195. Cambridge University Press, Cambridge.

Trostel, B.
1994   Household Pots and Possessions: An Ethnoarchaeological Study of Material Goods and Wealth. In *Kalinga Ethnoarchaeology: Expanding Archaeological Method and Theory*, edited by W. A. Longacre and J. M. Skibo, pp. 209–224. Smithsonian Institution Press, Washington, D.C.

Tschopik, H.
1950   An Andean Ceramic Tradition in Historical Perspective. *American Antiquity* 15:196–218.

Tuckson, M., and P. May
1975   Pots, Firing, and Potters in Papua New Guinea. *Australian Natural History* 18: 168–173.

Turner, C. G. and L. Lofgren
1966   Household Size of Prehistoric Western Pueblo Indians. *Southwestern Journal of Anthropology* 22:117–132.

Van de Velde, P., and H. R. Van de Velde
1939   *The Black Pottery of Coyotepec, Oaxaca, Mexico*. Southwest Museum Papers 13. Los Angeles.

Vaughan, J. H., Jr.
1970   Caste Systems in the Western Sudan. In *Social Stratification in Africa*, edited by A. Tuden and L. Plotnicov, pp. 59–92. Free Press, New York.

Vavilov, I.
1926   *Studies on the Origin of Cultivated Plants*. Institute of Applied Botanical Plant Breeding, Leningrad.

Wahlman, M.
1972   Yoruba Pottery Making Techniques. *Baessler-Archiv* 20:313–346.

Watson, V.
1955   Pottery in the Eastern Highlands of New Guinea. *Southwestern Journal of Anthropology* 11:121–128.

Weigand, P. C.
1969   *Modern Huichol Ceramics*. University Museum Mesoamerican Studies. Southern Illinois University, Carbondale.

Westphal, E.
1975   *Agricultural Systems in Ethiopia*. Center for Agricultural Publishing and Documentation, Wageningen, the Netherlands.

Wilson, D. C.
1994   Identification and Assessment of Secondary Refuse Aggregates. *Journal of Archaeological Method and Theory* 1: 41–68.

Index

Page numbers in *italics* indicate figures.

Abélès, M., 10, 19
agriculture of Gamo region, 6, 10–12, 21, 23, 27
Arnold, D. E., 52, 53, 55, 136, 138
Arnold, P. J., III, 3, 4, 5, 52, 92, 100, 136, 138, 140
Aronson, M., 2, 5, 6, 8, 31, 53, 55, 71, 72, 136, 137
Arthur, J. W., 4, 5, 7, 34, 103, 138
Atherton, J., 102

Bankes, G., 3, 92, 100
baso (lowlands), 10, 20, 46
beer jars, 84, 93, 113, 114, 118, 119, 126, 128, 129, 133
Behura, N. K., 51, 135
Binford, L. R., 140
Birbir pots and potters, 14, 59, 61–63, 68, 93, 137
Birmingham, J., 3, 73, 92, 100
Blurton, T. R., 51, 135
Bodo market, 13, 21, 27, 64
Borada, 6, 14
Bowser, B. J., 51
Brandt, S. A., 10, 11
Braun, D., 2, 7
Brumbach, H. J., 5
Bureau, J., 19
burro, 15. *See also* caste system

Calder, A. M., 102
Cannon, A., 5, 51, 121, 140
Cartledge, D., 10, 15, 18
caste group analysis, 64–65, 82–86, 95–96, 110–15, 125–29
caste system, 1; ceramics in, 6, 51, 53; and economic rank, 67; and pottery production, 6; social organization in, 15–16, 64, 138; and vessel reuse, 120; and vessel volume, 85
Castro, A., 2
ceramics: form, 7–8; instruction, 30, 51, 135; lifecycle of vessels, 8, 66, 121; placement of, 7, 89; primary-use, 7, 73–91; reuse, 2, 3, 7, 102–20, 139; rim type, 7–8, 31, 40, 42; use-life, 2–3, 92–101, 129, 138; vessel volume, 8, 96, 97, 98,

99, 114. *See also* primary-use pottery, spatial location of ceramics
ceramic vessels: cost, 5, 7, 57, 60, 63, 69, 92, 93, 101; decoration, 44–46, 72; discard, 2, 3, 121–34, 122, 139; distribution, 2, 55–72; drying, 42–44, 43, 53; firing, 47–50, 48, 49, 53, 103; formation, 35–42; function, 138; mending, 2, 102–20, 139; reuse, 2, 3, 102–20, 139; shapes, 31, 35, 36, 37, 38, 39, 40; storage of, 79, 86, 110, 119, 123, 133, 140; types, 12, 35–42, 93, 94, 95, 95, 100, 108–9, 121–22, 126–28; use-life, 3, 92–101, 129, 138; volume, 8, 96, 97, 98, 99, 114, 128. *See also* pottery
Cerulli, E., 15
Chávez, K. M., 55
Chinese porcelain, as replacement for ceramics, 73
clay: mining of, 31–34, 33, 52, 136; mixing of, 30, 34, 34–35, 36, 53, 113, 114; preparation, 34–35, 35, 36; proximity to village, 31, 32, 51, 52, 53; selection of, 34–35, 53; temper, 31–35, 136; types of, 34, 52, 53
coil-and-scrape method, 35, 37, 40, 41, 42, 135
Cowgill, G. L., 2
Crossland, L. B., 89, 137
Curtis, F., 53
Cushing, 1

David, N., 2, 3, 15, 51, 90, 92, 100, 102, 135, 137
Davison, P., 52, 136
de la Torre, A., 3, 92
Deal, M., 2, 3, 5, 51, 73, 90, 92, 100, 102, 119, 121, 132, 133, 135, 138, 139, 140
DeBoer, W. R., 2, 3, 5, 92, 93, 100, 102
decoration, 31, 44–46; comb-stamping, 31, 45–46; rippling, 44–45
Deetz, 2
dega (highland region), 10–11, 23, 27
degala caste, 6, 15, 20, 25, 27, 64, 65
DeWalt, K. M., 2
diet, 18–19, 67; and ceramic vessels, 16–19, 73, 77, 83, 137; wealth and, 18–19, 86, 90
Dietler, M., 90, 137
Dumont, L., 15

enset, 10–11, 18, 21, 138; rope from, 15, 42, 105, *106*; vessel mending, 104–6, *106*
Etello village: census information, 6–7; location, 6, 21, 27; use of ceramics, 74–75, *76*
etema, 18, 48, *48*, 105
Evans, C., 52, 53, 102, 136
Ezo Shasha potters, 52–53
Ezo, 13, 78; market at, 13, 23, 25, 27, 60, 62, 64–65, 68

Fattovich, R., 11
Fewkes, J. W., 1
Foster, G. M., 3, 51, 92, 100, 135, 138
Frank, B. E., 51, 135
Freeman, D., 19, 20
Friedel, D. A., 73
fuelwood, 8, 46–47, 53, 64

Gamo people: characteristics of, 4, 46; demographics of, 10
Gamo potters, 29–35, 46, 51–53, 71, 78, 135; geographic distribution of, 55
Gamo region, 4, 5; agriculture of, 10–12; geography of, 10–12
Gamo society, 2, 51, 138; political organization, 19–20, *20*
Garrow, P. H., 140
Gelbert, A., 51, 135
Goody, J., 2
Gosselain, O., 2, 5, 55
Gould, R. A., 5
Gupta, S. P., 51, 135
Guyla potters, 32, 49, 55, 60, 92–93
Guyla village: census information, 6–7; location, 6, 21, 23; purchase of pottery, 55–57, *58*; use of ceramics, 76; wealth of, 67

Haaland, R., 52, 136
Haberland, E., 15
Hagstrum, M. B., 2, 102, 119, 139
halaka, 19–20, 23, 25
Hally, D. J., 73
Halperin, R., 19
Hamer, J., 15
hand-building method, 35–42, 135
Handler, J., 53, 136
Hard, R. J., 89
Harlan, J. R., 11
Hasen, A., 10
Hayden, B., 5, 51, 121, 140
Hendry, J. C., 51
Hennig, H., 2, 3, 90, 92, 100, 102, 137
Henry, S. L., 140
Herbert, I., 51, 135
Herbich, I., 51, 90, 135, 137

highland region, 138. See also *dega*
Hill, 2
Hill, R. M., II, 3, 6, 52, 121
Hocart, A. M., 15
Hodder, I., 90, 137
Hosford, J., 52, 136
Huffnagel, H. P., 10
Hutton, J. H., 15

Jackson, R. T., 13, 14, 25
Jarvenpa, R., 5

Kakubayashi, F., 53
Kalinga (Philippines), 51; potters, 71–72, 100, 133, 136
Kent, S., 140
Kia potters, 69
King, J. A., 140
Kramer, C., 6, 51, 55, 70, 90, 100, 135, 137

Lackey, L., 53
Lake Abaya, 10, 32, 37, 46
Lathrap, D. W., 2, 5, 90, 102, 137
Lauer, P. K., 53, 136
LaViolette, A. J., 51, 135
Leach, E. R., 15
LeBlanc, S., 7
Leesha, 25; market, 13, 23, 25, 59, 60; potters, 14
Levine, D. N., 15
Lewis, H. S., 15
Lewis, O., 2
Lindahl, A., 3, 121, 132, 133, 140
Linton, R., 1
Lofgren, 8
London, G. A., 51, 102, 135
Longacre, W. A., 2, 3, 5, 51, 53, 73, 92, 93, 98, 100, 133, 138
lowlands, 138. See also *baso*
Luo (Kenya), 51, 135

mala caste, 6, 15, 20, 22–23, 64, 83, 135
mana caste, 6, 15, 20, 22–23, 25, 64, 83, 135
Maquet, J., 15
market economy, 55. *See also* market system
market system, 55–56, 71, 137
markets, to buy and sell ceramics, 12–15, 71, 93, 139; local, 13, 57, 69; regional, 13. *See also individual markets*
marriage patterns, 29, 51, 62, 64, 68, 135; and economic status, 66, 67
Matenga, E., 3, 121, 132, 133, 140
Matson, F. R., 1
May, P., 53
Maya, 51, 89, 90, 120, 132, 133, 135, 139
mayla, 16, 55. *See also* patron-client system

McBride, K. A., 140
McBride, W. S., 140
Menelik II, 13
metal vessels, 4, 74–75, 90
Miller, D., 2, 3, 6, 70, 138
Miller, H. M., 90, 140
Mitchell, W. P., 51, 135
Mohr Chávez, K. L., 89
Moran, G. P., 140
Mount Tola, 10
Mudar, K. M., 3, 92

Nelson, B. A., 2, 6, 7, 8, 71, 89, 100, 137, 138,
	140
Neupert, M. A., 53, 136
Nicholson, P. T., 29
non-pottery-producing villages, 55–56, 72, 136,
	137, 139

Ochollo district, 20–21, 61; potters, 22, 57, 92
Okpopo, A. I., 3, 92, 100
Olmstead, J., 10, 19
Otto, J. S., 2, 138, 140

paddle-and-anvil method, 35–37, 135
Pango market, 25, 27, 62, 65, 69
Pankhurst, A., 15
Papousek, D. A., 53
Pastron, A. G., 100
patron-client system, 15, 52, 55–56, 60, 64, 65, 68,
	70, 71, 72, 75, 137
Patterson, H. L., 29
plastic containers, use of, 5, 74–75, 84
Plog, S., 7
Posnansky, M., 89, 137
pottery: cost, 60, 63–64, 67–68, 72, 75, 100;
	decoration, 44–46; distribution, 70, 71; firing,
	46–54; lifecycle of, 1–2, 82, 88, 110, 121, 125,
	133, 139; mending, 102–20; procurement, 29–
	35, 52, 72, 98, 136; production, 2, 7, 35–44, 60;
	proximity, 27, 55, 61, 64, 65, 71, 72, 73, 75,
	137; strength, 8, 48, 71–72, 136; use-life, 92–
	101. See also ceramics, ceramic vessels,
	primary-use pottery
pottery-producing villages, 55–56, 136
primary-use pottery, 73–91; frequency of, 75–77,
	75, 86; spatial analysis, 78–82; 79, 80, 81, 86,
	88–89; storage of, 82, 86, 89; types of, 75,
	77–78, 83–84, 86–88; vessel volume, 85–86,
	88

Reid, K. C., 3, 92
Reina, R. E., 3, 6, 52, 121
resocialization, 51, 136
Rice, P., 1, 3, 8, 100, 138

Rift Valley, 4, 10, 21
rim type (ceramics), 7, 31, 40, 42
ritual sacrificer, 69, 84–86
Rye, O., 52, 53, 102, 136

sacred forests, 46, 53
Sargent, C. F., 73
Sassaman, K. E., 7
Sauer, C. O., 11
Schiffer, M. B., 2, 53, 55, 140
Senior, L. M., 119
Shack, W. A., 10, 11, 15
Shepard, A., 1
Shona, 132, 133
Shott, M. J., 3, 92, 93, 100, 138
Shutler, M. E., 53
Sillar, B., 51, 135
Silverman, R. A., 15, 51
Simmons, F., 11
Sinopoli, C. M., 6, 140
Skibo, J. M., 2, 4, 53, 55, 73
Smith, J., 53, 138
Smith, M. F., 15, 90
social status: within caste system, 84, 128, 135;
	and ceramics, 82, 85, 86, 90, 96, 100–101, 110,
	137, 139
Solheim, W., 102
spatial location of ceramics, 3, 102, 110, 114–15,
	119, 123–25, 129–32. See also spatial pattern-
	ing
spatial patterning, 66, 102, 112, 116, 117, 120,
	123, 124, 125, 130. See also spatial location of
	ceramics
Spencer-Wood, S. M., 140
Sperber, D., 10, 18, 19, 20
Stanislawski, B. B., 51
Stanislawski, M. B., 2, 51, 100, 102, 119, 139
Stark, M. T., 6, 51, 52, 55, 135
Steponaitis, V. P., 7
Sterner, J., 15, 102
Stevenson, M. G., 133, 134
stockpiling, of ceramic vessels, 6, 71, 137

Tani, M., 6, 8, 71, 92, 93, 98, 100, 137, 138
temper. See clay
Thompson, R. A., 51, 135
tobacco, use of, 35, 36, 78
Todd, D., 15
Tomka, S. A., 133, 134
Trostel, B., 90, 138
Tschopik, H., 102
Tuckson, M., 53
Tuka market, 12, 13, 14, 23, 25, 27, 62, 74, 75, 83
Turner, 8
Tzeltal Maya. See Maya

Van de Velde, H. R., 53, 136
Van de Velde, P., 53, 136
Vaughan, J. H., Jr., 15
Vavilov, I., 11
vessel. *See* ceramic vessel, metal vessel, plastic
    containers, wooden vessel

Wahlman, M., 53
Watson, V., 53
wealth: and beer production, 88, 90, 118; and diet,
    18–19, 137–38; diversity of vessel types, 86;
    land holdings, 67; livestock, 67; number of
    wives, 66–67; number of occupations, 67. *See
    also* social status

Weedman, K. J., 4, 5
Weigand, P. C., 3, 51, 102, 121
Westphal, E., 10
Wilson, D. C., 138
women, in Gamo society, 15, 29–31, 125; as
    potters, 29–31, 51, 135
wooden vessels, 78, 84, 89, 109, 138, 139

Zada potters, 14, 60, 69, 92
Zuni potters, 1
Zuza potters, 31, 50, 55, 69, 92, 136
Zuza village: census information, 6–7; demo-
    graphics, 22; location, 6, 20–21; use of
    ceramics, 76